REMARKABLE
FEASTS

——

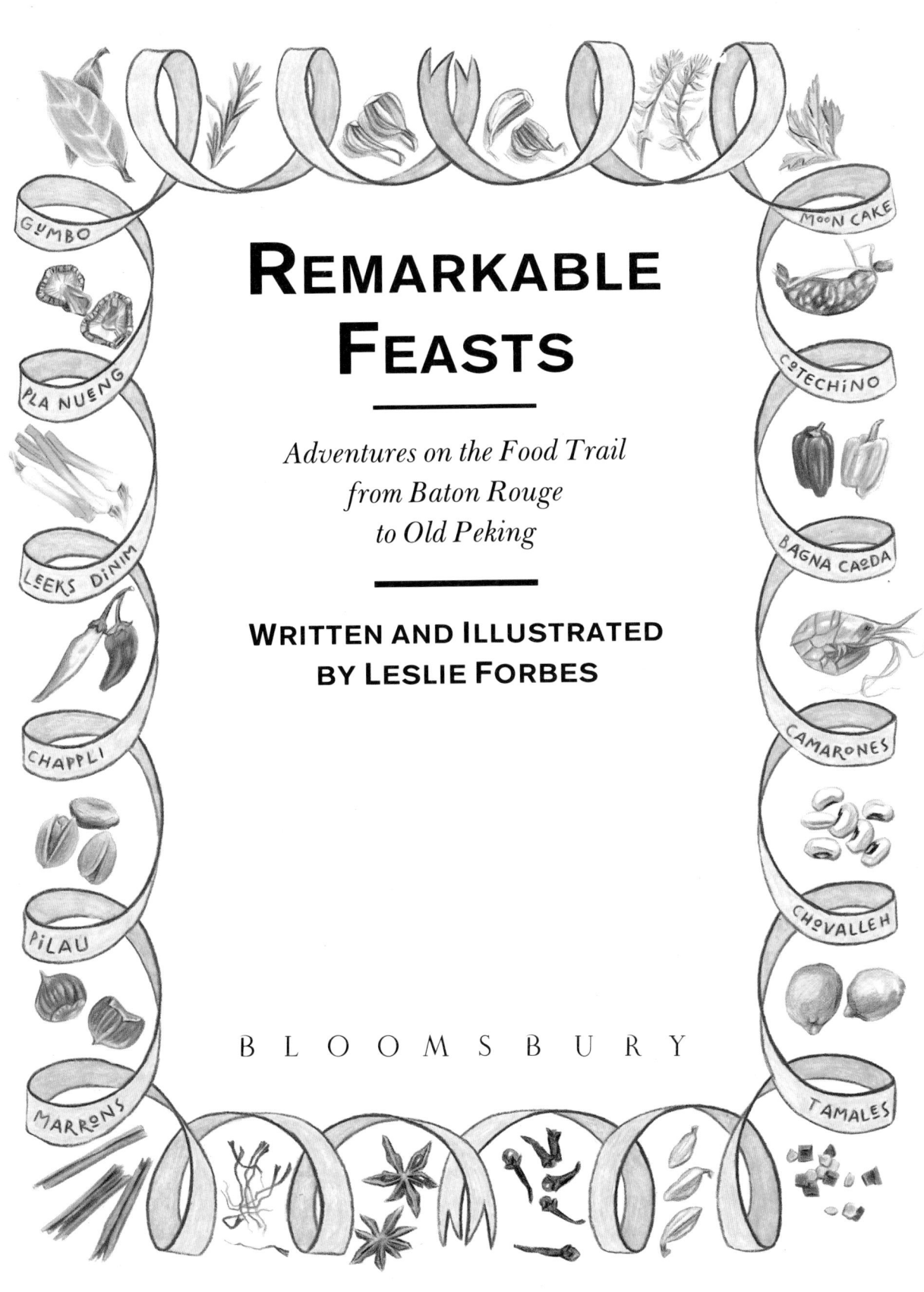

REMARKABLE FEASTS

*Adventures on the Food Trail
from Baton Rouge
to Old Peking*

**WRITTEN AND ILLUSTRATED
BY LESLIE FORBES**

BLOOMSBURY

First published in Great Britain 1990
Bloomsbury Publishing Limited, 2 Soho Square, London W1V 5DE

Text and illustrations copyright © 1990 by Leslie Forbes
The moral right of the author has been asserted

A CIP catalogue record for this book
is available from the British Library

ISBN 0–7475–0653–1

10 9 8 7 6 5 4 3 2 1

Designed by Fielding Rowinski
Typeset by Bookworm Typesetting, Manchester

Produced by Mandarin Offset
Printed and bound in Hong Kong

CONTENTS

————

To Andrew Thomas, again,
and to all the people and countries
who made their feasts mine

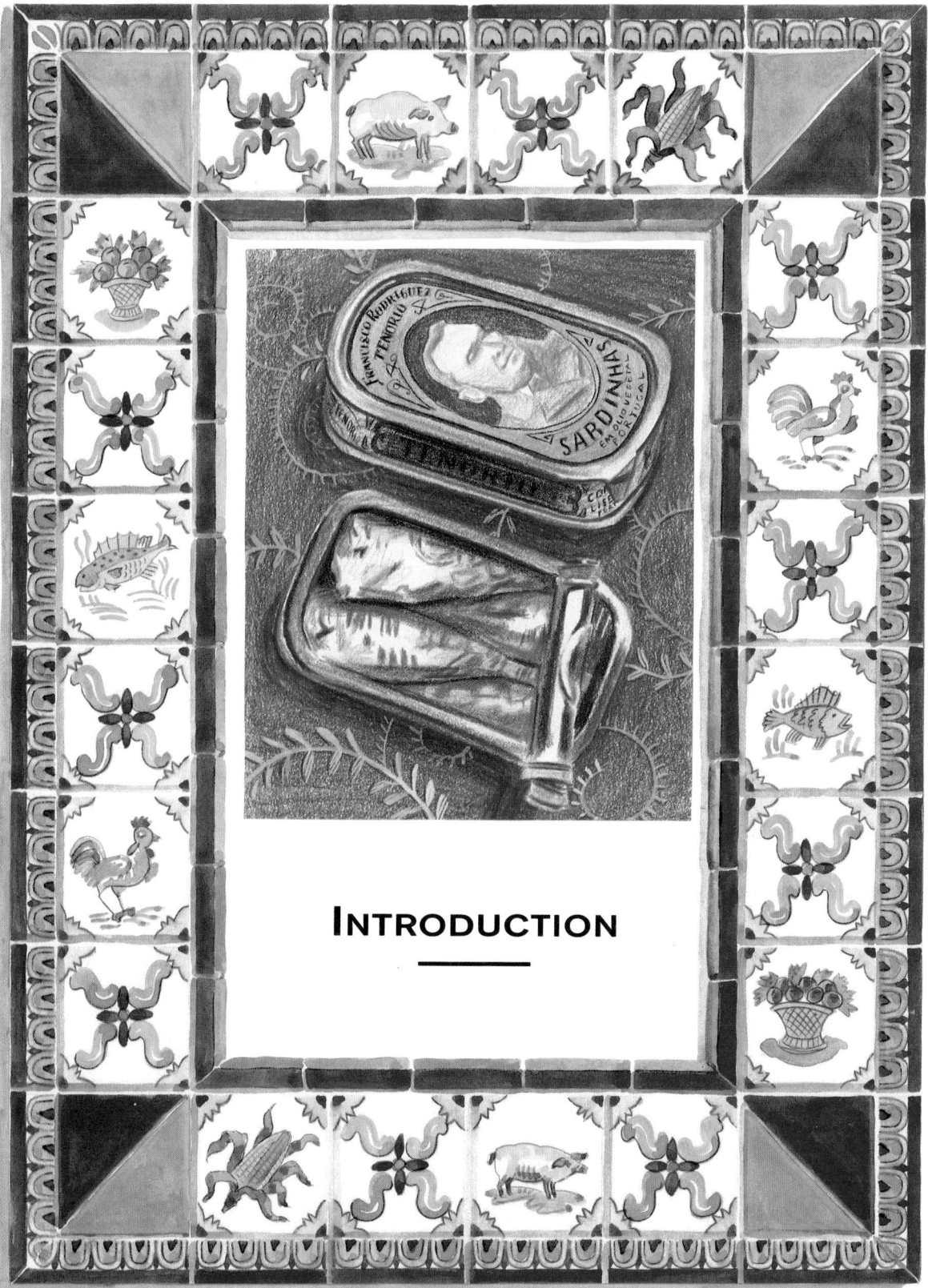

INTRODUCTION

In the winter of 1987 two things happened which crystallized an idea I had been working on for a book: I saw a movie called *Babette's Feast*, and read *Honey from a Weed*, an account of fasting and feasting in Greece, Tuscany and Spain by Patience Gray.

My idea had been conceived on a damp June day in Tuscany when I sat in the huge old kitchen of the country's best restaurant, shoulder to shoulder with its twenty-strong staff.

I don't remember now what we ate – something simple and vivid like focaccia bread smeared with olive oil and garlic, some fresh noodles under a basilly tomato sauce, slices of wild boar prosciutto; nothing resembling the highly evolved dishes served in the dining room. But it was undoubtedly a feast – what does my dictionary call it? – a movable feast that recurs on different dates; a gratification of the senses; a sumptuous meal.

Aldous Huxley once said that feasts must be solemn and rare or else they cease to be feasts. No doubt the old misery would have approved of the Japanese, who congregate every autumn to compose solemn poems to the moon. In Mexico's villages, not a month goes by without a fiesta, and they are no less festive for being often repeated.

Some people need little excuse for a party, and others find it easier to let go of gold than of sobriety. In two years of travelling I met both kinds. This book is a collection of drawings, menus, recipes and recollections of their daily life and their celebrations: a cook's diary, a stock pot of scrap memories.

The recipes come from a variety of sources – hand-written by friends, scribbled down by me under a camel's shadow, typed out neatly. They have all been adapted, more or less depending on the source, to fit my kitchen. The flaws are mine, not the original cook's.

If unable to discover the local name for a dish, I have simply given a loose English description, and in almost all cases the recipes offer suggestions for substitutions where ingredients are difficult to find.

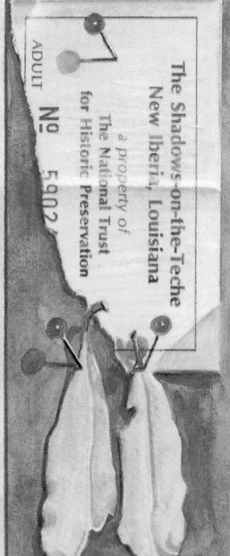

THE DAY ITSELF
AIN'T NUTHIN

Mardi Gras in Louisiana

There is a man in New Orleans, swears he's graded every
oyster he's eaten since 1930. Mounted on a plaque in his
office, the shell of the best ever:
                April 7, 1957 at The Pearl

There are two Cajun friends I know, said, 'Someone's going to
make money out of a Cajun musical, why not us?' Wrote:
    First you take your flour and drop it in your oil
    Stir it stir it rich and brown as soil
    Secret's in the stirring, in the wrist
    No sense in hurrying through that onion-scented mist.
Not just a musical, but the first Cajun Cooking Musical – the actors
make gumbo on stage.

You can't get away from food in Louisiana. Like jazz and corruption
and Mardi Gras, it pumps the pulse in the state's veins. The French
have always rated their stomachs right up there close to their hearts,
and there are three French cultures in Louisiana: the Cajuns (the word
comes from Acadians – sailors and farmers of Breton stock living in
Nova Scotia in the seventeenth and eighteenth centuries, exiled for
reasons of religion and politics), who tempered their French fiddle
music and country cooking in the Louisiana swamps; the Creoles, of
French/Spanish descent – haute society and haute cuisine; and the
Creoles' former slaves from the West Indies and Africa, whose
influence, both culinary and musical, spread up the Mississippi delta as
far as slavery.

In the two centuries since the slaves arrived, the three cultures have
mixed more than cuisines. Mardi Gras (or Fat Tuesday) – the day of
feasting before the Lenten fast – was not observed with such
enthusiasm in France; not in Spain, not even in Venice (where they do
like a party). Only in Rio and Trinidad does it have a more pagan beat.

Mardi Gras in New Orleans begins sedately enough with a de-
butante's ball on Twelfth Night. From then until the midnight before
Ash Wednesday the number of parades and parties – sponsored by
secret men's clubs called Mystick Krewes – increases daily. Most krewes
are run by the city's prominent white businessmen, although the krewe
of Zulu is black (and, most bizarrely, 'blacked up' in their parade), and
there are mirror events organized by loucher elements of society.

The last ninety-six hours of Mardi Gras is one continuous night of
frenzied barbarity. Or Good Clean American Fun. It all depends where
you're standing when the parade passes by. A hundred years ago,
people in the parades threw flour, then gold coins. Now it is thousands
of dollars' worth of metallic doubloons, fake pearls, silver-painted
coconuts and plastic 'Go' cups to fill with bourbon or Diet Coke.

On Louisiana's rice prairies, and out in the swamps near the Gulf of Mexico, the celebrations are entirely different.

I flew in over the Mississippi River delta to write about Mardi Gras. I had a head full of jazz and eyes clouded by a decadent, sensuous legend: the romantic South – like a painted gauze curtain over a stage set, blurring the edges.

I found a feast and a story on every corner.

ONE

It was late January in New Orleans, but the weather was all magnolia blossoms and venetian blinds drawn in the afternoon. You could taste mint juleps in the thick wet air.

The handsomest man in Louisiana had invited me to a party and I felt like Blanche Dubois, only younger. I wanted to put on seamed stockings with a tear in them, and a silk dress the colour of old roses: portent of falling petals and fallen women. I wanted to catch a streetcar named Desire.

The handsomest man in Louisiana lived in the busiest part of the city, and the streetcar didn't go there. I took the bus instead.

None of my friends could tell me about the bus system in their city. 'The *bus*,' they said, shaking their heads: another quirky foreigner dies on the public transport system. I expected criminals at the very least, but the people just looked very old, or very poor, or both. A tall black man got off with me at the end of the Canal Street line. When I told him I was going to walk to Jackson Square he said 'What you wanna walk faw? Y'awl *paid* for a transfer – aw'll show ya where to get the streetcar. Aw believe in gettin' ma money's wuth.'

I said he had a nice town.

'Y'awl must be a tourist to say that, hon'.'

The handsomest man in Louisiana is considered quite bohemian by his society friends. In some New Orleans circles a bohemian is anyone who voted for Dukakis instead of Bush.

His guests sat at a picnic table on the nineteenth-century balcony of the first apartment block built in America, a place of curving stairs and high ceilings and light wells onto moon-dappled courtyards. Beyond the balcony's black ironwork, Jackson Square shimmied through a Mississippi rivermist. It all looked too ridiculously romantic, like a Whistler canvas, or the opening credits to a forties film.

From somewhere below came the husky voice of a saxophone, singing of sex and solitude, and the teasing, tropical smells of warm drains and damp sheets. At our backs, French windows opened into a

huge golden room filled with the glow from an old chandelier. The chandelier was the size of my bedroom in London.

The table was covered in old copies of the *Times-Picayune* and piled a foot high with freshly boiled Louisiana crawfish, crab and new potatoes, bought from Captain Sid's in Buck-town, on Lake Pontchartrain. Everything was a deep rusty pink with the hot spices used to cook the crawfish. We ate with our fingers, dipping the potatoes in sweet melted butter, pulling the heads off the crawfish and sticking our tongues in to suck out the juice, cracking the tail for the succulent flesh. After a while the spices and salt made your lips pucker like someone who has been too long in the water, but you kept on eating.

There was talk of how New Orleans' relaxed attitudes lead not only to good music and tolerance, but to laziness and drug trafficking and crime. It's a good place to be a lawyer. Or a criminal.

'It's ingrained in the system, a certain amount of corruption,' said the handsomest man in Louisiana. He had the kind of voice you could strike a match on.

After dinner, the more decadent of us went to the Old Absinthe Bar on Bourbon Street for some cold beer and a feel of the street.

The walls of the Old Absinthe were covered in yellowing business

cards. From the ceiling hung enough football helmets for a decade's Superbowls, and there was a non-stop sports channel on the four-foot TV screen. Outside the bar, the 'Lucky Dog' man was selling soft drinks and boiled weiners from a six-foot hot dog. Bourbon Street was packed with drunken revellers and honky-tonks and girlie shows and tacky souvenir shops and men dressed as women and crowds shouting 'SHOW YOUR TITS! SHOW YOUR TITS!' to girls on balconies. If enough plastic beads were thrown, some of them did.

A woman walked down the street carrying a huge placard which read 'GOD IS COOL – MAINLINE JESUS'.

I could see that Bourbon Street at any time was a great pond for fishing lost souls. At Mardi Gras it must be very like a strict Baptist's vision of hell.

TWO

Jackson Square, another day. Young black boys were working the more obvious tourists in the crowd.

'Hey lady – I can tell you where you gotcha shoes – wanna bet?' So they bet him, laid down their five dollars' worth of naïveté on the guillotine of his street-kid smile.

'You gottem right here right now in Jackson Square N'Yawlins, lady, thass where you gottem – pay me my fi' dollahs!'

In the French Quarter there was free street music everywhere. A Cajun band called Jambalaya sent crowds second-lining round an outdoor dance floor, waving their umbrellas in the air behind a massive black lady in a stretch pink tracksuit. She had haunches that shook against the beat, and dyed blonde hair parted in the middle and combed over her head like a water buffalo's horns.

'Second lining?' I asked. 'What's that? Why second?'

'Secon' linin' is what black folks do at their funerals, dollin'. Foist line out slow an' lonesome, secon' line back fast an' jazzy.'

Everybody in New Orleans told me, 'You gotta go to K-Paul's to eat the best Cajun food in N'Yawlins.' I tried to get in but all the tourists in the city were there ahead of me. So I dived into the Acme Oyster Bar on Iberville Street for a dozen of their best and a couple of Dixie beers – 'Eight dollahs, hon' – and sat slurping down the ozone, with my feet on the crazy-paved lino. I put Patsy Cline on the jukebox to sing her 'Sweet Dreams' and read yesterday's headlines by the light of old neon beer signs and a plastic lamp in the shape of a bunch of grapes.

When I came out an hour later, the temperature had dropped 14 degrees to 10°C. A man walked by in black fishnet tights, a leather jock strap, and a pink satin cape.

The New Orleans Mardi Gras season was just warming up.

Sooner or later in New Orleans you have to go to the Café Du Monde, drink chicory café au lait and eat three beignets for $1.65, and watch the Everests of white icing sugar off the crisp doughnuts sift through the wrought-iron table onto your clothes. Twenty-four hours a day of non-stop sugar and caffeine fix. This is New Orleans' image of itself.

I shared my three warm beignets with Henry Schmidt – 'Call me Sunshine, dollin', everybody does' – at the table where he always sat so he could watch the pretty girls without getting the sun in his eyes. He had a cataract in one eye, 'An' I don't see so good outta the othah.' He is seventy-four. They call him the Mayor of the Quarter.

Henry put my arm through his and took me on a tour.

'Now Gallantine Street, that useta be a real bad part of town. Old roomin' houses, lottsa seamen, lottsa gamblin', lottsa moidahs. Forty-five French Market Place useta be the gamblinest place in New Orleans. Funny thing, nevah had one Frenchman. They was all Italians. People useta bring the wild game they shot, their fish, to sell to the restaurants an' the rich Creoles' cooks. But those days are long gone, dollin'.'

Restaurants have their supplies trucked in now. The rich go to their local supermarkets. The Italians have moved into delis.

In the Market, most of the traders were black, the balance of trade slanted towards tourists more than locals: pecan pralines and earrings and antiques mixed up with okra and Louisiana sugarcane.

'Me, I shop local, dollin',' said Henry. 'I like my beans – navy beans, red beans, lima beans – *any* kine o' beans. I put in some thyme an' some bay leaf – you know we got those flavahs from the Injuns, dollin'? An' some of that slab bacon, or some pickled pawk tips; mebbe that ham hock – it's good seasonin' for beans. I boil' em a long time so they real tender, mebbe with a pound o' those plump fleshy tomatoes chopped in 'em; might stir in some onions stewed with butter at the end. That's *good* eatin'! Then I might come down the Kwawtuh, get me some nice plump ersters to eat with radish an' lime.'

At Tipitina's that evening I had my first red beans and rice, free with the $4 entrance fee. Tipitina's is where Dennis Quaid supposedly romanced Ellen Barkin in *The Big Easy*. Ex-restaurant, ex-whorehouse, now the best music club in New Orleans, it is in the kind of area where the least offensive person on the street is a drug-addict, and the crumbling dwellings are ominously called 'shotguns'.

Some shotguns can have a certain old-fashioned charm. Around Tipitina's they are just old, not fashioned in any way. Outside are vehicles of no identifiable genealogy assembled from pieces broken off other people's cars.

'Fais-do-do' is what the Cajuns used to say to their children when they sent them off to bed before the dancing started in the front room. The Sunday Fais-do-dos at Tip's start at 5.30. There were college kids drinking caffeine-free Diet Coke (you may die from the saccharine, but calmly), and old couples with iced tea, and lots of clean-cut middle-aged types in pressed jeans standing around politely sipping Dixie beer, all waiting for the music.

A few degenerates in knotted headbands and studded leather belts lurked around the edges, but they were in the minority.

Then the band started to play, a real sweaty, gumbo-stirrin', elbow in that stranger's ear, fingers in his groin, get drunk, get beat up, get left in a heap for the vultures out-of-control Cajun jitterbug.

I danced with a washboard-player on his night off from the Bourbon Street Cajun Cabin, with a Cajun dance instructor who has his shoes bronzed and hung up at Mulate's (The World's Most Famous Cajun Restaurant), with Fred, the best dancer in the world, with an unemployment insurance rep who told me about New Orleans' high rate of illiteracy, with Fred again, with one of the degenerates,who held me so closely I could read the fine print on his tattoos.

Suddenly the doors burst open and a parade of half-naked drunken masked men streamed in throwing strings of fake pearls and plastic roses, and wearing stockings and high heels, and bras like horses' nosebags. Their band took over the stage for a while and played Mardi Gras tunes and old-time Armstrong jazz. Then the whole parade wandered off into the night.

Up on the wall, a huge poster of the late great Professor Longhair (who ensured his immortality in this carnival-crazed town by writing a Mardi Gras song) beamed down beatifically on the action at his old home base.

Another nice quiet night at Tip's.

THREE

On Monday I had breakfast at Sweickhardt's Drugstore. The waitress poured me some strong black coffee and cut thick slices of pink ham fresh off the bone. 'Y'awl like that chicory cawfee?' she asked. 'Chicory a root, y'know, hon' – brings out the cawfee flavah. Thass strickly N'Yawlins – Cajuns don' use it. Hey! Y'awl take ma pitcher with ma head in the dishes? You gonna heah from ma lawyer!'

Sweickhardt's hasn't changed since it was built in the 1940s, and still sells everything from ice-cream sodas to surgical trusses. I kept waiting for Mickey Rooney and Debbie Reynolds to appear and do a tap dance on the soda counter.

'Flo' shook her head at a new arrival. 'You gotta get up earlier than this you wanna taste my biscuits, hon'.' She picked up my plate, where minute traces of ham and eggs were still visible.

'What's wrong – y'awl eat too much las' night?'

I asked her about Mardi Gras and she smiled. 'Y'awl talkin' to the wrong lady, sugah.' She told me to go talk to Mizz Chase at Dooky's.

'Don't take no wooden nickels on the way, hon',' she said as I left. The laconic charm of New Orleans.

At Dooky Chase's I had my second taste of red beans and rice. Dooky's was in an area where a white face stood out like a hard-boiled egg in a bowl of gumbo. When they talk about a murder a day in New Orleans, this is where they mean: the notorious 'projects'. Illiteracy runs almost as high as crime here. Inside the pretty green-shuttered building, everything was infinitely respectable. Mrs Chase herself was as neat as a swept room; at sixty-four, her years of working twenty-hour days were scarcely visible. I got the feeling she knew what was good for me. I might not like it, but I'd get it anyway.

'I'm such a renegade. Boys come to our short-order section, tough boys from the projects, y'know? But I've known their families a *long* time. I say, "God, look at your hair – I bet your Maw is ready to die." They say, "Yes, Mizz Chase", real polite. "Well you can't come in here," I say. "You too raggedy for me." '

Mrs Chases's father-in-law, the original Dooky, was a door-to-door lottery vendor. When he got ulcers in 1939 from the pressure of too many big-time hustlers, he and his wife opened a corner shop with a bar one side, selling beer and sandwiches and lottery tickets over the counter. Then he borrowed $600 and opened a restaurant.

'You gotta know that before the 1940s there was nowhere nice black families could go – they sorta had to be homebodies. Dooky's was *it* for black people for many years.'

In the forties and fifties, before desegregation, it was illegal for blacks and whites to mix in public. But they have always mixed at Dooky's. White politicians met black leaders, musicians, theatre people; the sugar union met here, in an integrated room upstairs.

Mrs Chase's parents were country people from Martinique; she grew up in a Madisonville farm across the river from New Orleans. Her daddy raised hogs.

'An' boy, that pork fat made the best pie crust ever!' She smiled ruefully. 'Course we didn't think about cholesterol in those days – just good eating.'

They had access to all of Louisiana's plentiful game: venison to roast or stew or barbecue, quail, rabbits and squirrels for deep-crust pies.

'My daddy grew strawberries – he made the *best* strawberry wine – and when those quail was eatin' the berries you jes' got a gun and banged 'em outta there. Used to stew them in that wine so they had berries in and out. Or split 'em, brown 'em in butter, coat 'em in plum jelly and let 'em simmer in a little water. Then serve 'em with grits.'

They seasoned the game with her father's garden onions and garlic and lots of sweet green peppers, and with thyme, bay leaves and chillies laid out to dry in the hot Louisiana sun. They used wild juniper berries 'pounded *real* good' to marinate the rabbit and venison. They melted chicken fat and beat it with fresh eggs to use instead of mayonnaise for the creamiest potato salad. There were elderberry pies and elderflowers simmered with sugar for cough syrup; and parsley and garlic soup (her daddy had a lot of garlic): you took two good big handfuls of parsley, washed and roughly chopped, then softened lots of sliced garlic in bacon fat. Salt, pepper; sometimes you added a spoonful of flour, or a couple of chopped potatoes. It was covered in water and boiled until it thickened, the parsley added last, just for a few minutes. A *good* soup. And they stewed wild purslane with onions and served it like spinach, with hard-boiled egges sliced on top.

'They eat wild purslane in France too, y'say? God, I didn' know anyone else knew about that. We used to be kinda shamed – eatin' weeds, y'know?'

'Holidays we always had a gumbo, of course, and always a chicken fricassee stewed in brown gravy after midnight Mass on Christmas Eve. Then . . .oh we had roast pork jes' *stuffed* with garlic, and baked apples all around it – y'know? And fresh oyster dressing for the turkeys.'

At Christmas there were fruit cakes 'for weeks', because people in the country went around to each house for cake and a glass of wine, even if they hadn't seen each other all year. Her daddy served his Cherry Bounce: little cherries soaked for months in whisky and cane sugar. You scooped the drunken cherries out of your glass with a spoon.

'The river was our entertainment in the country, but Mardi Gras my aunts took us into New Orleans, everyone on the back of a truck. Only thing you came to the city for – babies, school and Mardi Gras.'

They took sandwiches and fried chicken, bought street food – corndogs, fried fish, sweet potato pies – along Claiborne Avenue, lined then with beautiful oak trees. Now it is an expressway. That fast food was Mrs Chase's favourite, ''Cause any other time my maw would kill you roundly if you had food in your mouth while you were walking. You can still get good sweet potato pies on the street, and the meltingest coconut pies – Mr Williams, he pushes his cart around.'

'Y'awl like Dooky's, dollin'?' The black cabbie grinned into his rear-view mirror. 'It's good, but ain't as good as Shay Hulleens – y'awl bin there? Et some o' Austin's stuffed swimps an' berled ersters? Now they *good*!'

'Sounds as if you like food.'

'I know what's good, hon'. My wife's a cook, a real Creole lady ... parlay that French y'know? But me, I likes Austin's *soul* food best.' He rolled the words around in his mouth like baby oysters dripping with butter and garlic.

On Mardi Gras morning he and his wife would be up at 4.00, making a picnic to take down the river and watch the all-black Zulu parade dock its boat at 6.00. He said he wouldn't risk taking the kids up Canal Street in the crush later.

'They some real funny people there these days – stomp a kid's hand soon as drink a Dixie.'

I asked him why the Zulu parade came in on a boat, and he gave me a long cool look in the mirror.

''Coz that's the way us black folks came in from Africa, dollin'.'

The laconic charm of New Orleans always has an edge to it.

That night I was invited to a parade party in the suburbs, and had my third taste of red beans and rice. By now I was getting the hang of it: Monday, right? Beans – am I right?

The hostess asked me to pick up a traditional icky-sticky King Cake from a bakery called Mr Wedding Cake.

The original Kings' Cakes in France – Gâteaux des Rois – were light pastry or brioche with almonds. They had a bean buried inside, and the person who found it was king for a day.

New Orleans' King Cakes are sugary brioches iced in the Mardi Gras colours of purple, green and gold, a combination which seems somehow ill-advised for anything edible. They contain small pink plastic babies – anyone who finds a baby is supposed to give the next King Cake party. So many people have started lying about it recently, hiding the baby in their pocket, swallowing it, that bakers have been asked to increase the number of babies per cake.

The instinct for indolence and inertia runs deep in New Orleans. '*Laissez les bons temps rouler*,' they say. '*Laissez-faire*,' they mean.

The parade was all-American, as parades always seem to be. Pre-pubescent majorettes in brief shorts bumped and ground and twirled batons. Marching bands of small boys in blue uniforms with outsized gold epaulettes rolled their eyes and smiled at familiar faces while their lips kept that pucker and blew: echoes of a young Louis Armstrong, leader of the band.

The floats were not up to the standards of the uptown krewes' gross bad taste but there were as many plastic beads thrown, and the shouts of 'Throw me somethin', mistah!' were just as loud, if less threatening. You don't want to mess with some of the people jostling you for beads at the big parades.

I caught fifteen plastic necklaces, three purple plastic 'Go' cups and four green aluminium doubloons. I could have caught more if I'd held up a child – 'Something for the baby, mistah!' – or if I'd shown some cleavage. 'Anything to attract their attention. Those ole boys on the floats get *awful* bored after three hours throwin'.'

The price of carnival 'throws' has remained steady, even with inflation.

A white male elite runs the big parades. There are fifty-odd Mardi Gras krewes, but the most socially prestigious, Rex and Proteus and Momus and Comus, are so exclusive that even Huey Long, the most powerful governor Louisiana ever had, never got invited to one of their balls. They reek of privilege and power; membership in them depends on the insistent presence of money. Their history hinges on lesser French and Spanish gentry, drunken socialites, Creole intrigues; grand dukes, infatuation, an actress and a silly song; segregation, Zulus, gay balls, movie stars, secret societies.

Secret krewes hold secret meetings in secret rooms to elect who will lead their processions along a parade route whose start is so secret it is surprising the parades begin at all. Everything related to Mardi Gras krewes is not so much veiled as draped, canopied, quilted, cocooned, shrouded in secrecy.

The kings elected by their krewes are kings of industry who have performed some high-profile (definitely *not* secret) volunteer work during the year; their queens are debutantes chosen because of their fathers' social or industrial prominence. The identities of Rex's king and queen are kept secret until Mardi Gras day. The identity of Comus's king is never revealed.

The emperor's new clothes exist all right: The King of Rex wears a pageboy wig, a gold crown, mock jewels, white tights and a stomach (his own) usually as prominent as his business. In New Orleans, it is the empire that is a delusion.

FOUR

On Tuesday I tried to get into K-Paul's for lunch, but every tourist in Louisiana was there in line before me.

I went instead to Chez Helene in the tough district north of Louis Armstrong Park. Friends that swam confidently in the white mainstream had warned me, 'Oh, y'awl don't want to go there *alone.*' Implying murder, mayhem, rape, the need for a crack team of paratroopers; people won't look like you.

There was an old man leaning against a lamp outside a bar in the sleepy, peeling neighbourhood. I rolled my car window down three or four millimetres and asked him the way.

'Jes' follah that truck ovah theah, dollin'. He goin' to Hulleens.'

After the truckdriver failed to overturn my car and mug me, we both stopped opposite a brick building, covered in red and white signs: THE BEST FRIED CHICKEN IN N.O, WE HAVE LOBSTER NOW. BREAKFASTS LUNCHES SEA FOOD. Only two small black boys on skateboards stood between me and the restaurant. They made no overtly hostile moves.

Austin Leslie sat inside Helene's at a bar crowded with good smells. 'Come on in, dollin'. Sit anywhere you like.'

Beyond was a café with checked tablecloths, its walls hung with strings of hot chillies and old newspaper reviews.

A little basket of white cornmeal muffins arrived first, nutty-tasting from a well-tempered pan, then a bowl of lip-tingling gumbo with chunks of smoked sausage and shreds of fresh crabmeat. There was a choice of shrimp étouffée – 'Jes' a thick tomato and sweet pepper sauce, hon' – or treacly barbecued ribs; blackened redfish, some garlicky mustard greens cooked with pickled pork tips, jambalaya (everything left over in the kitchen mixed with rice and sausage), the inevitable red beans and rice. They have always been traditional Monday food, simmering away all day while housewives did their chores.

'Thass jes' what we calls pot food,' said Miss Helen, namesake of the restaurant. 'What black folks ate, like catfish fried in cornmeal, stewed gizzards, pigs' feet, black-eyed peas an' greens. Didn' useta be no *white* folks eatin' catfish – *no* way.' She shook her head. 'But then Austin useta cut a chicken in twelve pieces before he fry it. Now even the black folks is gettin' fussy, won't eat no chicken wingtips.'

She gave me a bowl of caramel-coloured bread pudding, stiff and creamy and sweet with pineapple and raisins. Some potent rum sauce had been ladled generously over the top.

'Now bread puddin' y'see, that useta be somethin' the black folks made with leftovers. My Ma useta work for white folks. They might give her their stale bread.' Austin Leslie grinned at me. 'She might jes' help herself to a little brown sugah, a little spice.'

'You can't make this,' said Aunt Helen. 'Its all in the bread. An' don't ax me for no recipe, hon', I make that puddin' in a pail. I mix it with my hands.'

'I can tell who made the puddin',' said Austin. 'I can tell if Mizz Helen made the gumbo – jes' by the nose. Jes' like a bricklayer, he stops layin' bricks at noon, he can tell nex' day where the other fellah started.'

Aunt Helen started her first restaurant in 1942 – called Howard's Eatery after her husband – in a place just south of Canal Street.

'I went to a funeral in Texas an' got this intuition I could do somethin' for myself. Stawted with pennies, didn' throw away nuthin.'

Blacks didn't go to Canal Street then, nor to the Quarter unless it was to work. As long as you were in work clothes, you were OK.

Rampart Street was for blacks what Bourbon Street is now for whites: gambling, honky-tonks and sex. 'Lotta people wantin' my biscuits and greens – you eat greens, you gotta have biscuits with 'em.'

In 1964 Austin and Helen opened Chez Helene – Austin cooking twelve-hour night shifts, his aunt twelve-hour days.

'Austin, he laffin' an' grinnin' with the bums, the thieves. I ain't braggin' or nuthin', but he kep' things smooth, made this a nice place for folks to come.'

From the very beginning both blacks and whites came to the restaurant. 'Never bin no big division like in other southern states,' said Helen. 'Italians useta have delis in the black neighbourhoods even during segregation. They was no what you call real ghetto here.'

But Mardi Gras then was different. Claiborne Avenue was for the blacks, as was the Zulu parade. There were stands selling homemade food on Mardi Gras day down the boulevard in the middle of Claiborne, in what New Orleanians call the Neutral Ground. (Sounds like a battleground, I said. 'It was sortta that,' said Helen. Or a cemetery, I said. 'That too sometimes,' said Austin.) Not the corndogs and caramel corn you find now, but red beans and rice – those beans again – and hot sausage like Spanish chorizo, and sweet potato pies and fried chicken and ribs.

'It's the comin' of Mardi Gras that's always been the thing,' said Austin. 'The day itself ain't nuthin – jes' the feast before the fast.'

'I remember Mizz Mary,' said Helen. 'She *liked* her beer. Drank so much one Mardi Gras, said she'd give up drinkin' Regal – her favourite brand – for Lent.' Helen laughed. 'Drank Jax instead.'

FIVE

On Wednesday I had an oyster loaf and pecan pie at Casamento's. What Sweickhardt's is to soda fountains, Casamento's is to oyster bars.

On the counter next to the Bowling League Trophy was an old ice-box stuffed with fresh oysters. If you had 'A Dozen in the Hand and a Bud $5.70 at the Bar', the shucker just slapped yer ersters down on the counter next to yer beer. No plate. No lemon. Or you could sit at the melamine tables and have an old black waitress with orange hair take your order. Oyster Stew: $5.55 a dozen or $3.80 a half. Oyster Loaf: a whole baton of fluffy French bread scooped out, oysters dipped in the resulting crumbs, deep-fried, and heaped back into the bread. You went crack, crunch, squish, squirt with every bite.

After the oysters I tried to talk to K-Paul in the kitchen behind his restaurant. He was too busy: all the tourists in America were waiting for him to autograph their copies of his latest cookery book. So I talked to his brother Abel instead.

'We're real proud of Paul,' said his brother, a little bullet-headed gnome with a big smile. He had a grocery in Opelousas for twelve years, then was thirty years in the oil business before being laid off. Now he ran the meat side of the K-Paul empire, producing hot sausage and tasso (Cajun spiced pork) and boudins for the kitchens.

'People in Louisiana don't make boudin in the French way no more, with blood, 'cept mebbe at one o' them grandes boucheries out near Breaux Bridge. Too difficult. When the hawg is killed you gotta see the blood doesn't clabber – you know what clabber is, sugah? It kinda seizes up, an' if it clabbers it don't eat so good. Some folks do it for themselves – put vinegar in to stop the clabbering. But on a big scale it ain't practical.'

Abel's Cajun parents spoke French at home, but few of the numerous Prudhomme siblings know more than a few words.

'They useta fuss us too much at school if we spoke French, sugah. 'Cept for Paul now; he's the youngest an' he speaks it real good. We're real proud of our little brother.'

At the table his little brother, his vast thighs rippling like lava under his white chef's outfit, was puffing his Krakatoa puffs as his boudin fingers swallowed another autograph pen. 'Good eatin', Good livin', and Good lovin', Paul.'

He writes it in all the fans' books.

SIX

The Friday before Mardi Gras anyone who wants to be seen to be somebody goes to Galatoire's for lunch. By 11 a.m., the restaurant had a half-mile queue of people out the front – old friends already – drinking Michelob and Bud from the bar opposite. The man at the front had been waiting on his Keep-Kool box since 9 a.m., saving a place for someone more important; looked like he was ready to storm the Bastille.

I went to Antoine's, where there was a stag party for an elite krewe in one of the back rooms. Unlikely-looking nuns kept tiptoeing demurely through, their arrival greeted by raucous laughter, and red-faced socialites staggered in and out, leering drunkenly at single women. But the restaurant had awe-inspiring potato puffs (the simplest recipe lost me after the fifth paragraph), and great bread.

I read in the paper that David Ernest Duke, ex-Grand Wizard of the Knights of the Ku Klux Klan, was campaigning for a seat in Jefferson Parish's 81st House District. He might lose, not because of his past, but because people questioned whether he had lived long enough in the area before entering the race.

It was time to leave the city for the open space.

There was a traffic jam out of New Orleans, backed up behind a three-storey house travelling West on a flat-bed lorry. Three men stood on its roof, lifting traffic lights over the chimney.

I turned off the main road in Baton Rouge and drove like a lunatic, breaking speed limits through a series of parking lots the size of Spain, to try and beat the house to the Dunkin' Donuts crossroads. But the police were stopping traffic, and I wound up behind the house's garage, which was travelling separately on the back of a smaller truck.

Fortunately the house and its garage turned off at the next corner. I kept on driving down Interstate 10.

Just outside Gator-Mix Cement in Opelousas I finally managed to ease around the edge of my automatic zip-lock safety belt enough to tune the radio to the local Cajun station ... 'WAH WAH WAH something something Two step de L'anse à Paille WAH WAH'. I missed out Mulate's in Breaux Bridge, The World's Most Famous Cajun Restaurant, keeping it in reserve, and drove on through Eunice, Louisiana's Prairie Cajun Capital, to Mamou, home of world-famous Fred's Lounge.

Fred's is a bar built like a public lavatory. Every Saturday morning at 9.00 for the past forty-three years, they have been broadcasting a live Cajun music radio show, and throwing cornmeal down on the bar room floor to mop up the Michelob and Bud and make it smooth enough to dance the two-step or the Texan one-step on.

When I drove into Mamou it was still a little early for Fred's, but things were hopping at Jeff's Coffee House. The tables were full of men wearing checked shirts and truckers' hats and talking French and English – the kind of French and English they talk in Louisiana.

'We talk more pure French here t'an t'ey do in Breaux Bridge,' said one of the Fontenot brothers. 'Over t'ere t'ey don' talk lak us – t'ey bin here longer. Last t'ing t'at was put in t'e pot, t'at was us. Hey – tu parles Cajun? Tu es après manger un 'tit?'

There were baking-powder biscuits for breakfast, and good raunchy bacon tasting strongly of pig; chilli peppers soaked in bottles of vinegar on the tables. On the board: 'Today's Specials $3.75 – Smothered Porkchops, Tasso & Sausage Picante, corn, fried okra, donut'. Or you could have the gumbo/chicken and sausage and a slice of sweet dough pie. I had some of the pie, made with cream and cinnamon and sweet potatoes, and coffee, black as David Duke's past.

Fred's had a nice lived-in feel to it: garlic breath and stale beer and

the smell of a communal bag of warm boudin that was sitting on the bar.

Sue, Fred's ex-wife, was there, since remarried but still running the bar as a business interest; and his sister Essie, in the chair where she has been sitting every Saturday morning for twenty-five years, with her leg up on a stool since she had the tumour removed from her spine a few years ago. 'I got news for you, Doc,' she is reputed to have said to the doctor who told her she'd never walk again. 'I'll *dance* again!'

She's a survivor, is Essie. But then they all are here – goers and stayers and survivors – the place was full of unemployed oil workers and characters with Stories to Tell. 'If I was a writer ...' they said, or 'My life would make a book ...'

A man in his early fifties, with GEORGE spelled out in brass on his cowboy belt, asked me to dance. 'It's bad now and getting badder, chère. Lucky we grow beautiful rice down here. Rice done keep us up.'

I was invited to come to Mamou for Mardi Gras. Twenty thousand people come to dance all day in the street to a band playing on the back of a flat-bed truck. Masked men on horses gallop out in the morning, stopping at farms across the country, asking '*Voulez-vous recevoir les Mardi Gras?*' And if you do, they sing the Mardi Gras song and then demand that you give them 'une 'tite poule grasse' so they can make 'un gumbo gras'. The ill-fated chicken gets chased through the stubble, caught and thrown onto a pile of others with its neck wrung.

'All t'e girls get together to mek t'at big gumbo. T'ey brings t'eir own roux an' adds it to t'e pot. Everyone gets to eat, no charge. Y'awl come back now, chère, eat all t'e gumbo, dance all you want.' Regrettably, I had other plans.

New Iberia is a small sprawling town between Mamou and New Orleans. In the old part, where the Spanish moss hangs thickest on the banks of Bayou Teche, is a beautifully proportioned 1834 manor house. Shadows on the Teche; even its name sounds like the ghosts of summer nights. Thanks to one man, it has not been swagged and ruched into the Disney parody of Scarlett's Tara that is the fate of so many of the South's antebellum homes.

Weeks Hall was one of those tragic little eccentrics – heavy drinkers, men of genius, homosexuals – that rise every so often out of the swamps and the palmetto groves of the Old South's glorious, crumbling past. He abandoned his impoverished aristocratic background in Louisiana to study art in Paris in the early years of this century. The playwright Sherwood Anderson recalled when he returned: unpredictable, incapable of doing anything healthy, he would get blind drunk, pick fights with anyone bigger than himself, insult women.

Then in the early 1920s Weeks Hall inherited an unexpected fortune that enabled him to begin restoring his great grandfather's old plantation home. The windfall changed his life. Until his death in 1958, he poured all his energy into Shadows on the Teche, to revive its former beauty and its tradition of hospitality. He became a famous host: such celebrities of the time as D.W. Griffith, Cecil B. De Mille, Henry Miller, H.L. Mencken, among many others, were all guests. When he died, he passed on his life's work to the US National Trust.

In the days before Weeks Hall came into his legacy, he was dominated by a wealthy dragon of an aunt, Patty Torian, whose only concession to his poverty was an occasional invitation to attend one of the sumptuous Creole dinners she often gave.

First there would be 'Sazerac' cocktails – a measure of bourbon, a half-measure of vermouth, a dash of orange bitters, all shaken with crushed ice and poured into heavy, chilled glasses with a few drops of absinthe – on and on until guests were left weak-willed and legless, or frenzied with hunger. One woman remembered eating a banana first before attending any of Mrs Torian's affairs.

When the uninitiated had despaired of ever soaking up the alcohol with anything more solid than a twist of lemon, the feast would arrive. A great fish simmered in a positively Mediterranean broth of olive oil and garlic, green peppers, tomatoes, thyme and parsley and saffron; boiled and hotly spiced Louisiana crawfish on a big platter; a wickedly creamy omelette of sweetbreads (ordinary Americans still ate offal then); perhaps some red snapper cooked in an intricate Creole sauce. And almost always there would be Aunt Patty's favourite 'daube glacée', rich jellied beef laced with crushed peppercorns, bay leaf and cloves.

Those were the days when caution and gastronomy did not sit down together at the same table.

Aunt Patty would eat doggedly and greedily, oblivious of her guests' waning appetites. She worked through course after course, one of them wrote, 'with the precision of a surgeon'.

Mrs Torian's obsessive interest in food is evident in Shadows' extensive files of her recipes. There are at least eight for the sugary pastry fritters called 'oreilles de cochon'. There is a letter to her from Taxco, in Mexico, with a recipe for 'Rice à la Valenciana'. There are six gingham-bound cloth cookery books on whose covers are naive watercolour paintings of her various black cooks. Their names – 'Toinette and Memene, Tante Calixte and Mauricia, Raphaele and Tante Melanie and Carmelita – reveal their West Indian slave roots even more than do their recipes for pickled pigs' feet and fermented pineapple 'Bière Creole'.

From the start, those black cooks with their Indian ways with chillies and spices made the local dialects sing. Even the black longshoremen gave English a swing that had the Caribbean in every syllable. *Streamin'* meant a boat going upriver. *Slicin' time* was saving time. *Hip the jive* was to be careful of incautious talk.

The women selling hot lunches and pies along the wharves were *bucket women* or *pan ladies* because they sold their wares from buckets, huge flat pans or baskets. Meat was *bullneck*, bread pudding *heavy devil*, doughnuts *elephant ears*; lunch for a longshoreman might be a *stage plank* (a flat ginger cake) and a dipper of water.

Here is a recipe for Creole Coffee from one of Mrs Torian's cooks (typed neatly into a gingham cookery book):

> Jess wait..to you I'm goin to shoh..
> Buy fresh-pawched coffee at coffee stoh
> Put three big spoon in drip', you knoh
> Not percolate..oh..no, no..
> Poh boil'n water by leetle floh
> And hear de drops fall..dep..dep..slow..slow
> Nah..dreenk eet hot as 'down Beloh'
> As black as davils in a row
> As sweet as engels..Nah..you knoh
> Meck 'Creole Café' good..for shoh.

When Weeks Hall began to restore Shadows, Aunt Patty moved in – crippled and blind by then, but still a force. He organized the house around her, and typed an extraordinarily detailed set of instructions to his servants, complete with black and white photographs.

'Iced tea will be used far more than wines. At lunch, serve always in summer. Add a finger of ginger-ale to each glass, & a very little crushed fresh mint. It is not made *too* sweet.'

When Weeks Hall's grandfather died in 1834, the Old South was at its peak. There is a story of a plantation owner, Gabriel Valcour Aimé, so rich he was known as the Louis XIV of Louisiana. Bragging to a gourmet friend in New Orleans one day, he promised him a dinner 'that you yourself will admit is perfect, every item from my own plantation'.

'I do not doubt that you can supply a dinner from your land,' said the epicure. 'But a perfect meal – impossible.'

They wagered $10,000.

Valcour Aimé served his guest dishes of terrapin, shrimp and crab, snipe and quail, breasts of wild duck, salad, exotic fruit; then coffee, cigars and wine.

'What say you?' asked the host.

'The dinner was indeed perfect. But I think you lose,' answered the New Orleans man. 'For no man can supply me with bananas, coffee and tobacco grown in Louisiana.'

Then Valcour Aimé showed him the conservatories.

The ghost of this grander South haunts the pages of Weeks Hall's severe little 1939 edict. After a 'light supper' of sherry, turtle soup, escalloped oysters, creamed mushrooms, round potatoes, salad, frozen Creole cream cheese with lady fingers and coffee, he recommended that a three-shelf cake stand be brought in with the port. On it:

(1) TOP shelf: *Always* small plates: Sheffield gadroon-edged or china; cocktail napkins; butter knives
(2) MIDDLE shelf: *Always* the three shell compartment for spreads, preserves, cheeses etc
(3) BOTTOM shelf: Either Sheffield biscuit box for wholewheat crackers, or Sheffield-edged plate for whole-wheat crackers or cakes.
The middle three-compartment dish might contain: roquefort paste, strawberry preserves, almonds, small dried herrings, ripe olives, Bar le Duc, sharp cheddar, pickled kumquats, pecans, dry crisp bacon, guava jelly, Cheddar.
On the bottom plate were: hot breads, covered with a napkin, sliced layer cake, raisin bread cut thin, bacon twisted in biscuit dough, little hot buttered biscuits, Oreilles de Cochon, Tidewater Thin cookies.

Aunt Patty had taught her nephew well.

SEVEN

Back in New Orleans the Mardi Gras spirit was picking up momentum with block parties and drinks parties and more parades – twice, three times a day. The old timers in Miss Mae's, been there so long they're like fungus growing off the bar, had their hangovers disturbed by the overflow from a college kids' party opposite.

The St Charles streetcar clanged and rumbled its way amiably through New Orleans' Garden District. Flags hung outside some of the houses (beautiful Greek Revival buildings that made the White House look self-effacing), homes of the ex-kings of Mardi Gras krewes.

On the Sunday before Mardi Gras I got to flash credit cards at twenty paces with these tropic zone aristocrats. They like to take their families for brunch at Commander's Palace, to have Mimosa cocktails and 'Our World Famous Garlic Bread Topped with Romano Cheese' (in Louisiana I kept feeling that the whole world had read some book I'd never heard of. That book was world-famous too) and turtle soup, with big chunks of turtle meat floating up when you dig your spoon in. They eat 'Eggs Sardou' – a cushion of creamy spinach sitting on an artichoke bottom, all of it covered in nutmeggy bechamel. You can taste the money: the trout drowned in pecans and butter; even the bread pudding had been made into a raisin-studded soufflé with rum sauce.

The men at Commander's were Gatsbys without the tragedy, Gatsbys twenty years on, working on their first cholesterol-induced heart attack. The women were working on their charities and their cellulite.

Mr Williams had been up half the night cooking the five kinds of pies he was selling from a table in the French Market. They are his mother's recipes – she was cook and pastry-maker to a rich French Creole family called Colomb.

'Ahm Seventh Day Adventist, hon', can't staht til aftah sundown on Satiday. Bin doin' it toidy-five yeahs now – useta sell'em up an' down the wharves on the riverfront. Fifteen cents each educated mah kids.'

Pecan and sweet potato are the city's favourites, creamy and not too sweet, with crisp, feathery crusts.

'Nobody tops this crust,' said Clement Williams. 'Even Brennan's (the family that owns Commander's) sends out to buy from me. Secret is ah use vegetable shortenin', cause animal fat jes' don't hold up. An' mah wife cook her own fillin' – put in good fillin', it jes' melt in yo' mouth.'

New Orleans may be one of the 'Most eatin' places in the US', but with the oil slump and the port no longer humming, Mr Williams' business has been dropping off. On Mardi Gras he would be pushing his cart around for the extra cash. 'Ah'll tell you why you can't miss me, hon', ah'm the only person sellin' homemade pies. Bin that way fah toidy-fah yeahs. Ah'll be lookin' fah you, Mizz Leslie!'

That night I stood for four hours on Canal Street watching the Bacchus parade with its giant Bacchusaurus float, warming my hands on 'po'boy' sandwiches 'wit' everyting on 'em' from Mother's in Poydras Street. The temperature had dropped another fifteen degrees, but the lords of the city, hidden behind pagan Ku Klux Klan-style masks, kept throwing beads and doubloons, and we kept chanting 'Throw me somethin', mistah'. I was plugged into the primitive parade beat now with everybody else.

TOURIST SHOT TO DEATH BY MUGGER AFTER PARADE ran a headline the next day in the *Times-Picayune*. You get this buzz all the time in America; that old 'it could have been me' shiver down your spine. After a while you need a bigger and bigger fix.

EIGHT

The Proteus Ball reminded me that I was living in Scarlett O'Hara land. Beaux and belles and plantation manners; dewy debutantes in Ice Queen tiaras and virginal gowns like christening robes on the arms of masked men in King Arthur doublets; engraved 'call-out' invitations: you got the privilege of dancing with one of the krewe members; it was a great honour to receive one – non-exchangeable. It made me feel like one of the wicked stepsisters at Cinderella's ball. I just knew the glass slipper would never fit.

Here is the tableau: first the fillies paraded, then everyone stood for the Queen of Proteus. People said later, 'You didn't stand for the Queen – you would stand for your *own* Queen wouldn't you?' 'Well . . .' I said.

Then the veils screening the stage slowly parted to reveal: the King and Queen of Proteus standing in a giant clam shell! Then the really lucky people, all the prime sirloin of N.O. Society, queued up to kneel and receive the Protean blessing. The band played 'Chicago, Chicago – it's my kind of town!' and everyone danced.

An ex-Cinderella wired into all the society circuits, forty-year-old veteran of many Mardi Gras balls, voiced her cynicism for the events. 'Oh yeah,' she said, biting the hand that bred her. 'All those little ole balls are pretty dumb. But I still like the night parades with their torchons, and the truck parades where Mom and Pop and the kids get together to decorate a neighbour's truck. Too many balls I've gone to, honey, where the men stumble outta the back room aftah drinkin' an' shootin' craps. There you ah in your $600 dress, waitin' fah romance [she said roMAyance, her milk-chocolate voice dragging three syllables out of the two], waitin' fah champagne breakfast aftah the ball. An' all your Prince Charmin' wants to do is spew up an' sleep.'

Later I went to Phillip's Bar, where the down-and-outers were drinking fruit gelatine laced with pure alcohol. Called them Jello Shots, the alkie's cocktail, so viscous they could have been hepatitis injections. Great with grits.

NINE

On Mardi Gras morning the sky was overcast and the wind down Esplanade blew straight from Alaska. The bus into town got stuck behind 350 trucks filled with people wearing foam hats in the shape of alligators and crawfish; some were dressed as bottles of Tabasco. A motorcycle policeman stopped to pick up a string of fake pearls and loop them over his bike.

The joyful, jumping, sexy jazz of the Zulu parade could be heard long before the first blacked-up black man appeared wearing a grass skirt and throwing silver-painted coconuts and plastic spears. The crowd was going wild for these most prized Mardi Gras souvenirs: you had to have murder in your soul and the skill of a basketball player to catch a coconut.

I saw Mr Williams from a distance and waved, but lost him behind Snow White and the Seven Dwarves.

The phwat phwat of the horns and the long whoonsh of the saxophones got your toes tapping. I thought of Aunt Helen saying, 'We second-lined, *ah* second-lined – when you get that ole time jazz, your body jes' gets more into it.'

Everywhere were bare bosoms and bellies and buttocks.

I went to the Central Grocery Store on Decatur Street for lunch, where they were selling food from a booth set up across the door.

The Central Grocery stocked all the flavours of Louisiana – chicory coffee, wild rice and popcorn rice, Yogi crab and shrimp boil (the best), a shelf of hot sauces – but the aroma was pure Neapolitan back street. Their Muffelatta sandwiches were round, dense loaves split in half crosswise, then bathed in olive oil and stuffed with a moist salad of garlicky salami, chopped olives, slices of sweet peppers, onions and

pickled cauliflower. In Italy they would call it *pan bagnat*, in Nice *pain baigné* – like salade niçoise in a giant hamburger bun. The salad juice ran down my chin and dropped into my 'Go' cup of bourbon.

The Garden District doors had tasteful woven wreaths in subdued Mardi Gras colours, as tasteful as purple, lime green and gold could be. Families lined the streets along Canal and St Charles, waiting for the next parade and keeping the kids quiet with Keep Kool boxes stuffed with food. Down Bourbon Street they kept on shouting 'SHOW YOUR TITS, SHOW YOUR TITS' and taking fifteen-cent whiffs of laughing gas.

That night I returned to the Mardi Gras madness of the French Quarter and the tourists staggering from one smouldering bar to the next, in search of more fun and sin and degradation. It wasn't hard to find; you just had to stand still long enough.

At midnight everything stopped. I caught a cab in Jackson Square as all the crystal coaches started to turn back into pumpkins, just before a phalanx of mounted policemen began to sweep up the dregs of humanity down Bourbon Street; in time to see the Lucky Dog man pushing his six-foot hot dog home down Decatur, as the GIRLS GIRLS GIRLS LIMITED sign above him went dark, bulb by flashing neon bulb.

TEN

The next morning all the dropped beads and crushed beer cans were gone from the gutters. Mardi Gras had been swept up: the streets were as echoing as an empty whisky bottle. I left Hangover City and headed out to the gator-stompin', crawfish-eatin' bayous of southern Louisiana.

'We use a lotta swamp bay in the cookin' here,' said the owner of the Indian Catfish House at Honey Island Swamp.

'Choctaw Indians used to eat the fan palm – base tastes like celery. Still good survival food to remember if you ever lost inna swamp.'

I had a choice of alligator étouffée or fried catfish and hushpuppies for lunch. Or frogs' legs. Sometimes they go frogging here on hot and humid swamp nights. Catch croakers big as kittens, the meaty legs – looking disturbingly like human limbs – floured and fried, tasting of sweetest chicken.

'Gotta watch out for them ole water moccasins though. But gators won't hurcha – 'less you try an' pettem!'

Driving down Bayou Lafourche you notice the signs first: FOR SALE: HOGS HEAD CHEESE; HAVE YOU HUGGED YOUR WIFE TODAY?; THE FAMILY THAT PRAYS TOGETHER STAYS TOGETHER; COOTER'S LIVE MUSIC AND DANCING; PROPER DRESS AND PICTURE ID REQUIRED. Then the names on the mailboxes: Le Blanc, Thibodeaux, Broussard, Guitry, Cheramie.

Daisy Guitry worked for Cote Blanche Productions (or *was* Cote Blanche, in the absence of its founder), a small film and Cajun mail-order company in Cut Off. Glenn Pitre, a Harvard film graduate, started making films in Cajun French in his home town; put an ad in the local paper: 'Come Be in a Movie'. When the films were shown locally people came whose last trip to the cinema had been to see *Citizen Kane*. An old woman in one of the cinemas said it was the most popcorn she ever sold. Glenn's Cajun French films outsold *Star Wars*.

When Daisy was in school, kids were expelled if they spoke French in class. Her mother and father only got to third grade because of the language barrier.

'But we've always bin French here. Started when people on the coast lost everything in a bad hurricane in 1893. They floated their houses up the bayou to here and then couldn't even afford a coat of coloured paint for 'em. So everything was painted white. Riverboat captains called the area Cote Blanche ever since on account o' that.'

Daisy's father had been out in his boat collecting oysters that morning – illegal to take farmed ones, but these were wild. Or so he said. We dipped them in his homemade hot sauce and swallowed them, cool as beer. There was corn soup then, with the taste of pickled pork. They use pickled pork here where other places might use beef. Daisy had browned an onion in oil for the soup, added a little homemade tomato sauce, some potatoes, whole cobs of corn in each bowl.

She laughed. 'Jes' real simple when ah think y'awl a cookery writer. Kinda vegetable gumbo. Ah doubt you'd find a household in the area goes a week without some kind of gumbo.' She made hers with shrimp, rice, hard-boiled eggs, oysters, spicy smoked sausage and a pinch of filé – but not so much that it thickened the soup like bayou mud.

'An' you gotta have potato salad wit gumbo. It's jes' one o' those things you gotta do.'

Loulan Pitre, Glenn's father, is famous for his cooking around here. When he and Robert Duvall were in Glenn's Cannes entry film *Belizaire the Cajun*, all Duvall wanted to do was eat Loulan's food. 'Had me in the kitchen teachin' big high-class chefs at Patout's in New Iberia how to cook lima beans. Beans! An' them serving dishes so fancy – man, I thought they was jes' starters.'

He said his beans were easy: first you made a light roux, then you added chopped onions, parsley, spring onions, salt, pepper, garlic (but not too much, unless it was the last meal of the day), and you cooked those beans down until they were tender. 'Same as we do with cabbage for New Year's, 'cept then we use salt pork. Cabbage is lucky for New Year's, y'know? 'Cause it's green like greenbacks. You break it up with oil and salt pork, then you jes' smother that sucker down.'

They eat everything over rice in southern Louisiana – 'Hell, we probably eat bread over rice!' – and not as spicy as around Lafayette. At Christmas they have 'dirty rice' (fried rice with shrimp and onion), gumbo, ham and candied yams, baked turkey with rice dressing, and melting orange-scented shortbread filled with walnuts and dusted with icing sugar. They call them cocones, or sandies, because of the texture.

Loulan taught Robert Duvall how to make Fish Court Bouillon (now a big hit in Hollywood). 'Redfish is best, but they limit them now, people fished 'em out so much for that blackened stuff. But anything is good long as it ain't bony.'

Duvall's wife learned to make 'Freeco', with potatoes cubed and sautéed in oil, then simmered with onions, shredded beef, a little water. 'I kep' tellin' her how to do it, finally she said, "I see Lou – what you're saying is: first you burn it, then you boil it." ' I knew the origins of this dish better than Loulan did. In French-speaking Canada they call it 'Fricou' and make it with meat, potatoes and dumplings, seasoned with a big bunch of summer savoury stuck upside down into the simmering stew, the stems held by the weight of the pot's iron lid.

Robert Duvall keeps coming back. They say around here that once you taste that bayou water, you can't stay away from it. And it is true that Cajun families are miserable when separated; the students fret when they must leave to go to university.

They sent me to Dufrene's Bakery in Golden Meadow to buy sandies and custard tarts and the best French bread on Bayou Lafourche. I waited next to a fisherman named Jasper Cheramie. He told me how to make 'popcorn' shrimp. 'You dip 'em in t'at hot Cajun mustard an' t'en you fry 'em in real hot oil. Or you can make dirty rice wit' 'em, y'know? You let t'ose lil shrimp cook in fat till t'ey turns red an' t'e water runs out, t'en lettem stick an' scrape t'e pan an' stir in t'e rice.'

They told me you gotta eat at K-Paul's, and I never did. But I talked to Paul's brother, I drank jelly shots at Phillip's Bar and second-lined down Decatur. I saw the Zulu boat come in and watched the sun go down over the Gulf of Mexico. And no one can ever tell me again, you shoulda bin here last week; at least not in New Orleans. But perhaps in Mamou.

RECIPES

First You Burn It, Then You Boil It

Roux: Every Louisiana cookery book begins, 'First you make a roux.'

Basically a roux is flour browned in fat – butter in the case of Creoles, oil, lard or bacon drippings in Cajun dishes. Cajuns use oil because it can be cooked longer without burning, and the essence of their roux is the long, slow cooking which breaks down flour molecules and gives a characteristic toasted walnut flavour.

The Cajun prelude to cooking almost everything owes much to the Spanish 'sofregit', in which herbs and aromatic vegetables are finely chopped and simmered in oil before you add meat or fish. In Louisiana the herbs are thyme, bay leaves, parsley; the vegetables, onions (both white and spring green), garlic, celery and sweet green peppers.

This is the point of departure for most Cajun recipes, and not a few Creole ones. Joints of chicken, rabbit, or wild duck may be browned first in the oil, with an *andouille*, or smoked sausage, if the dish is to be a gumbo; or with crushed tomatoes (simmered slowly until their liquid evaporates), bay leaves, thyme and lots of cayenne for a *sauce piquante*. More or less liquid can be added – water, wine or beer – to transform the base into courtbouillon or *étouffée*. In a classic Cajun *étouffée*, the yellow 'fat' from crawfish heads is melted with the oil in the roux, tomatoes cooked down with it, and the fleshy crawfish tails added at the last minute.

Filé Powder: Choctaw Indians of the Louisiana swamps collected, dried and ground sassafras leaves to make filé powder. It is used mainly to thicken gumbos, added at the last minute and sparingly (not least because of its high cost). Too much will turn the gumbo into glue. Its presence in a gumbo is a possible clue to that thick soup's mysterious name: the Choctaw word for sassafras is *kombo*.

Okra is used in gumbos where filé is absent for its earthy flavour as well as its thickening properties. Unlike filé, it should be added in time for its peculiar sticky sap to bind the sauce. Gumbo may have another derivation: 'guin-gombo' is an African word for okra.

Spices: Both cayenne and Louisiana hot sauces add piquancy, cayenne at the beginning with the other aromatics, hot sauce as a last-minute spice. Tabasco is perhaps the best sauce, as it contains only vinegar and hot Louisiana chillies aged in salt – giving the purest 'bite'.

CHICKEN AND SEAFOOD GUMBO WITH OKRA

(serves 6)

Serve with rice and hushpuppies or cornmeal muffins. You may substitute rabbit, wild duck or squirrel for the chicken.

1 lb/500 g fresh raw shrimps in their shells
1 onion stuck with 6 cloves
2 bay leaves
2 garlic cloves
pinch of thyme
6 tbsp vegetable oil
1 free-range chicken, cut into 8–10 pieces
½ lb/250 g smoked sausage (Polish is good)
5 tbsp plain white flour
1 large onion, finely chopped
2 sticks of celery, chopped
1 green pepper, cored and coarsely chopped
3 garlic cloves, finely chopped
1 lb/500 g fresh okra, trimmed
several sprigs fresh thyme, or 1 tsp dried
1 tsp Tabasco or cayenne pepper
2 bay leaves
1 tsp salt plus extra to taste
½ tsp allspice
(optional) 1 dozen oysters, or mussels, in the shell
3–4 spring (green) onions, finely sliced crosswise

(1) Shell and clean the shrimps, and put the shells in a pan with the least meaty bits of chicken, the cloved onion and the seasoning. Cover with 3 pt/1.7 l water. Bring to a low boil, simmer 30 minutes and strain. Heat 6 tbsp of oil in a large heavy pot and brown the chicken and sausage on all sides. Lift out with a slotted spoon and reserve.

(2) In a separate frying pan, heat the remaining 2 tbsp of oil and cook the onions, celery and garlic until the onions are golden. Reheat the oil in the first pan (making sure you still have over 4 tbsp left), add the flour and stir constantly over low heat until the roux turns a deep caramel brown, scraping the pan well and adjusting the heat so the roux does not burn. Slowly pour in a teacup of hot water, stirring to stop lumps forming, then add all remaining ingredients (except shrimps, okra, oysters and spring onions) with 2½ pt/1.5 l shrimp stock. Bring to a low boil and simmer for 1 hour.

(3) 30 minutes before the end of cooking, add the okra and shrimps, and 20 minutes later open the oysters and add them with their liquid. If the liquid in the pot is too thin – it should be quite thick: running rather than standing, like a thin stew rather than a thick soup – add a pinch of filé powder. Serve from the pot with the spring onion scattered over the top.

GUMBO Z'HERBES

(serves 8)

A piquant, deep-green, creamy soup with smoky depths.

6 tbsp butter or bacon fat
1 medium onion, finely chopped
2 garlic cloves, finely chopped
1 green pepper, cored and finely chopped
2 rounded tbsp flour
2 pt/1.25 l strong homemade stock/broth
1 lb/500 g fresh spinach, washed well and trimmed
1 lb/500 g spring or collard greens, washed well and trimmed
1 tsp sugar
1 lb/500 g pickled pork*, drained, rinsed and chopped
salt (about 1 tsp), ½ tsp nutmeg, lots of black pepper

(1) Melt the butter in a large, heavy saucepan and soften the onions, green pepper and garlic in it. Stir in the flour until it is lightly browned and add the stock a little at a time. Add the greens and sugar, cover and simmer 10 minutes.

(2) Purée the greens and return to the pot with the pickled pork, simmering for another hour, or until mixture has reduced to a thick, creamy purée. Add seasonings about 10 minutes before the end of cooking. Serve with hot buttered baking-powder biscuits and lots of Dixie Beer.

LOUISIANA PICKLED PORK

Used in all dried-bean dishes, and to add punch to stewed turnip greens. This is nothing to do with the English version, which is salted to preserve it.

1 lb/ 500 g fleshy pork spare ribs, chopped in 2–3 in/5–8 cm chunks
2–3 tbsp coarse salt
2 tsp black peppercorns, crushed
1 dried bay leaf, crumbled
4 hot red chillies, chopped
enough cider vinegar to cover (about ¾ pt/400 ml)

Put the ribs in a bowl and sprinkle with spices. Pour over the vinegar, cover tightly and refrigerate for 24–48 hours.

If you don't have time to wait for the pork to marinate, and still want to gain its character in a bean dish, even 2–3 hours' soaking in vinegar and spices will add a certain Louisiana flair.

Bread, Rice and True Grits

Louisiana bread is chewy, crusty and shaped like a small submarine.

They will tell you in New Orleans that *po'boys* – French loaves as long as arms, filled with everything from oysters to meatballs, were invented during the 1920s streetcar strike, and used to cost a nickel.

Real *oyster loaves*, if you can find them, are survivors of those nickelodeon days. The loaves are halved lengthwise, hollowed out and brushed with melted garlic butter, then baked a crisp brown in the oven. Freshly shucked oysters are fried after being dipped in beaten egg and the reserved crumbs. Finally, the oysters and the two halves of warm bread are sandwiched together, perhaps with a little more melted butter, some salt and Tabasco, a few chopped olives and pickles.

Weeks Hall used to call po'boys 'peace-makers', because errant husbands would stop at a café after a late-night binge and bring one home – very hot and very fresh – to their wives. 'The effect of these somewhat tangible manifestations of guilt had to bee nicely calculated,' he said. 'Everything hung upon the wife's appetite.'

BREAD PUDDING WITH MERINGUE TOPPING

(serves 6)

Stale bread is turned into *bread pudding* – Austin Leslie baked his slowly, taking it out after the first hour to beat it. An outrageously rich old-fashioned pudding, especially good with the rum or whisky sauce on page 39.

9 fl oz/250 ml thick cream
18 fl oz/500 ml milk
4 tbsp dark rum
1 scraped vanilla pod/bean (save the seeds for meringue)
3–4 oz/90–125 g stale French bread, broken up
4 oz/125 g stick butter
3 egg yolks
6 oz/180 g white sugar
2 apples, coarsely chopped
2½ oz/75 g raisins
juice and grated zest of 1 lemon

Meringue
5 egg whites
5 oz/150 g icing sugar
scraped seeds from 1 vanilla pod/bean

(1) Preheat oven to 350°F/175°C/gas mark 4. Heat the cream and milk with the vanilla pod until just below boiling, remove from heat and leave to steep for 30 minutes. Remove pod and pour milk over bread. Lift bread out when soft and put in a greased baking dish (breaking the bread into even smaller pieces). Beat together butter and sugar, and when smooth and light, beat in liquids. Stir fruit and butter/egg mixture into bread. Bake for 1 hour and allow to cool.
(2) Preheat oven to 375°F/190°C/gas mark 5. Beat the egg whites until they are stiff, then gradually beat in the sugar and vanilla seeds. Spread the meringue over the pudding to cover completely. Bake 10–15 minutes until meringue is well browned. Serve warm.

BREAD PUDDING SOUFFLÉ WITH WHISKY OR RUM SAUCE

(serves 6)

This is a lower-cholesterol version of the Commander's Palace soufflé.

Base of soufflé
2 tbsp plus 1 tsp plain white flour
¼ pt/150 ml milk
2 oz/60 g plus 1 tbsp white sugar
4 whole eggs plus 2 egg whites (save extra yolks for sauce)
1 tsp vanilla essence
3 tbsp bourbon or rum
grated zest of 1 lemon
handful of raisins
3 oz/90 g (about 1 small loaf) stale French bread, soaked in water, squeezed out and crumbled
½ tsp cinnamon
icing sugar to finish

Whisky or rum sauce
2 egg yolks
2 oz/60 g white sugar
juice of 1 lemon
5 fl oz/150 ml bourbon or rum
2 fl oz/60 ml water

(1) Preheat oven to 200°C/400°F/gas mark 6. Butter a 2½ pt/5 cup soufflé dish* and sprinkle with sugar to give the soufflé a crisp crust.

(2) Lightly whisk together the flour and milk until smooth, then whisk in sugar. Bring to a boil in a saucepan over medium heat, continuing to beat (to prevent lumps). After 30 seconds, remove from heat and beat for another minute.

(3) Separate the eggs one by one, dropping the whites into a large clean bowl, and beating the yolks into the flour mixture (except for the last two).

(4) Whisk egg whites stiff, adding a pinch of salt and 1 tbsp sugar halfway through. Mix remaining base ingredients into yolks. Add a quarter of the whites to lighten it, then fold the remaining whites in with a metal spoon and pour into the dish. (At this point, if necessary, the soufflé can stand for about an hour without falling.) Place the dish at the bottom of the oven and turn down the heat to 375°F/190°C/gas mark 5. After 20 minutes, sprinkle the top liberally with icing sugar and continue cooking for another 15 minutes.

(5) To make the sauce, boil the alcohol, sugar, lemon juice and water in a small pan for several minutes, then pour slowly into the eggs while beating vigorously. Pour the sauce back into the pan over very low heat and continue whisking until it begins to thicken. Immediately remove from heat. Serve the soufflé as soon as it comes from the oven, with a little sauce poured over each portion.

*The soufflé mixture can be poured into individual soufflé dishes as they do at Commander's.

Cornmeal began as the native Indians' staple. Baked into pan breads and skillet cakes, it fed farmers; dried corn fed their livestock, and the dried cornshucks – plaited – were used to weave chair seats, hats and mule collars. It is still the poor man's French bread – New Orleans' back-o'-town food in black family cafés.

Hardened Louisiana veterans eat hominy grits (boiled, ground maize kernels) for breakfast, unadulterated, with a little melted butter (and a lot of black coffee) to sluice everything down. They are best with lashings of butter and grated cheese stirred in off the heat when the grits have finished cooking. A favourite Creole combination for a festive brunch is grits and *grillades* – thin squares of beef pounded flat, dredged in flour, salt and pepper, browned in oil quickly, and finally simmered in a coarse, vivid, tomato sauce made with chopped celery, green peppers, garlic (lots) and onions.

Leftover grits can be sliced and deep-fried the next day and served under stews and fricassees, or brushed with a little oil and chargrilled (the best, the *only* way to eat grits, I would say, not being a Southerner) so they are crunchy and smoky outside and creamy within.

HUSHPUPPIES/CORN FRITTERS
(makes 6–8 as a side dish)
A recipe based on a 1908 one from Avery Island, where Tabasco sauce is made. Delicious with fried fish, shrimp étouffée or jambalaya.

1½ cups plain white flour
2 tsp baking powder
1 tsp salt
2 medium eggs, beaten
5 tbsp milk
1 tsp Tabasco sauce
1 tbsp melted bacon fat or butter
2 cups tinned corn niblets, drained, or 6 ears of fresh, grated fat for deep-frying

(1) Sift together the flour, baking powder and salt. Beat the eggs with the milk, Tabasco and fat. Add the flour a little at a time and then stir in the corn.
(2) Heat the fat to 365–375°F/190°C/gas mark 5, or until a chunk of bread turns brown in about 60 seconds. Drop the corn batter in by spoonfuls and fry for 3–4 minutes, turning once. Serve while still warm.

CORNMEAL AND BACON MUFFINS
(makes 8–12 depending on size of pan)
Serve hot and buttered with a main course (great with Hoppin' John, page 43) – and for breakfast with smoky sausages.

¼ lb/125 g streaky smoked bacon, coarsely chopped
4½ oz/140 g plain white flour
1 tbsp baking powder
4½ oz/140 g plus a little extra fine yellow or white cornmeal
pinch of salt
2 tsp sugar
1 egg, beaten
½ pt/300 ml milk
3 tbsp butter or bacon fat, melted

(1) Preheat oven to 425°F/220°C/gas mark 7. Fry the bacon until starting to crisp and use the rendered fat to grease either an American muffin or English 'fairy cake' tin. Dust the pan with the extra cornmeal and heat it for at least 10 minutes before baking to crisp the muffins.

(2) Sift together flour and baking powder and stir in all remaining ingredients, including the bacon, mixing well. Fill the muffin tins two-thirds full and bake for 20–25 minutes until golden brown and cooked through.

Variations: Soften 1 large chopped apple in the melted butter and stir into the muffin mix; or 3 finely chopped jalapeno chillies, for a spicier touch. Or pour the batter into a greased loaf pan and slice it like bread – serve buttered with maple syrup poured over for breakfast.

BAKING-POWDER BISCUITS
(makes 12)

In Louisiana these are served with chicken and ribs in the same places you find cornbread. The dough may also be rolled out and used as a crust on beef or chicken stews. Cook the stew as usual, then slip the biscuit dough on top – pinching it around the edges to seal – and bake it for 15 minutes in a 450°F/230°C/gas mark 8 oven.

The less you handle the biscuits the lighter they will be.

12 oz/350 g plain white flour
4 tsp baking powder
½ tsp salt
1 tbsp sugar
4½ tsp butter, 4½ tsp shortening/Crisco
about 4½ fl oz/125 ml/8 tbsp milk

(1) Preheat oven to 450°F/230°C/gas mark 8. Grease a metal baking tray. Sift together the flour and baking powder into a bowl. Stir in the salt and sugar and cut in the fat with a knife or pastry cutter. Sprinkle over the milk a little at a time, stirring it in just enough to make the flour stick together. Roll into a ball and knead lightly.

(2) Flour a work surface and roll out the dough to about ¾ in/1.5 cm. Cut circles in it with a 2 in/5 cm cutter. Lay the dough on the baking sheet and bake in the oven for 15 minutes, or until pale gold and well risen. Serve hot with butter.

Rice

The Louisiana paddies stretch out flat and shimmering as a mirage around the town of Mamou. Rice is a profitable crop – more than one ex-oilman has thanked his Cajun grandfather for throwing handfuls of the grain to grow at will in his ditches and ponds. Some rice finds its way west to Houston to become Budweiser beer; more winds up in Louisiana cooking pots. It is usually American long-grain, but sometimes the Cajuns have 'popcorn' rice, so called because of the smell.

Cajuns thicken their gumbos and boudin sausages with rice; cooked with suitable seasonings – chopped onions, garlic, green pepper – it stuffs turkeys and vegetables.

Black Creoles used to make for breakfast a yeast-risen rice sponge mixed with eggs and butter and deep fried in a skillet. These were the 'cala' vendors, who cooked their fritters in the streets of New Orleans. One of the last chanted this song:

We sell it to the rich, we sell it to the poor,
We give it to the sweet brownskin, peepin' out the door.
Tous chauds, Madame, tous chauds!
Git'em while they're hot! Belles calas!

RABBIT AND SAUSAGE JAMBALAYA
(serves 6)

A sensational dish – vivid, colourful and full of earthy flavour. Also very good with
wild duck instead of rabbit.

> *4 tbsp bacon fat or vegetable oil*
> *1 whole rabbit, skinned, cleaned, and cut in chunks,*
> *neck and gizzard etc. reserved for making stock*
> *1 medium onion, finely chopped*
> *2 sticks of celery, chopped with leaves*
> *2 garlic cloves, finely chopped*
> *1 14 oz/400 ml tin of whole Italian plum tomatoes*
> *9 fl oz/250 ml homemade stock/broth or water*
> *9 fl oz/250 ml dark beer*
> *2 cloves*
> *4–5 big sprigs of fresh thyme or 1 tsp dried*
> *1½ tsp salt*
> *6 small spiced garlic sausages, cut in ½ in/1 cm chunks*
> *2 green peppers, cored and sliced in strips lengthwise*
> *1½ tsp Tabasco sauce or cayenne pepper*
> *10 oz/300 g uncooked long-grain rice*
> *handful of fresh flat parsley*
> *1 peeled garlic clove*
> *grated zest from a lemon*

(1) Heat half the oil in a large, heavy pot and brown the rabbit well on all sides.
Lift out with a slotted spoon, add the onion and celery to the pot and stir until the
onions are soft and golden, adding the garlic a few minutes before the end (add
garlic later than onions because it burns more easily). Pour in the tomatoes, liquid,
cloves, thyme and salt and bring to a gentle boil. Return the rabbit to the pot, cover
and simmer for 35–40 minutes, or until the rabbit is tender. This will depend on
whether it is wild or tame.
(2) While the rabbit cooks, wash rice under cold running water until the water
runs clear. Drain. Heat remaining oil in a pan and brown the sausages. Add the
peppers and rice to the pan, stirring until the rice is slightly transparent. When the
rabbit is almost tender, add the rice, sausages and peppers. Bring liquid back to the
boil, cover pot and reduce heat.
(3) After about 20 minutes, when all the liquid has been absorbed, remove from
the heat and let stand for 10 minutes to harden the rice. Spoon the jambalaya out
onto a large serving dish, arranging the rabbit pieces on top, and sprinkle over the
parsley, garlic and lemon, finely chopped.

RED BEANS AND RICE
(serves 6–8)

Earthy, warming Monday food. If you had a ham
bone from the Sunday feast, you would throw that
in too. The pickled pork (page 37) gives the dish
an extra depth. Great with char-grilled boudin and
apples fried in butter (or olive oil) and
cinnamon.

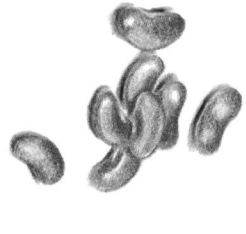

1 lb/500 g red beans
1 large peeled onion stuck with 8 cloves
2 tbsp brown sugar
4 tbsp bacon drippings or vegetable oil
1 large onion, finely chopped
1 green pepper, finely chopped
2 garlic cloves, finely chopped
1 celery stick, finely chopped
2 bay leaves
½ lb/250 g pickled pork, diced or 1 lb/500 g ham hocks
4–6 oz/125–180 g American long-grain rice, cooked
1½ tsp salt
2 tsp black peppercorns, coarsely crushed
handful of fresh parsley, finely chopped

(1) Put the beans in a big pot, cover with plenty of water, bring to the boil and boil hard for 5 minutes. Turn off heat and leave to soak for 2 hours. Drain, cover again with water (it should be at least 1 in/25 mm above beans), and add the clove-stuck onion, brown sugar and bay leaves. Bring to the boil, reduce heat to very low, cover and simmer gently for 2 hours.

(2) In the meantime, heat the bacon drippings and fry the onion, green pepper, garlic and celery until softened. After the beans have cooked for 1 hour, remove the clove and onion, and add these seasonings along with the pickled pork. Ten minutes before the end, add the salt and pepper. Serve over rice and scatter the top with chopped parsley.

All beans taste better if left overnight and reheated the next day. They also benefit from the use of homemade stock instead of water (hence the hambone). You can try maple syrup instead of sugar, add cayenne with the other seasonings for more bite, drizzle some warmed olive oil over the rice – or use the butter the apples have cooked in.

HOPPIN' JOHN/BLACK- EYED PEAS WITH RICE

(serves 8)

Hoppin' because of the beans or the cayenne? I don't know – the name is an old one. Serve it for brunch with grillades, or for supper with smoky grilled sausages sliced on top.

2 tbsp vegetable oil
½ lb/250 g streaky smoked bacon, chopped
1 medium onion, finely chopped
2 green peppers, finely chopped
2 celery sticks, chopped
4 garlic cloves, crushed
bunch of fresh thyme or 1 tsp dried
1½ tsp cayenne pepper
1½ tsp salt
1 tbsp cider vinegar
2 bay leaves
3½ pt/2 l strong homemade stock/broth*
¾ lb/350 g dried black-eyed peas/beans, well washed
4 oz/125 g American long-grain rice

(1) Cook the bacon for 3–4 minutes in a deep heavy saucepan with the oil. Add the onion, green pepper, celery and garlic and stir frequently until the onion is golden.
(2) Add all the remaining ingredients except rice and salt, bring to a rapid boil and boil hard for five minutes. Reduce heat to very low, cover tightly and simmer 60 minutes, skimming off any foam occasionally.
(3) In the meantime, wash the rice under cold running water until the water runs clear. Twenty minutes before the beans have finished cooking, add rice. Cover tightly and finish cooking, adding salt just before the end. Allow to sit for 10 minutes to firm the rice before serving.

Never add salt to any dried beans until about 10 minutes before the end of cooking as it tends to harden them.

*Double up the liquid needed for cooking the boudin meat (page 45) and use this in the beans.

From Sea and Swamp

If a good roux is the heart of Cajun cooking, crawfish is its soul. They look like a cross between a lobster and a shrimp but locals claim they taste better than both.

Like early Cajuns, the crawfish build mud chimneys for their homes (thus earning the local name 'mudbug'); these mushroom-shaped chimneys burgeon like fairy rings in the low-lying areas around swamp cypress.

September is peak egg-laying season. Cajuns say that the female crawfish, with the eggs carried briefly on her abdomen making her look like a blackberry, is 'in berry'. Eggs hatched in autumn are edible crawfish in time for Mardi Gras.

Louisiana's fresh fish, shellfish and crustaceans are the centre of every feast, not surprisingly, considering the sheer quantity and quality of what is available – oysters; crawfish and shrimps; meaty white fish called pompano ('en papillote' – cooked in an envelope of waxed paper with a mushroom and crabmeat sauce); redfish, bluefish, catfish, trout; 'Buster' crab, which bust their shells at a certain time every year, thus becoming entirely edible – they are dipped into egg batter and deep-fried; turtle, and alligator (like a cross between a fish and a pig).

Louisiana cooks are blasé about this natural bounty. They use fresh oysters and shrimps as a flavouring as Europeans use lardons or bacon.

GOOD STOCK OR COURT BOUILLON

For a good broth to use as a base for any fish or shellfish recipe, break the tails off a dozen or so crawfish (reserve for another dish). Soften a chopped onion, a clove or two of garlic and half a celery stalk in two tablespoons of olive oil, add the crawfish heads and brown for a couple of minutes. Pour in 7 fl oz/200 ml white wine or cider and 1¾ pt/1 l of cold water with a bay leaf, a tsp salt and a handful of parsley. Bubble for about 20 minutes and strain before using. For a more intense flavour, reduce this over medium-high heat until it thickens.

If you simmer this mixture for an hour with a chopped sweet pepper, a can of good plum tomatoes and a healthy spoonful of cayenne or Tabasco, then slip a fish into it 10 minutes before the end, you will have one version of what passes for 'court bouillon' in Louisiana.

Pickled Tips & Grandes Boucheries

Pork is far more important than beef in southern Louisiana. The 'Boucherie' or weekly slaughter used to be an excuse for 'fais-do-dos'. Sometimes as many as twenty or twenty-five families might attend a 'grande' one. They ensured fresh meat in the days before refrigeration.

Pigs' heads would be simmered in broth in a big iron kettle with bay leaves, juniper berries and fresh thyme, the tender meat from them stripped, after cooling in its own liquor, to make hog's head cheese – even better when wine or beer had been added to the pot. Whole families would grind the fattier cuts of meat into boudin, or spicy andouille (more like Spanish merguez sausage than anything resembling French andouille); the feet and rib tips would be pickled in vinegar to give a bite to beans and greens; fatty skin and tails flung into a pan to make crisp 'cracklins'. The pig's lard would be conserved in a cool place to make pastry, or to spread on thick slices of bread with a sprinkling of coarse salt.

After a big barbecue of the ribs and innards, each family could take home some of the more precious cuts for use in the week.

Hams were smoked, then cooked slowly in water or beer until tender; or parboiled, wrapped in parchment and baked. An hour before the end of cooking, the paper and pork rind was removed, the fat scored and studded with cloves. Cane sugar might be sprinkled on and the ham basted with rum for the remaining time, and served with slices of orange or apple cooked in the pan liquor. The rags and tatters left on the bone would go into next day's gumbo or jambalaya.

These days Boucheries are not so frequent. But there is still a Grande Boucherie in St Martinville on the Sunday before Mardi Gras.

BOUDIN/SPICY LOUISIANA SAUSAGE
(about 3–4 lb/1.5–2 kg, or 10–12 large sausages)
An earthy-tasting country sausage, wonderful simmered slowly with cabbage or beans, or brushed with melted butter, grilled, and served with Cajun/Dijon mustard, potato and pineapple pancakes (page 46) and cinnamony cooked apples.

1¼ lb/600 g lean pork loin
12 oz/350 g pork liver, cleaned
8 oz/250 g pork back fat
2 tsp salt
10 green/spring onions, chopped, half reserved
big handful fresh parsley, finely chopped, half reserved
2 tsp ground cloves
1½ tsp dried thyme
handful of celery tops, finely chopped
3 garlic cloves, finely chopped
1 tbsp black peppercorns, coarsely cracked
1 tbsp sugar
1½ tsp cayenne
7 oz/200 g American long-grain rice, cooked
large sausage casings

(1) A day or two before you want to cook the sausages, finely chop the meat and fat, mix with everything except the reserved onion, parsley and rice, and grind coarsely in a mincer or food processor. Cover and refrigerate at least 24 hours to allow to absorb the flavours.

(2) The next day, soak the sausage cases in lukewarm water for 30 minutes and run water through them to check for any holes. Mix remaining ingredients into the

spiced meat and fill the casings, knotting about every 8 in/20 cm to make the sausages. Do not fill too tightly or the sausages will burst in cooking.

(3) Prick the sausages with a needle several times and cook for 2–3 minutes in simmering water, then grill until well browned, or cook with beans or cabbage.

A Vegetable Feast

Creole cooks, especially black Creoles, are fond of rich mixtures: yams baked to a melting sweetness with sugar and lemon, turnip greens stewed with pickled pork, okra simmered with ham.

Yams, plantains, sweet potatoes are baked in a medium oven until just tender, then peeled and sliced into a buttered baking dish. Orange or lemon juice is squeezed over (about 1 lemon per pound/500 g of vegetable), the top is sprinkled with brown sugar, salt and pepper, a little cinnamon or vanilla, dotted with butter and baked for a further 20–30 minutes in a hot oven. Or the cooked, sliced yams are layered with vinegar, sugar and herbs as a pickle – excellent with spicy foods.

The Guitrys on Bayou Lafourche cooked sweet potatoes with pickled pork or ham, sautéed green onions, parsley and garlic – just as they would have cooked lima beans (see page 14), and put the deep orange yams into a stew instead of potatoes.

A great favourite at Antoine's and Galatoire's are the salted *Pommes de Terre Soufflées* in which starchy potatoes are peeled, sliced 3 mm thick, washed and dried, then plunged first in moderately hot fat, to cook them, and just before serving into a second pan of very hot deep fat (it should be at least 375°F/190°C/gas mark 5) which puffs them up.

Another favourite are *potato pancakes*: peeled raw potatoes coarsely grated, with chopped chives, an egg, 3 tbsp of pineapple juice, and ¼ lb/125 g of flour to every pound/500 g of potatoes, salt and pepper. Mix thoroughly together and fry crisp and brown, first one side, then the other, in bacon fat. Good with boudin and spiced apples.

Wild Game

The best gumbos are made with smoked venison sausage and wild duck; a wild rabbit gives an altogether raunchier flavour to jambalaya than does its tame equivalent. In the swamps and bayous of Louisiana, a freezer well stocked with the benefits of successful weekend hunts – supplemented by pickled pork, crawfish and 'wild' oysters – can make the difference between profit and loss for a restaurant.

A TEAL DUCK ROASTED PLAIN

Picked, singed, wiped and trussed three fine teal ducks. Roasted in a hot oven 14 minutes. Arrange with 6 slices of fried hominy and a little watercress.

MRS MCILHENNY'S CANARD PRESSÉ

(The McIlhennys own Avery Island, the protruding 100-foot tip of a 50,000-foot salt 'iceberg' sunk in the bayous off the Louisiana Gulf Coast, where Tabasco sauce has always been produced.)

Wild ducks best but tame will do. In the first place ducks must be strangled. This leaves them with a rosy breast. Roast them about 10 minutes. Mash livers to a paste with 1 part cognac and 2 parts Madeira, salt, black pepper. Slice the breast, broil legs and serve them with lettuce salad. Carcass is put into a press to get the juice, which is poured over the slices of breast with the liver sauce and a dash of lemon juice, the whole placed in a chafing dish and cooked until the sauce thickens, the meat being continually basted with the sauce.

Beginnings and Endings

Many Louisiana sweets centre on native pecans – scorned at first by the French and Spanish cooks accustomed to making pralines and *tarte aux noix* with almonds and walnuts. But local pecans gradually replaced the expensive imported nuts in classic European recipes – thus walnut tart became pecan pie, suffering not one whit in the process.

MR WILLIAM'S SWEET-POTATO PIE

Shortcrust pastry for 4 4 in/10 cm tarts or a 9 in/22 cm pie
1 large sweet potato about 12 oz/350 g
3 medium eggs
4 oz/125 g brown sugar
6 fl oz/185 ml/³/₄ cup thick cream
3 oz/90 g butter, melted
1 tsp vanilla
1¹/₂ tsp cinnamon
¹/₂ tsp nutmeg plus extra to sprinkle
pinch of salt
whipping cream for topping

(1) Either peel the sweet potato, cover in water and boil until tender, or wrap in foil and bake in 350°F/180°C/gas mark 4 oven for 1 hour. When tender, push through a fine sieve. Roll out the pastry, prick with fork, par-bake under beans etc.
(2) Preheat the oven to 350°F/180°C/gas mark 4. Beat together the eggs and sugar until pale and smooth and then stir in the remaining ingredients. Fill the pies and bake for 30–40 minutes until a toothpick inserted in the centre comes out dry. Cover the top with sweetened whipped cream and grate over some fresh nutmeg.

AUNT PATTY'S PAIN PATATE

Sweet-potato cake with pecan praline
A sweet-potato flan to eat with dollops of cool whipped cream.

4 oz/125 g butter, softened
4 oz/125 g brown sugar
3 medium eggs, separated
1 lb/500 g sweet potatoes, cooked and finely sieved
9 fl oz/250 ml/1 cup lukewarm milk
1¹/₂ tsp cinnamon
pinch of salt
Pecan praline
1 tbsp water
1¹/₂ oz/45 g white sugar
1 oz/30 g pecans

(1) Preheat oven to 400°F/200°C/gas mark 6. Cream together butter and sugar until light and fluffy. Whisk in egg yolks, well beaten, and potatoes, and gradualy stir in milk, cinnamon and salt. Beat the egg whites stiff, stir a quarter of them into

the batter to lighten it, and fold in the remaining whites. Pour into a round greased pan and cook for 15 minutes, or until the liquid begins to set. Lower the oven heat to 325°F/165°C/gas mark 3 and continue cooking for another 50–60 minutes, or until firm. Cool before unmoulding.

(2) While the flan is cooking, make the praline. Heat the sugar, water and pecans together over medium heat until the sugar bubbles into dark caramel. Pour out onto a greased metal pan. When completely cool and hard, roughly pound the praline into little pieces. Serve the flan at room temperature with the crushed praline scattered over the top.

Coffee – The Ending and Beginning

Weeks Hall wrote that there was always a rite peculiar to southern Louisiana – the early morning coffee, 'purest of virgins, black as the devil and hot as Hell', brought up to your bedroom just after dawn. Coffee continued throughout the day, offered in all business and social contacts, 'whether in the heavy china of the cabins or in the silver pots of the planter'; the grand finale to every feast.

Community Coffee, brewed in Baton Rouge, is the one that Cajuns carry to homesick relatives and friends around the world.

CAFÉ BRULOT (FAMOUS CRESCENT CLUB RECIPE)

(serves 12)

peel from one orange, broken up
4 in/10 cm cinnamon stick, broken up
12 cloves
4–6 whisky glasses of cognac
12–14 lumps of sugar
10–12 demitasses of strong hot coffee

Heat the cognac first. Place all the ingredients except coffee in a deep bowl and pour a little hot cognac into a warm spoon, light it and use it to light the rest. Stir for 30 seconds and then pour coffee in slowly. Serve at once in demitasses.

From a turn-of-the-century Louisiana cookery book comes the idea of a moulded coffee jelly with the remains of Café Brulot. Top with cream and orange zest.

A VISUAL FEAST

---

*The New Year Water
Festival in Thailand*

I know a man who spent a year sampling the whores in all the whorehouses in the world (or as many as one man could be expected to sample in 365 nights), and lived to write a book about it. Between one massive penicillin injection and the next he told me that the girls in Thailand were the most fun-loving, beautiful, feminine and willing of his lengthy research.

'Go to Thailand,' he told his friends. 'It's not just the women, it's all the people, the food, the country itself. Go to the Songkran New Year festival in Chiang Mai and you might understand.'

The word 'songkran' comes from the Sanskrit for a move or a change; in Thailand, the beginning of the solar new year – 13, 14 and 15 April – is assumed to be the date of the sun's entrance into Aries.

There is a great trade in live birds and fish at new year in Thailand. They are bought in the days before Songkran and then released during the festival to earn their purchasers religious merit. The custom stems from earlier times when the country's central plains suffered great floods. As the floods dried, they left pools of fish behind – trapped until the next Songkran rains released them into the canals and rivers.

Songkran is when the rains begin, even if only metaphorically. The Ancients believed that mythical serpents called the Nagas brought rain by spouting water from the seas. Modern Thais take matters into their own hands.

ONE

On the plane to Bangkok there was a man sitting next to me who had never been to Thailand, but, like a cheap greeting-card company, had a cliché to suit every occasion.

'Oh yeah – Thailand,' he said, and leered. 'The Land of Smiles, *The King and I*, great girls.'

Like all clichés this one had an element of truth. Thailand is full of smiling people and temples and monks and beautiful girls and *The King and I*. It is also full of opium, middle-aged hippies, diamond smugglers, the smell of fresh fish and old canals, the noise of tuk tuks (three-wheeled motor-rickshaws) and glorious, spicy, remarkable food.

TWO

In the lobby of the Bangkok Oriental a string quartet of elegant golden men wearing tailcoats and white gloves were playing 'Over the Sea to Skye' while slim Thai girls in silk brought Earl Grey tea and scones to ferociously dyed-blonde guests. The air-conditioning kept the temperature at a steady 16°C. It seemed perfectly feasible to work up an appetite for lunch by walking half a mile to Thanying, the restaurant I had heard was owned by a member of Thailand's royal family.

One foot outside the Oriental's doors the temperature rose to 38°C. I tried to avoid the hovering mock-Gucci vendors and five other tuk tuk drivers rushed forward shouting '*Tuk tuk leddi tuk tuk*'. A man held up a ripe mango. I tripped over a Siamese cat as thin as a plucked grouse. Someone waved lottery tickets in my face. The sultry, damp hand of Thailand reached out. Suddenly half a mile seemed a lot further.

You could tell when you were close to Bangrak Market by the sharp smells of fresh coriander and pickled garlic, and the ripe drain odour of cut durian – that huge prehistoric dinosaur of a fruit.

Bangrak Market was the city's digestive tract – through it coursed both the best and the worst. Butchers' stalls were piled with the bleeding carcasses and internal organs of unidentifiable mammals, while the butchers waited to buy fresh honey waffles off a young girl's spotlessly clean brazier. Vegetables were of extraordinary variety: green and baby-pink bamboo shoots threaded neatly in rows onto narrow whips of dried bamboo, clusters of grape-sized aubergines arranged with bouquets of seedpods and twenty different types of basil folded into leaf 'wallets' – all the greens together on an earth-coloured woven bamboo tray lined with banana leaves. Winter melons sliced crosswise to show the creamy flesh wheeled around a mound of peeled chunks of green squash. Bunches of garlic chives and the fresh herbs for prawn soup – kaffir lime leaf, lemon grass, orange-skinned Siamese ginger – were lashed together with

green thread and laid beside little plastic bags of green chillies tied with orange, next to pinky-orange squash and furry piles of red-orange rambutans.

While photographing an old lady's pyramid of baskets, each with its perfect fan of silvery fish inside, I used two of my ten words of Thai.

'*Dee mark!*' 'Very good!' I said inadequately, pointing at the fish.

The old lady beamed and tucked a banana flower between two baskets for a better effect. The juxtaposition of complementary colour and form was not accidental, but carefully considered – an outward manifestation of the joyous appreciation of beauty that even the poorest Thai peasant seemed to possess.

'Thanying' is the Thai equivalent of 'duchess' or 'princess'. The owner of the Thanying restaurant was the nephew of the old Queen of Thailand. His Royal Highness Sorut Visuddhi ('Ask for Mr Jack,' he had said on the telephone) had the calm and tranquil face of a very young man who has never had to sweat. He was forty-two. He sat under a banana palm in his garden, feeding dainty morsels off a china plate to a pair of brilliant green Indian parrots with scarlet beaks.

'This is one of the dishes my mother used to cook for the Emperor of Japan, thirty or forty years ago when he was Ambassador to Thailand and came often to the palace.'

A waiter glided up with a pierced brass tray. In the middle was a porcelain bowl of rice and scented ice-water with jasmine blossoms floating in it. I picked up the twin of what Mr Jack had been feeding to his parrots: a fragile, flower-shaped pastry cup about an inch across, filled with a teaspoon of minced fresh corn, shrimps, garlic and green chillies. It looked like something from a dolls' picnic.

'*Gahtong tong,*' he said. 'Gold Cups; gold for good luck.'

Next to the Gold Cups were a few balls of shrimp paste the size of large marbles, wrapped and steamed in thin pieces of kale leaf. Then two small chillies stuffed with spiced pork and rolled into a lacy net of crisp egg threads. A bowl of sweet cured beef shreds. Five or six strips of candied turnip. Two perfect 'leaves' carved from slices of green mango. A tablespoon of carp smoked over coconut. Four shallots that had been stuffed, dipped in egg batter and deep-fried, the crisp egg trailing off like the wispy tails of ornamental goldfish.

Stuffed *shallots*, I thought. Only a tiny, perfect people with even tinier fingers could imagine stuffing a shallot.

'You must first have a spoonful of the rice and scented water,' said Jack. 'Then balance the blandness with a bite of spice, a bite of sweet.'

This collection of dishes was called 'Khao Chae Chao Wang' – 'The Court Iced-Water Rice', a feast for the hottest months. The dishes were invented by ladies of the palace during the reign of King Chulalongkorn (son of *The King and I*) from 1868 to 1910. Ice was then an unthinkable extravagance for any but the wealthiest, a rare luxury imported by ship from Singapore.

The dishes were only mildly spicy, not at all what I had expected from Thai food.

'It is only the common people's food that is really hot,' said Jack. 'And very sweet too to disguise poor ingredients. Royal dishes are much milder. Where peasants might eat one bowl of curried rice or noodles, in the court there would be many dainty things to tempt jaded appetites. The more elaborate the preparation, the better.'

A savoury custard of sliced chicken and coconut cream would be steamed and served in a carved coconut bowl. The crispy sweet noodles and shrimp mixture called 'Mee grob', offered to monks at the palace, would come in its own deep-fried noodle basket. Lychee-sized eggplants to dip in a sweet-sour tamarind sauce were halved and filled with coconut custard. All the fruits were carved into intricate shapes so that they would not shame royal chefs by appearing to be what they actually were: a watermelon must be carved to resemble a chrysanthemum; a green mango like a rose leaf; a guava like a lily.

'My mother cooked for her sister, the old Queen, for thirty years. When the Queen died four years ago, everything changed. All the people who used to work with my mother came here, to cook the very same things they had once prepared in the palace.'

Cooking has always been considered a royal art in Thailand. During King Narai's reign in the mid-seventeenth century, a certain Lady Vichajen served him such delicious sweets that he gave her a feudal levy of money, and the title of head of his kitchen. Narai had strong French allies, and Lady Vichajen was the first to teach Siamese women how to cook new French dishes, later part of traditional Thai cuisine, just as earlier Portuguese influences of the sixteenth century resulted in many new Thai sweets.

Mrs Anna Leonowens wrote in her 1872 *Romance of the Harem* of Lady Thieng, a beautiful woman of thirty who had given the King four sons and eight daughters, and was ranked as head wife, the queen consort being dead:

All these considerations entitled her to the lucrative and responsible position of superintendent of the royal cuisine. Thieng had two houses. One was her home, where her children were born and brought up. In the other, adjoining the royal kitchen, she spent the greater part of each day in selecting, overlooking, and sometimes preparing with her own fair hands many of the costly dainties that were destined to grace the royal table.

When I mentioned Anna Leonowens to Jack, he said she was a very silly woman who had misrepresented both the King and Siam.

'Did you know that the king who employed her spent twenty-seven
years as a monk before accession? And that he not only knew Latin and
English, but also read the Buddhist scriptures in Pali [Sanskrit]? Did
Victoria do as much?'

Jack's mother still comes to the restaurant from time to time. One day
during Songkran, all sixty of the staff came out of the kitchen and
prostrated themselves on the floor before their old mistress.

'Our foreign guests stopped eating in disbelief,' said Jack, in his sweet,
soft voice. 'I think it is not quite what you are used to back home?'

THREE

It was already dark when I got to my guest-house in Chiang Mai after
the flight from Bangkok. The room was so hot that I took a sheet and a
pillow to the open roof. By the light of a street market in the distance I
could see the curled golden roofs of a score of wats piercing the night,
and not a hundred yards away tiny bats swooped and fluttered around
the stone spire of a ruined temple rising like an unlaunched rocketship.
Within an hour I had twenty-nine mosquito bites on my left leg, but I
didn't grudge the blood.

At dawn I walked into town along a dusty road lined with old teak
houses. An orange-robed monk carrying a pink paper parasol was
walking ahead of me. I followed him as far as the Chiang Mai Gate.

In the street the drivers of old wooden bicycle rickshaws were sitting
in them having breakfast from the jumble of fast-food stalls. Women
crouched almost under their wheels, cooking food on portable clay
braziers.

Standing at one of the kiosks were three men dressed in baggy knee-
length black skirts, turquoise knee socks and fuchsia-pink tunics. They
had grass cloches on their heads, and three or four woven cloth shopping bags of goods each slung from straps around their foreheads. One
of the men was eating a honey waffle. When he saw I was drawing him,
he smiled, showing teeth stained black and worn almost to the gum in
the front from chewing betel nut.

'They are Meo,' a Thai boy behind me said. 'Nomadic hill tribe
people come for shopping before Songkran starts.'

The King of Thailand had just returned from the Chiang Mai hills,
where he had been trying to convince these tribes to grow legal
peaches, asparagus and radicchio instead of illegal opium poppies. The
USA has donated money to the project. I asked the student how much
success they were having.

'Many success,' he said. 'Now they grow opium where not visible.'

'But surely they are running a big risk?'

He rubbed his fingers together suggestively. 'Very big risk, very big

money. Everybody want opium. Not many people want lettuce. And
our government does not really enforce law – except when US Ambassador visiting Chiang Mai.'

The tribesmen walked off with the measured strides of people used
to covering long distances before lunch. The Thai student gestured to a
brazier lady, who poured rice and coconut batter into a cast-iron plate
with a circle of round hollows in it. She set the plate over hot coals and a
minute later sprinkled over some chopped spring onions and lifted out
eight perfect miniature custards, golden brown where they had pressed
the iron pan. Her pretty daughter shook on some coarse sugar and arranged them on a banana leaf that was folded and fastened with two
bamboo slivers to make a tray.

From another woman in a hat shaped like a wastepaper basket the
student bought a small cane cage with a bird in it, a thin basket of dyed
bamboo filled with six oval golden fruits, and a long paper banner
painted with bright pictograms. He gave me the bird and the fruit,
ignoring my protests.

'The bird you must set free tomorrow – good luck for Songkran. This
fruit is also traditional. We call it Mah prang – child's cheek – for its
smoothness. You must offer it to the monks at Tai Peh Gate in the
morning. Very important for ladies to make merit this way as they cannot be monks.'

'And the banner?'

'That is to decorate my jedi. A jedi is like a sand castle. During Songkran we carry buckets of sand to the wat and cover them in flowers
and flags to help raise the temple grounds above wet season floods.'

'Songkran marks the start of the wet season then?'

'Definitely,' he said, grinning broadly. 'Take tuk tuk to town this afternoon and the rains will certainly fall.'

The covered market at Chiang Mai Gate was on several different levels:
the higher the floor, the lower the quality of the goods. It was impossible to get a wide-angled view: everything was too close. Slipping side-
ways along congested aisles, I kept losing my way and passing the same
people. A small boy sold me a tin of jasmine paste, 'for scent water on
Buddha', while his grandfather slept, head cushioned on a bowl of rice.
The second time round the boy sold me some betel nuts. Three different old women cooked bananas ten different ways. Small hard
bananas of the north were threaded six to a skewer, slashed and slightly
flattened, then grilled until golden. Some were simmered whole in coconut cream; others dipped in rice and coconut batter, deep-fried and
rolled in syrup and sesame seeds.

Everywhere I asked, 'For Songkran?', people smiled and pointed to
their own or another's stall. Candied sticky rice Songkran sweets –

galamae – coloured caramel with burnt coconut, each square topped with half a toasted peanut. A painted paper banner. A packet of crispy rice cakes with a fudgy mixture of palm sugar and jasmine water swirled on the top. These are khao-tan, traditional to offer to the monks; a savoury version is a popular hors d'oeuvre to dip in spicy chilli paste before the big family lunch on Songkran Day.

Chiang Mai is famous for its Burmese-influenced food – especially for the noodle dish called Khao Soi. The chef at one Khao Soi café used to cook at the French embassy and still spoke his own charmingly frac-tured version of the language. There was a Khao Soi stall at Chiang Mai market, and another by Tai Peh Gate, but the most popular was the Sutha Sinee house near the night bazaar.

A person in a red satin mini-skirt took my order. She had a shadowed jaw, a husky voice and a pronounced Adam's apple.

The buxom chef had the arms of a Sumo wrestler. In front of her were three immense woks – one with boiling water, one with a sim-mering coconut and chicken curry, one with hot oil – and a big bowl of freshly cooked egg noodles which she topped up from time to time. As orders came she would fling a handful of cooked noodles into a bowl with a scoop of chicken curry, a handful into the deep fat, lifting the deep-fried noodles out a moment later and crumbling them over the curry with a little fresh coriander. On a separate plate she gave each customer some shallots sliced very thinly, a generous spoonful of pickled cabbage with red chillies, a quartered lime, and a condiment set of sugar, salty fish sauce and chillied vinegar. With a plate of smoky barbecued satay, it cost me the price of coffee at the Oriental.

I left in a tuk tuk, past the Khaithong restaurant:

THE ONLY RESTAURANT IN THE WORLD THAT SERVES SNAKE STEAK!
WE ALSO SERVE OTHER KINDS OF STEAK: BEEF, CHICKEN, PORK,
RABBIT, LAMB, VENISON, CROCODILE ETC'

I loved the 'etc.'.

FOUR

There was a drum contest at the Tai Peh Gate that night. Two stages had been set up, one at either end of the square outside the gate, the edges defined by the inevitable rows of fast-food braziers.

One old lady poured small circles of rice-flour batter onto a hotplate over glowing coals. When the batter crisped she folded it quickly into a mini taco and filled it with sweet pickled cucumber or shrimps stir-fried with fresh ginger.

Another woman ladled smoky noodles and bean sprouts into a

banana leaf, sprinkled them with chilli sugar, crushed toasted pea-nuts, a splash of vinegar and a few shredded chillies. On top she laid two long garlic chives, a wedge of lime and some chopped cabbage, folded the leaf like an origami boat and fastened it with a bamboo pin. Next to her elbow were wedges of sticky rice fried golden and crisp in hot oil, to dip in another banana-leaf boat of peanut and coconut sauce. Thai fast-food vendors fold everything from soup to goldfish in leaves. It means that all the litter is biodegradable.

The drum contest was more inscrutable. Four men on the wooden stage beat what looked like a long-handled frying pan. A man with a paint-whitened face hunched over beating to Ta TA TA tata on some cymbals, and a sixth man thumped out POM POM dePOM on a long horn-shaped drum. They shuffled off to scattered applause.

Seven men then shuffled on carrying a drum strapped to a bamboo pole. The man in front of me in a tartan skirt and red baseball sneakers nodded and smiled knowingly. Two men holding the drum went BUM 1pit BUMpit; the man with cymbals hit them, two more with a wok on a string went PING. Pit BUM pit BUM CRASH POM ping.

Suddenly a rock band at the other end of the square drowned everything out with their rendition of 'Satisfaction'. I never really got to grips with Thai music. I blame it on Mick Jagger.

FIVE

At 6.00 the next morning the streets were lined with kneeling people offering bowls of food to passing monks.

Two boys on bicycles stopped behind one monk and held out a plastic bag. He turned calmly and emptied all his food into the bag.

'It is very simple,' said a Chiang Mai friend. 'Monks do not have enough bowls to keep all food separate, so they eat just a token and pour rest into big pots to fry up later. In North we sometimes make this dish, call it "Gang hoh" – means "put everything together".'

'Sounds like a dog's breakfast,' I said.

'Oh no,' said my friend. 'Mostly people offer only three types of food: a hungley or curry, some spicy sai ua sausage, and bean thread soup called Wun sen. So it is not really breakfast for dog.'

The crowds at the Tai Peh Gate were offering a lot more to the monks: packs of Campbell's Cup-a-Soup, Mars bars, boxes of lychee juice. One small boy walked behind each monk carrying a plastic bag. 'This

is modern way,' said a local girl. 'Package foods are easier to keep.'

I pressed my palms together to greet two young monks. The smallest one forgot himself and grinned.

Su, the receptionist at my guest house, had invited me to her auntie's home for Songkran breakfast. We had to wait while a parade of Thai girls in silk dresses cycled past, each girl holding an open umbrella.

Breakfast was tea in fragile cups from Lamphung province, and a tray of Chinese doughnuts like swollen butterflies, and round sesame-coated shortbreads, pale green from pandanus leaf or pale pink from a local flower.

After breakfast we sat on the floor with Auntie in the middle on a teak table, two large silver bowls of water next to her scented with jasmine and coloured golden with saffron, and edged forward one by one on our knees to pour water over her hands and receive a blessing.

I spent the rest of the morning perched on the wheel guard in the back of a Toyota pick-up with tiny boys and girls who had naughty Siamese-kitten faces and punk rocker haircuts, our faces smeared with white jasmine paste. 'Minz good ruck,' said one little girl as she slapped more paste on me.

Between us we had two oil drums full of water, and we criss-crossed Chiang Mai heaving water at anyone brave enough to venture out, drenching and being drenched by other blue-clad water guerrillas. Even the old people took the dousing in good part – resignedly muttering '*Khop khun maak*' – except when hit by lumps of ice that had been slipped in to make the cleansing of the unwary soul that much more painful.

That afternoon there was a three-hour parade of Buddhas past the governor's residence and all through the city to the great Wat of Pra Singh. Hundreds of Buddha statues had been carried from wats all over the province. As they passed, the crowd blessed them with splashes of water.

The statues were pulled by hill people in tribal clothes, some staggering drunk from bottles of whisky passed through the line, some red-eyed and weaving from drier intoxicants. Interspersed were amateur beauty queens and flocks of shaven-headed young monks in snowy robes, each living baby Buddha clutching a wax-perfect white lotus bud. The inscrutable drummers thumped their own inscrutable time. The sun beat down, sending a haze of steam off wet clothing, and flashed off a Gold Buddha, a Jade Buddha, an Emerald Buddha, a tiny Crystal Buddha with a solid-gold base; there was the smell of jasmine and smoking oil from the fast-food woks, and very occasionally the pungent Western odour of deodorant. The hairless Thais, however closely pressed together, never seemed to smell of anything worse than charcoal smoke and mild garlic.

SIX

Officially, Songkran lasts for three days, although for several weeks on either side of that time if you take a bus or train through the north you are likely to get soaked.

In the late afternoon of 14 April the courtyard around Wat Pra Singh was full of charcoal braziers and hawkers.

Young monks sat listening to another drum contest, their eyes following the movements of the more immodestly dressed foreign girls. On the building behind them a sign read, 'No ladies please'.

Buses kept degorging families carrying damp sand from the river to

build their jedis. The pile of sand pyramids was now twice as tall as me.

On the morning of the 15 April this wat would be crowded with people carrying trays of food prepared the day before for the monks, who would eat a token and bless the dead ancestors and their living relatives. Then everyone would go home to lunch. Time in Thailand is punctuated not by seconds and minutes, but by meals, snacks, tea-breaks; a mouthful of coconut cake, a slice of ripe mango.

'Our lunch on the fifteenth used to be served on big wooden or brass trays with four to six people seated round – called Kang Dtok,' said the Dean of Education at Chiang Mai University, who showed the usual Thai willingness to talk about food. 'Now this happens only in rural areas. But we still have the same food: sticky rice; Lab, a curry made with crispy pork skin; Nam phrik num, chilli and pork dip served with crisp rice; and always one or two yams or salads – maybe young jackfruit, which is in season, pounded with spices and fried.'

There are oranges for dessert and the little northern bananas, and lots of Mei Kong whisky. Later, people go to pay their respects to their elders with gifts and fruit. Rural monks come to the city's senior monk, the dean's students come to him, each faculty goes to the university president. 'So it goes, up and up,' said the Dean. 'Making a mountain of fruit.'

On the final day all the chiefs of the district bring gifts to the governor of Chiang Mai in a long parade of fruit pyramids and whole garlic trees and mountains of fried chillies.

I left in the late afternoon to take the night train south, but not late enough to avoid a small boy who ran out from a doorway to tip a ladle of ice-water over me in the tuk tuk. The last I saw of Chiang Mai was his gleeful form waving a long-handled wooden ladle in the air like an Indian waving his tomahawk after a successful scalping mission. He was shouting 'Goo'bye leddee! Goo' Ruck!'

The rains had indeed fallen.

SEVEN

The monastery at Suan Mokh, built in the jungle on the narrow isthmus that becomes Malaysia a couple of hundred miles further on, is known wherever there are Buddhists. Several times a year the Oriental Hotel sends its staff there, twelve hours by train from Bangkok, for a four-day seminar. They sleep on wooden floors, sharing wooden water barrels to wash in, and rise at 4.00 a.m. to walk a mile into the jungle for two hours of lectures and meditation. It is the Thai answer to job satisfaction training.

I went to Suan Mokh to see what the staff of the most luxurious hotel in Thailand could get out of the monastery. To see the fast after the feast.

A white flower the Thais call Mrs Protector bloomed beneath the stilts of the teak dormitories. 'It is auspicious that it blooms – good luck,' said Khunvina, the woman who had initiated the first trip to Suan Mokh. She had a degree in French literature from New York University. A six-foot lizard wrapped its tail round a tree next to her and blinked a blood-red eye.

'Jungle lizard – very poisonous,' said one of the Oriental's chefs, a wiry brown woman with a street kid's cynical grin. 'Not so auspicious.'

We went to pay our respects to the head monk, who was famous in Thailand for his interpretation of the Buddha's teaching. He had a snowy crewcut and sat cross-legged on the ground supporting his substantial bulk with an old stick, talking to us almost absent-mindedly in a low voice. He was dying of diabetes but continued to lecture.

Nuns with shaved heads and white smocks served the monks. Buddhists say that woman is the hind legs of the elephant that is man – nuns may serve, but, unlike the monks, may not teach. One of the nuns at Suan Mokh was a university professor and senior government official.

At 4.00 the next morning the clearing in the jungle was only visible by the gleam of the moon. Monkeys chattered and landed with loud thumps in the bushes. Khunvina told me that the first time she was here she heard a jaguar cough. There are poisonous snakes as well but no monk has yet been bitten; or if they have, it has not been reported.

Three different monks lectured over the four days, interpreting the head monk's vision. The essence was that people neglected spiritual health and happiness for physical and mental satisfaction.

'We have hospitals for the body and the brain but none for the spirit,' said one of the monks, an MBA graduate from Bangkok University. 'Buddhism is medicine for the spirit.' He was very thin and looked like a cross between Gandhi and a Roman emperor.

'You must learn to be free from desires,' he told us. 'Addiction to desires is worse than addiction to drugs. Do not always ask for salary increases. Decrease your spending on cigarettes, alcohol and women and it will seem like an increase. Try sleeping on the floor and going without a meal.'

'He suffers terribly from high cholesterol,' Khunvina said.

We did not go without any meals at Suan Mokh. Breakfast was Chinese doughnuts spread with thick condensed milk, or Khao tom, a Thai soup made with rice and chicken broth enriched with pieces of pork liver and flavoured with fresh coriander, fried garlic, shredded chillies and fish sauce.

Lunch was under a makeshift tent in the thriving community that had grown up outside the monastery walls. Dinner was a superb spread of curries and tiny fresh vegetables that would have done justice to any restaurant.

It is traditional that supplicants at Suan Mokh should offer the monks their main meal in the morning, to teach about giving and receiving. The monks sat in a long half-circle while the sun came up through the trees. Each monk held out his bowl, keeping his eyes lowered, and we gave them rice and green curried vegetables, handfuls of crisp water spinach and slabs of melon, and folded pyramids of banana leaves filled with steamed rice and sweet bean paste.

So much for the fast—in Thailand, even the monks eat well.

RECIPES

Read the list of dishes for a traditional Thai meal recommended by the Oriental Hotel's Cookery School, and you realize that in Thailand every meal is a feast:

Khow (cooked rice)
Gaeng Jued (soup)
Gaeng Ped (curry)
Krueang Kiang (condiments or side dishes)
Khong Nueng, Khong Thod, Paad, Khong Yaang (steamed, fried,
stir-fried, grilled dishes)
Yaam (herbed or spiced salad)
Krueang Jim (hot dip with vegetables and fish)
Khong Waan (desserts – one liquid and one dry)
Polomai (fruits)

Not everyone in Thailand eats like this, but even Thai street food has a vivid colour and harmony that lifts it out of the ordinary. The simplest bowl of noodles grabbed in a market comes in a banana leaf trimmed and folded as ingeniously as in origami, and is served with a little bowl of lime wedges, roasted peanuts to add crunch, a spoonful of shredded scarlet chillies, some fresh coriander leaves.

Royal feasts are elevated by their use of expensive ingredients and elaborate techniques.

'The mango to serve with sticky rice,' I was told in Bangkok's Thanying restaurant, 'would simply be peeled and mashed with the rice in peasant homes. But palace cooks would make sure it was peeled in at least twenty long strips to corrugate the surface.'

The common people make durian sticky rice with the cheap, pineapple-sized fruit – those that smell most pungently of drains – while in the palace the small, delicate, very expensive 'Man tong' is carved, and coated in coconut cream to whiten it.

Chali, in charge of the cooking school and the royal banquets at the Oriental Hotel, remembered the Queen of Thailand sending home for tiny carved coconuts to serve as bowls for a salad at a banquet in Los Angeles. If she had fruit in orange 'cups', she ensured that the oranges alternated orange and green. And the food offered to monks at Songkran by the court was just as carefully considered.

Street Feasts

PAD WUN SEN

Chiang Mai fast noodles (serves 4 as a light lunch with another dish or 6 as a side dish)
This recipe is a relaxed one, as befits a street recipe (it was served to me wrapped in
a leaf); the toppings should be put on the table for everyone to finish off their
noodles as they wish.

peanut, or other vegetable oil
3 garlic cloves, shredded
1 in/2.5 cm knob Siamese (or ordinary) ginger, peeled, shredded
6–8 shallot cloves, or 1 onion, finely sliced
¼ head white cabbage, finely shredded
7–10 oz/200–300 g fine jelly noodles, soaked 3 minutes, drained
2–3 eggs, beaten
5–6 oz/150–180 g fresh bean sprouts
2 tbsp nam pla fish sauce
2 tbsp rice vinegar
2 tsp sugar
Toppings
crushed dry-roasted peanuts, handful chopped fresh coriander,
3–4 small hot red chillies, seeded and finely sliced,
extra nam pla, sugar, vinegar

(1) Heat 5–6 tbsp oil over high heat in a wok. When smoking hot, add onions,
ginger, garlic, in that order, stirring rapidly to avoid burning. Add drained
noodles and toss rapidly for about 3 minutes. Reduce heat to medium and slowly
stir in the eggs. Immediately add all the other ingredients except the toppings and
stir for 2 minutes.

ARJAD

Cucumber pickle
A sweet and sour pickle to serve with satays (page 64) or other grilled meat, and as
a filling for the lime pancakes on page 64. It will last a couple of days if kept
covered in the refrigerator.

4 oz/125 g white sugar
1 tbsp salt
4½ fl oz/140 ml white wine or fruit vinegar
3 small cucumbers, shredded
2 small red, 2 small green chillies, seeded, shredded finely

(1) Heat sugar, salt and vinegar together in a small saucepan (not aluminium)
until sugar dissolves.
(2) Allow to cool, and pour over cucumber and chillies. Leave to marinate for
several hours before using.

KHANOM BEUANG

Savoury-sweet lime pancakes (serves 6–8 as a snack)

Thailand's answer to tacos – golden yellow and tasting delicately of lime. During the reign of Rama III, Thailand fought Vietnam and captured prisoners who brought this recipe with them. Now there are ladies up and down Chiang Mai making these on portable griddles.

6 oz/180 g rice flour, sifted with 2 oz/50 g mung bean or gram flour
1 large egg, beaten
3 oz/90 g creamed coconut mixed with 7 fl oz/200 ml hot water
1 tsp salt
1 tsp turmeric
1 tbsp brown sugar
juice of 2–3 big limes

(1) Mix together the flours, egg and just enough coconut milk to make a sticky dough. Knead for a few minutes and gradually add remaining coconut milk, then salt, turmeric, sugar, and enough lime juice (and extra water if necessary) to make a thick cream. Cover, leave 1 hour, sieve and stir.

(2) Heat a non-stick frying pan over medium low. Into the pan pour 3–4 in/7.5–10.5 cm circles (smearing them out to this size with a spoon so that they are as thin as possible). Cook them for 4–5 minutes, or until the edges pull away from the pan and the tops are dry. Lift out with a spatula and gently curve round to form little pockets. Serve with bowls of Arjad (page 63) and follow the recipe for coconut and shrimp filling below to stuff them.

KHANOM BEUANG YOOAHU

Coconut and shrimp filling

½ lb/250 g cleaned and shelled fresh raw shrimps
3 oz/90 g finely grated fresh coconut
3 tbsp vegetable oil
1 tbsp chopped coriander root (or stems)
2 garlic cloves, finely chopped
2 small hot red chillies, seeded and chopped
Seasonings: 2 tsp nam pla fish sauce, 1 tbsp sugar,
1 tsp salt, 1 tsp ground pepper
handful fresh coriander leaves

(1) Grind together shrimps and coconut to the consistency of coarse breadcrumbs in a food processor. Purée the coriander root, garlic and chillies. Stir-fry this spice paste in the oil over moderate heat until fragrant. Add coconut and shrimps and continue cooking until the shrimps are opaque. Season with fish sauce, etc., to taste. When ready to serve, stir in coarsely chopped coriander and use to fill the pancakes.

SATAYS

Grilled meats with peanut sauce (serves 6 with other dishes)

Satay stands selling these delicious strips of barbecued meat often park next to cafés in Chiang Mai so that the café customers can nibble while they wait for their main course. This recipe is loosely based on one from the Oriental Hotel, with a northern slant learned in Chiang Mai.

Satays
1 lb/500 g boneless raw chicken breast
1 lb/500 g boneless lean pork
8 fl oz/225 ml coconut milk
(3 oz/90 g creamed coconut mixed with boiling water)*
½ tsp ground turmeric
¼ tsp ground cumin
¼ tsp ground nutmeg
¼ tsp ground coriander
pinch of salt

Sauce
1¼ pt/700 ml thick coconut milk
(10 oz/300 g creamed coconut mixed with boiling water)*
3 tbsp red curry paste†
2 tbsp soft brown sugar
1 tbsp nam pla fish sauce
juice of 1 lime
3 tbsp ground roast peanuts or peanut butter

(1) Pound the meat until it is slightly flattened, then cut into strips about ¾ in/2 cm wide and 3–4 in/7.5–10 cm long. Mix together the coconut milk and spices and marinate the meat in this for at least an hour.

(2) To make the sauce, heat a cupful of coconut milk in a wok over medium-high heat until the milk begins to thicken. Stir in the red curry paste and fry it until oil begins to show. Stir in remaining coconut milk and continue cooking, stirring occasionally, until the sauce has the consistency of thick yoghurt, and then add the seasonings and peanuts and stir for a couple of minutes.

(3) Thread the meat onto skewers (wooden ones are best) and grill or barbecue the meat over high heat for a couple of minutes each side. Serve hot with the dipping sauce, and with a bowl of Arjad (page 63) for contrast.

*Coconut milk – made by blending fresh coconut meat with hot water and squeezing through cloth to extract. First squeezing is cream, second is milk. The coconut pulp can then be dried and burned on the barbecue – to add a subtle flavour to grilling meats. Fresh coconut milk when cooking has a delightful aroma, but is time-consuming to make. The following are some alternative methods:

Easiest – use tinned coconut milk (equivalent to thick coconut milk – the cream is usually on top, the thinner milk underneath). Or creamed coconut mixed with boiling water: 3½ oz/100 g/half a block of creamed coconut mixed with 7 fl oz /200 ml boiling water will make cream; 3½ oz/100 g of coconut with 14 fl oz /400 ml boiling water makes coconut milk.

From fresh coconut – liquidize chunks of fresh coconut flesh (remove brown skin) with a little hot water until smooth. Squeeze through some thin cloth to extract as much cream as possible. Liquidize the remaining pulp with about 1¼ pt/700 ml hot water, squeeze out again for the milk. Small coconuts yield about 6–7 fl oz/185–200 ml cream.

†Red curry paste – an excellent spicy paste that can be kept in the refrigerator for several weeks. Use it to coat chicken and duck before roasting, or mix with coconut milk and heat chicken, ground pork or beef in it for an instant Thai-style curry.

10 large dried hot peppers, seeded and soaked 5 minutes
3 shallots, chopped
4–8 garlic cloves, chopped
2 in/5 cm thumb of Siamese ginger (or ordinary ginger),
peeled and chopped
3 stalks of lemon grass, woody end only, chopped
(or grated zest from 1 lemon)
1 tsp salt
2½ tsp coriander seeds
1 tsp ground cumin
1 tsp dried kaffir lime skins, soaked and chopped
1 tsp shrimp paste

Purée all the ingredients, adding a little vegetable oil if necessary. The Thais would pound this in a mortar, which releases more herb oils. I admit to using a blender.

Thai shrimp paste does not smell very appetizing at first but it gives a rich depth of flavour to any dish in which it is used.

TOM SOM PLA

Sweet and sour fish soup (serves 4 with other dishes).
In Chiang Mai this soup was made with fresh river fish; in Bangkok and the south the fish came from the sea.

3 tbsp chopped coriander root or stems
½ tsp peppercorns
3 shallots
pinch of salt
¼ tsp shrimp paste
stems from 3 lemon grass stalks
3 tbsp peanut or other vegetable oil
10–12 oz/300–350 g boned firm white fish cut in big slices
4 tsp brown sugar
3 tbsp nam pla fish sauce
2 tbsp lime juice
4 finely shredded kaffir lime leaves
1 in/2.5 cm knob Siamese ginger, shredded
handful fresh mint or basil leaves, coarsely chopped
3 spring onions, finely cut crosswise

(1) Pound together or purée the coriander, pepper, shallots, salt, shrimp paste and lemon grass and fry in hot oil until fragrant. Cook the fish in this a minute each side.
(2) In a saucepan or wok big enough to hold all the ingredients, bring 2½ pt/1.4 l water to a boil, add the fish and the remaining spices and seasonings. Bring back to the boil, scatter over the fresh herbs and ginger, stir, and serve immediately.

A Songkran Feast at Home in Chiang Mai

A crucial element in old Chiang Mai was the 'Kan-Dtohk' brass tray of small dishes. Kan-Dtohk dinners were always arranged for the ordination of priests and for weddings and housewarmings. The trays would be set outside on bamboo mats with five or six people around each one. The trays are rare now, except in rural areas, but the feast dishes remain the same:

– sticky rice, very popular in northern Thailand
– a 'Lab' (meat curry, usually made with crisp pork skin)
– sliced spicy northern sausage called sai ua
– several of the spicy pork dips that are famous in the north (Nam phrik num – page 60) served with crisp deep-fried rice chips (below) and lightly blanched vegetables (broccoli, green beans) to dip in them
– cold salads, perhaps Yam Kanung On (young jackfruit boiled, pounded with spices and mixed with noodles), or Yam Thua (green wing bean salad – page 68)
– a big basket of fresh fruit – oranges, sapodillas and the little northern bananas – with plenty of fiery Mei Kong whisky to wash it all down.

KHAO DTANG

Sticky rice crisps (to make about 12 2 in/5 cm diamonds)

In Thailand there is always leftover pot rice to be dried in the sun and deep-fried for dips. I use a low oven to dry the rice – or press it out in a tray and leave overnight. Delicious to dip into the coconut and peanut sauce following, or to drizzle with sweet fudge (which in Thailand would be scented with jasmine).

7 oz/200 g Thai sticky rice
vegetable oil for deep frying

(1) Wash the rice in several changes of cold water until the water runs clear. Drain, wrap loosely in a cloth and steam for about an hour, until the rice has no hard centre.
(2) To make crispy rice, smooth it out in a greased baking tray to a depth of ½ in/ 1 cm. Dry for about an hour in a very low oven and cut into 2 in/5 cm diamonds. Heat the oil until a piece of bread browns in 50 seconds and fry the rice pieces in it a few at a time until golden. Be careful while frying as they may spit if they are still moist.

KHAO DTANG NA TANG

Sticky rice crisps with creamy coconut dip (6 as a snack)

In Chiang Mai each guest was served this sauce in individual cups of folded banana leaves held with wooden pins, and either quickly blanched fresh vegetables (tiny aubergines, broccoli, green beans) or a few crisp rice slices on the side to dip.

6 large kale or cabbage leaves
14 fl oz/375 ml thick coconut milk (1 tin, or see page 65)
4 garlic cloves, chopped
1 tsp shrimp paste
5 hot red chillies, seeded (plus 2, shredded, for decoration)
8 shallot cloves, chopped
10 oz/300 g ground pork
2½ oz/75 g ground roast peanuts or crunchy peanut butter
2–3 tbsp nam pla fish sauce
juice of 2–3 limes
1 tbsp sugar
fresh coriander leaves for decoration

(1) Make leaf cups as shown. Pound or purée the garlic, shrimp paste, chillies and shallots.

(2) In a wok or large frying pan stir-fry the coconut cream until oil begins to appear around the edges. Add pounded spice mixture, stir until fragrant, then ground pork.

(3) When the pork is no longer pink, stir in the peanuts, let them cook a little, then add fish sauce, sugar and lime. Pour into leaf cups or bowls and decorate with fresh coriander and shredded chillies.

YAM THUA PU

Wing bean salad (serves 4–6 with other dishes)

Wing beans are very long green beans available from many Chinese and Thai supermarkets. Normally one could substitute ordinary green beans, but to make this a special dish cooks tie the beans into decorative knots.

7 oz/200 g fresh wing beans
3 tbsp peanut or other vegetable oil
3 whole shallots, shredded
3 garlic cloves, shredded
3 fresh red chillies, seeded and shredded
(save some for decoration)
juice of 1 lime
2 tsp red curry paste (page 66) or
2 tbsp nam pla fish sauce
4 tsp sugar
salt to taste (about 1/2 tsp)
3 1/2 oz/100 g small cooked shrimps
3 1/2 oz/100 g shredded cooked pork
handful of crushed dry-roasted peanuts

(1) Cook beans for 5 minutes in boiling water, tie into knots while still warm and flexible, and plunge in iced water.

(2) Fry shallots, garlic and chillies in medium-hot oil until crisp and brown (but not burnt – start with the shallots, which take less time).

(3) Whisk together lime juice, curry paste (or fish sauce), sugar and salt and toss with the beans, shrimps, meat and shallot mixture. Scatter roasted peanuts and chillies over the top and serve immediately.

Offerings to Monks

GAENG CHUD WUN SEN

Vermicelli soup and spiced meatballs (serves 4–6)

This is very quick to make and has a delicious, delicate flavour. Do not break the long noodles, which are a symbol of long life in Thailand.

1/2 lb/250 g ground pork
3 garlic cloves, finely chopped
1 in/2.5 cm knob of fresh Siamese ginger
(or ordinary ginger), peeled and finely chopped
1/2 tsp salt
1 tbsp soy sauce
1 tsp ground black pepper
6 dried black Chinese mushrooms or shitake,

soaked in warm water for 15 minutes, sliced thinly
1 celery stalk, sliced thinly crosswise
7 oz/200 g rice vermicelli
3 spring/green onions, sliced thinly crosswise
about 3½ oz/100 g bean sprouts
1–2 tbsp fish sauce
handful of fresh coriander, coarsely chopped
2 small red chillies, seeded and shredded

(1) Mix the ground pork with the garlic, ginger, salt, soy sauce and pepper. Roll into 1 in/2.5 cm balls.

(2) Bring 3¼ pts/1.8 l water to a low boil. Add the pork balls, mushrooms and celery and simmer for 5 minutes. Add vermicelli, spring onions and bean sprouts, stir until the vermicelli is soft, season with fish sauce and top with coriander and chillies.

GAENG HUNGLEY GAI
Chiang Mai-style chicken curry (serves 4)

A richly flavoured curry with the Burmese-style spicing typical of food in the northwest. Serve it over boiled rice or thin noodles. If you use 1½ pt/800 ml of thin coconut milk at step 2 (instead of the thick milk), this dish becomes a version of Khao Soi, the Chiang Mai lunch soup – served in bowls over 12 oz/350 g thin rice noodles, a quarter of the noodles deep-fried after boiling and crumbled on top.

Khao Soi always comes with a selection of condiments – fresh lime, fish sauce, chilli vinegar and soy sauce.

2 lb/1 kg chicken
Curry paste*
7 large dried red peppers, seeded
6 shallot cloves or 1 onion, chopped
2 garlic cloves, chopped
2 in/5 cm lemon grass (white part), or 1 tbsp lemon zest
2 tsp chopped coriander root (or stems)
1 in/2.5 cm knob Siamese ginger, peeled and chopped
2 tsp Thai shrimp paste
1 tsp salt
1 tsp roasted coriander seeds
1 tsp roasted cumin seeds
½ tsp powdered nutmeg
½ tsp chopped preserved lime peel (or fresh)
3 tbsp mustard oil, or other vegetable oil
3½ oz/100 g bamboo shoots, shredded
juice of 2 limes
1 tbsp sugar
1 14 oz/400 ml tin coconut milk (or fresh – see page 65)
2 tbsp fish sauce
1 head of pickled garlic (optional)
Topping
2 red chillies, seeded and shredded
2 spring onions chopped
fresh coriander, chopped
(or cut the chillies and onions into flowers)

(1) Skin and chop the chicken (with bones) into 2 in/5 cm pieces. Purée all curry paste ingredients. If you use a food processor, pound the resulting paste for several seconds after to release natural oils. Heat the oil in a wok or frying pan and fry the spices until fragrant (about 5 minutes).

(2) Add the chicken to the pan and stir-fry for 1–2 minutes. Add shredded bamboo shoots and coconut milk and bring slowly to the boil. Stir in fish sauce, lime juice and pickled garlic and simmer gently, partially covered, for 15–20 minutes.

(3) When the chicken is cooked, serve it over the rice or noodles and scatter shredded chillies, etc. on top.

  *Curry paste can be made up well ahead of time and frozen.

MEE GROB

Sweet and sour crisp vermicelli (serves 6, with other dishes)

At the palace (and in the Oriental Hotel now) this was an exquisite dish served in deep-fried noodle baskets. The baskets are worth the effort to make (you will need 2 small enamelled metal soup plates), and keep for several weeks if tightly wrapped. If you can't be bothered, the crispy vermicelli noodles can be served in lettuce cups – lovely with any moist curries (like the previous recipe).

For noodle baskets
6 oz/180 g fine rice vermicelli
8–9 oz/250–280 g rice vermicelli for mixing
4 eggs, beaten
vegetable oil for deep-frying
(enough to completely cover metal soup plates)
4 oz/125 g/1 cake soybean curd, cut in tiny cubes
3 shallots or 1/2 small onion, finely chopped
6 garlic cloves, finely chopped
12 oz/360 g mixed pork and shrimps (or use just one meat)
3 tbsp preserved white soybeans (optional)
1/2 tsp salt
3 tsp rice vinegar, 2 tbsp nam pla fish sauce, juice of 1 lime
3 tbsp soft brown sugar
1 tbsp grated kaffir lime peel (or grated fresh lime peel)

For decoration
2 finely sliced pickled garlic cloves (optional)
2 small fresh red chillies, seeded and shredded
fresh coriander

(1) Cover the noodles in cold water and leave to soften for 15 minutes. Oil two small metal soup or pie plates, one inside and one out. Drain noodles and soak in the beaten eggs for 5 minutes – this stops them absorbing too much oil and keeps them much crisper. Drain again, reserving the eggs, and cover to keep moist.

(2) Heat the oil in a wok or saucepan until a piece of bread will brown in 50 seconds. Drape two layers of noodles over the outside of one of the soup plates, overlapping them in a criss-cross pattern. Trim them to the same size as the plate and press the other plate (greased inside) on top. Using a wire ladle, lower the plates into the hot oil and fry for 2–3 minutes, or until golden brown. Drain on kitchen paper.

(3) Deep-fry the remaining noodles (a few at a time – to stop them lowering the oil temperature and becoming too greasy) until golden in the oil. Lift out with a

slotted spoon and drain on kitchen paper. Crumble into small pieces – they can be stored for several days in an airtight container.

(4) Deep-fry the soybean curd until golden, drain on kitchen paper. Pour off all but 2 tbsp oil.

(5) Over medium heat, stir the onions and garlic in the oil until golden. Add the pork and shrimps and stir until opaque. Stir in the bean curd, preserved beans, salt, then the reserved eggs, a little at a time. Finally add the liquids, sugar and peel and stir until the mixture is very dry – about 7–10 minutes.

(6) Before serving, heat together the crisp noodles and the meat mixture and spoon into noodle baskets or lettuce cups, scattering the top with shredded garlic, etc.

GAENG KHIAW WAAN GOONG

Green prawn curry (serves 6)

The following recipe, based on one from the Oriental Hotel, is famous in southern Thailand. In the palace it was often cooked with baby squid that had been stuffed with pork, beef and fish, and would have been offered to monks on a big tray with other dishes.

> *15–20 tiny hot green chillies/phrig khee nu*
> *1 lemon grass stalk*
> *1 tbsp chopped kaffir lime peel*
> *1 in/2.5 cm stalk Siamese ginger (or ordinary ginger)*
> *1 tsp toasted coriander seeds, ground*
> *2 garlic cloves, 3 shallot heads*
> *1 tsp cumin seeds, toasted and ground*
> *1/2 tsp ground turmeric*
> *1 tsp shrimp paste*
> *9 fl oz/250 ml coconut cream and*
> *18 fl oz/500 ml coconut milk (page 65)*
> *3–4 tbsp nam pla fish sauce, 1 tsp soft brown sugar*
> *20 tiny aubergines (walnut-sized), halved*
> *1 lb/500 g uncooked prawns (weighed with shells),*
> *shelled and cleaned (or 12 oz/350 g chicken breast)*
> *2 stalks of fresh young peppercorns (if available)*
> *7 kaffir lime leaves, shredded*
> *5 tiny red chillies, seeded and shredded*
> *handful fresh basil or mint leaves*

(1) Pound or purée in a blender the chillies, lemon grass, kaffir lime peel, ginger, coriander, garlic, shallots, cumin and turmeric, adding the shrimp paste last. (This is green curry paste, the equivalent of the red curry paste on page 66, and can be used in the same way.)

(2) Bring the coconut cream to a boil and cook until it has an oily surface. Stir-fry the green curry paste in this until it is fragrant and thick. Season with fish sauce and sugar. Add tiny aubergines/eggplants (if available) and stir well, then prawns or chicken and stir for 2 minutes, gradually adding coconut milk.

(3) Just before serving, add green peppercorns, kaffir lime leaves, chillies and basil and stir for a minute.

YAM NEAU
Thai Beef Salad (serves 4–6 with other dishes)
A similar dish is still served at the Oriental Hotel.

black pepper
1¼ lb/625 g best beefsteak (tenderloin, rump)
2 tbsp vegetable oil
2 garlic cloves, 3 shallots, shredded
2 oz/60 g sugar
½ tsp salt
2 tbsp light soy sauce
juice of 2 limes
small handful fresh coriander leaves
3 spring/green onions, finely sliced crosswise
4–6 small hot red chillies, seeded and shredded
wedge of white cabbage, finely shredded

(1) Grind plenty of black pepper over the surface of the steak and grill on both sides until medium rare. Chill. Slice crosswise into thin strips.
(2) Fry the shallots and garlic in oil until brown and crisp but not burnt. Whisk together the sugar, salt, soy sauce and lime juice and toss with all the ingredients, reserving a few chillies and coriander to scatter over the top.

Royal Feasts
– miniature versions of everything, from fish soup cooked with stuffed baby squid to aubergines/eggplants the size of marbles hollowed out and filled with coconut milk.
– tiny water chestnut cubes stained blue and red, coated in cornflour and par-boiled, then plunged in syrup and served with coconut cream and ice (Siamese Gems). 'The Thais are a very playful people,' said Chali of this dish. 'They like to eat jewels.'

MEE GATHI
Herbed coconut vermicelli with prawns (serves 6–8)

This is an adaptation of one of Chali's recipes for a court dish served as a delicate lunch in the old days.

5 oz/150 g creamed coconut blended with 10 fl oz/300 ml hot water
4 whole shallots, shredded
1 in/2.5 cm thumb fresh ginger, shredded
1½ tbsp white preserved soy beans (optional)
½ lb/250 g raw ground pork or chicken
¼ lb/125 g shelled raw shrimps, ground, and
¼ lb/125 g whole shelled shrimps
1 bean curd cake, cut in little cubes
2½ tbsp sugar
2 tbsp fish sauce
2 oz/60 g creamed coconut blended with 6 fl oz/185 ml hot water
½ tsp ground red chillies or cayenne in 2 tbsp peanut oil
½–¾ lb/250–350 g rice vermicelli,
soaked in cold water 10 minutes, drained
about 4 oz/125 g fresh bean sprouts
fresh coriander, 2 small red chillies, shredded

(1) Heat the coconut cream over high heat until oil begins to show. Stir in the shallots, ginger and soybeans until fragrant. Add pork, shrimps and bean curd, cook until meat is opaque and season with sugar and fish sauce. Remove from heat and keep warm.

(2) Bring the coconut milk to a boil, add the chilli oil and turn and toss the noodles, and bean sprouts in this until well mixed. Serve topped with the sauce and garnished with fresh coriander and chillies.

KHAO CHAE CHAO WANG
The Court Iced-Water Rice

Of all the dishes served in Thailand, this one must surely be the most evocative of the country's spirit. Not really one dish, but a collection of titbits – carved fruit, stuffed shallots, sweet and sour beef, fragrant rice – with the centrepiece an earthenware pot of jasmine and smoke-scented ice water. You take a scoop of rice in scented water, and a few savoury-sweet morsels with every spoonful.

Khao Chae is traditional for the hot months of March and April, and is still served in the Oriental Hotel, Thanying and Bussaracum restaurants in Bangkok. I have given recipes for only a couple of the dishes – impossible to contemplate stuffing a shallot.

Rice in scented, smoked iced water
Stuffed sweet peppers in 'Golden Nets'
Shallot cloves, stuffed
with coconut cream and ground fish
Carved mango 'leaves', chilli 'flowers', cucumber 'flowers'
Salted Chinese radish
Crispy smoked catfish*
Deep-fried minced pork balls
Sweet and sour shredded beef†

*The catfish is smoke-roasted over coconut, filleted and dried in oven until stringy, and finally fried in oil for 2–3 minutes until crispy. On the way to the palace in Bangkok you can see huge ovens with men carrying baskets of catfish up from the river to be smoked.

†This salty sweet beef is made by massaging raw palm sugar, salt and nam pla fish sauce into the beef for 2 days. It is then shredded with the grain and fried or dried.

SMOKED FLOWER WATER

1 small beeswax incense candle
10 jasmine flowers
1 damask rose

Put flowers in the bottom of an earthenware lidded pot and fill the pot with cold water, leaving room at the top to float the candle. Light the candle and float it in a saucer on top of the water. Cover and leave to smoke. After an hour, remove the candle, recover the pot and leave to infuse for 6–7 hours or overnight. Add ice. To serve, spoon some rice into your bowl and top with smoked water.

STUFFED SWEET PEPPERS IN 'GOLDEN NETS'

The lacy nets that wrap these peppers are very pretty to fill with grilled chicken or shrimps instead, and much easier to make than they look.

4 garlic cloves
2 small hot red chillies, seeded
3 tbsp chopped coriander root or stems
1/2 lb/250 g ground raw pork
5 fresh raw prawns, shelled, cleaned and ground
3 tbsp fish sauce
1 tbsp sugar
1 egg, beaten
6 small pointed yellow Thai sweet peppers or
4 very small sweet green peppers

Golden nets
3 eggs, beaten

(1) Pound or purée the garlic, chillies and coriander and stir-fry in oil in a wok until fragrant. Add pork and prawns and continue cooking until opaque. Season with fish sauce and sugar, allow to cool, and mix with egg.

(2) Skin peppers over flame or under grill and slice them as little as possible down one side (just enough to remove seeds), leaving stems on. Stuff with pork mixture and steam for 5–10 minutes (or until tender to fork).

(3) To make the 'golden nets', heat a small non-stick pan over medium-low heat. Dip your fingers in the beaten egg and trail it thinly back and forth across the hot pan in a criss-cross pattern to make a lacy net. When the edges pull away from the pan and the top is set, lift out the net and repeat 4–6 times. Dry the peppers, wrap carefully in nets and serve at room temperature.

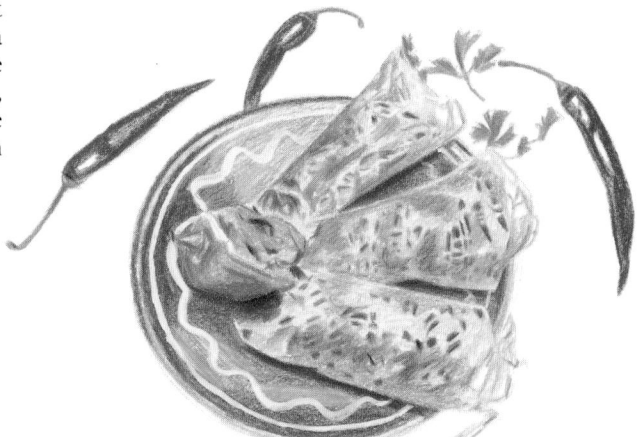

DEEP-FRIED MINCED PORK BALLS

¹/₂ lb/250 g ground pork
1 tbsp ground salted fish (or 2 tbsp fish sauce)
1 tsp ground pepper
fresh coriander leaves
1 egg, beaten
vegetable oil for deep-frying

Mix together the pork, fish and pepper and roll into 1 in/2.5 cm balls. Press a few coriander leaves into each, dip in egg and deep-fry in hot oil. May also be served as a condiment with curries.

PLA NUENG

Steamed fish (serves 4 with other dishes)
Exquisite-tasting and very beautiful – especially if you use a red snapper or pomfret.

1 medium whole pomfret (or red snapper or small sole)
4 dried Chinese black mushrooms,
soaked 15 minutes in warm water and sliced thinly
4 small hot red chillies, seeded
1¹/₂ tsp cornflour
2 tbsp soy sauce
¹/₂ tsp crushed peppercorns
2 garlic cloves, finely chopped
1 tbsp peanut oil
1 in/2.5 cm knob fresh ginger, peeled and shredded
2 pickled Chinese plums, or slices of pickled lime,
with a little of their juice, chopped (optional)
fresh coriander
4 spring onions
extra whole red chillies

(1) Slit the fish down its spine to remove guts and backbone (or have the fishmonger do it). Lay it on a shallow, heatproof dish and make 3 crosswise slashes down one side. Top, tail and seed 3 chillies and open them out flat. Slip these into the slashes leaving a scarlet rim poking out, and tuck some mushroom slices behind them.
(2) Mix together the cornflour, soy sauce, pepper, garlic, ginger, plums and 1 tbsp oil to make a sauce. Pour it inside and around the fish and stuff the fish with the remaining mushrooms. Steam it for about 20 minutes (depending on its thickness) until the flesh is opaque right through. I do this in a big Chinese bamboo steamer over a wok.
(3) Decorate with fresh coriander, spring onion curls and carved chillies.

YAM POLOMAI
Fruit salad

Toss together some cooked chicken and tiny shrimps with fresh fruits (rambutans, lychees, oranges, grapes), sliced water chestnuts, crisply fried shallots and garlic and almond slivers. Season with lime juice, sugar, salt, fresh coriander and shredded chillies and mound into hollowed out oranges, pineapples or rambutan shells.

MIANG KANA
Stuffed leaves with sweet and salty sauce (serves 6 with other dishes)

A very pretty do-it-yourself palace dish from the Thanying restaurant – trimmed leaves filled and topped with sauce. As with so many Thai recipes, the time involved is mostly in assembly.

Sauce
4 garlic cloves
1 small onion or 3 shallots
5 large dried red chillies, seeded and soaked in hot water
1 tsp shrimp paste
2 tbsp vegetable oil
3 oz/90 g boned white fish
1½ oz/45 g dried tamarind, in 4½ fl oz/125 ml boiling water
4 tbsp brown sugar
2 tbsp nam pla fish sauce

Fillings
vegetable oil for deep-frying
6 oz/180 g fatty pork, cut in 1 in/2.5 cm matchsticks
5 tbsp dried shrimps (optional)
12 big kale, spinach or collard green leaves, divided in half
2–3 big handfuls salted peanuts
2–3 limes, in ¼ in/0.5 cm dice
6 shallots, finely sliced
4 in/10 cm knob Siamese ginger, peeled and finely chopped
2–3 red chillies, seeded and finely sliced

(1) Make the sauce: purée the garlic, shallots, chillies and shrimp paste. Heat the oil and cook the fish in it on both sides until opaque. Lift out and flake. Add the spice paste to the pan and stir-fry until fragrant. Pour in the tamarind liquid and sugar and cook until reduced. Purée together with the cooked fish and fish sauce and pour into a serving bowl (or individual serving 'leaves').

(2) Heat the oil over medium-high heat until a cube of bread browns in 50 seconds, and deep-fry first the pork and then the shrimps (these do not smell wonderful when frying, but have a mysterious flavour), keeping them separate. Trim the leaves into 4 in/10 cm octagons or circles and arrange everything in little piles on a big bamboo tray, with the bowl of sauce in the middle.

Finally, take a leaf, fold it into a cone, add a few peanuts, shrimps, lime pieces; top with a spoonful of sauce and pop it in your mouth.

KHAO NIEW MAMUANG

Coconut steamed rice with mango (serves 4–6)

April is mango season in Thailand: in May there might be durian rice instead. The Thais say that if you eat three rambutans after durian, they will take away the smell of drains, but counter with the phrase 'a little bit of durian smell is a sign of wealth'.

4 oz/125 g sticky rice
12 fl oz/360 ml coconut cream (page 65)
2 tbsp sugar
1 tsp salt
3 mangoes, cut off their stones
3–4 tbsp dry-roasted peanuts, crushed coarsely

Cover the rice in water and leave to soak for 6 hours. Drain, wrap loosely in a clean cloth and steam for one hour. Spoon into a serving bowl and mix while still warm with 7 fl oz/200 ml coconut cream, sugar and salt. Cover in plastic film. (If you have access to jasmine, you can scatter a few flowers across the top.) Peel the mangoes and slice into bite-sized pieces (but keep in mango shape). To serve, take a few mango pieces and a spoonful of rice, coat it in more coconut cream and top with nuts.

GLUAY CHUEAM

Banana in lime syrup and coconut cream (serves 4–6)

6 oz sugar
1/2 tsp salt
juice and shredded zest of 1 lime
4–6 small hard bananas
9 fl oz/250 ml coconut cream (page 65)

Bring 18 fl oz/500 ml water to a boil, add sugar, salt and lime juice. Boil until reduced to a syrup. Slice the bananas in half lengthwise (and again crosswise if they are too long for the pot) and cook in the syrup until softened. Lift out onto a plate and spoon over some of the syrup, making sure you get some of the lime zest.

Heat the coconut cream until it thickens but does not separate and serve while still warm with the bananas.

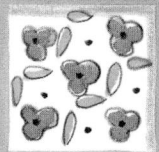
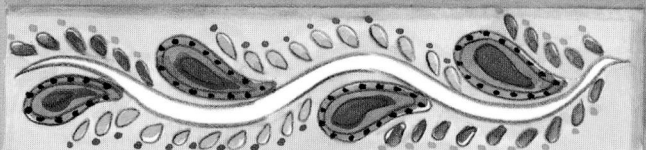

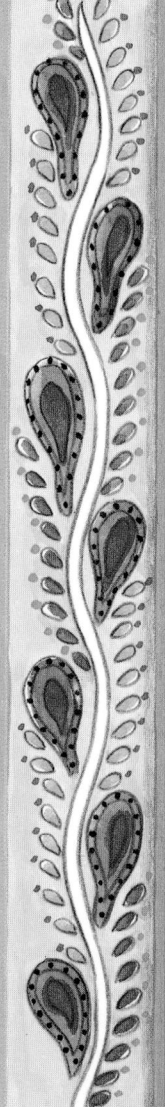

MADAME MORGENSTERN ET SES SACS

Jewish Passover in Nice

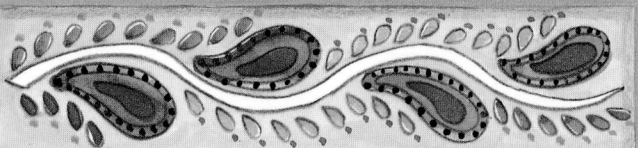

Passover remembers the last hurried supper the Israelites had in Egypt, and is roughly based on the description of that meal in Exodus 12:3–11. It is complicated now by the list of food laws that Moses passed on to his people, but essentially it remains a celebration of their flight, and of their final survival.

Traditionally, all the extended family and many generations are welcomed, as well as the poor of the community – 'Let all who are hungry come and eat.' Elijah is said to enjoy disguising himself as a beggar to see if he will be turned away from the Seders, the Passover dinners.

I went to Nice – a city of casinos and icing-white villas where Russian Grand Dukes lived in luxury before the Revolution and returned as waiters and chauffeurs after it – to spend Passover with the Morgenstern family. Jacques Morgenstern is a French physicist. I thought there could be no place on earth less likely to romanticize tradition.

Jacques Morgenstern's father was an Ashkenazic Jew from Warsaw, and his Sephardic mother came from Spain. During the Second World War Jacques was hidden from the Nazis and the Pétain supporters, first by nuns, and then in the homes of Christian friends. He never celebrated Passover. At university in Israel in the sixties he met Susie, an American from New Jersey. He turned up on her parents' doorstep one summer to visit her. Susie's mother took one look at the tall, imposing boy with the French accent and said, 'I can make a wedding in two weeks.'

ONE

To get to grips with the concept of Passover, I was told, you have to understand that the Hebrew word for Egypt stems from a root word meaning narrow, constrained, inhibited.

'To leave Egypt,' said Jacques, 'is to be reborn and revived.'

'So Passover is really a celebration of springtime then? New Year for the Jewish tribes?'

'A lot more than that.'

It is about a flight from narrowness and slavery into freedom – spiritual, emotional, psychological – and all that that implies, taking in ideas of movement: from chaos to order, from potential to actual, from womb to open world. The twin themes of exodus and creation run in parallel through the Passover disciplines.

'The food at Passover – the bitter herbs, the roasted lamb bone – they are symbols of this flight and rebirth then?'

'Yes and no,' Jacques said. 'The food we eat and the order in which it is served are not meant to be just ideas. We are to feel, each and every one present, that this is actually our last supper before fleeing Egypt.'

The origins of the Passover meal can be read in the Haggadah book that everyone is given at the feast: Haggadah, from the Hebrew 'to tell', the book of the legend. Four cups of wine, because of God's four promises to free the Israelites from slavery. Unleavened matzo, because the Jews did not have time to let their bread rise in the sudden flight from Egypt. Bitter herbs, like the bitterness of slavery. Greens, for the lack of meat – dipped in salty water to remember their tears.

'But these food laws, all those intricate rules about koshering, they are surely taken to extremes?' I asked.

'Perhaps,' said Jacques, physics clearly struggling with religion. 'But not if you believe in redemption through faith and discipline and respect for tradition.'

By the first day of Passover all leavened food in the house must be burnt. Not one hidden crumb should remain, even in your stomach.

In food cooked for the feast, potato starch and ground nuts take the place of flour; nutty-flavoured matzo meal replaces breadcrumbs. And all the china, cutlery, linen – anything to do with food – must be kosher. It means, really, having duplicate sets of everything just for Passover.

'All the old pots are exiled,' Susie said. 'If you have old salt, you throw it out and buy new. It takes weeks to get the house clean. While I am cleaning I have this dialogue with God, "Did you see? I even washed *that* cupboard corner!" You are supposed to go through on the last day with a candle and a feather to sweep up every last crumb.'

'And do you?'

'Well, I sort of go "Blah" with my hands instead. But the tension builds up to keep the two worlds apart. I have these islands of matzo kosherdom on my non-kosher kitchen table.'

'I hope God is watching and appreciating.'

Jacques grinned. 'I don't know. He is very busy, a little old and tired – and you know what it's like when you get old, you get forgetful.'

Before leaving London I had rung the head rabbi there to tell him I was researching the background of Passover and the koshering laws.

'That is not too difficult,' he said. 'There are many books.'

'And, of course, I want to find out why you celebrate in this way.'

'Ahh,' he said. '*Why* …why is another story. Why is much more complicated.'

There is one simple explanation. Three thousand years ago when Moses took his people out of Egypt in search of the promised land, the milk and honey were a long time coming. The Israelites wandered for forty years – if you take the Old Testament literally – or perhaps longer, if you see the forty years as a symbol. Most of the area they covered was hot and filthy.

Pork was most likely to breed worms and disease in the heat, butter and cream most likely to turn rancid – especially in contact with meat. So they were not to touch products of the pig, and 'Thou shalt not seethe a lamb in its mother's milk.' Both physically and emotionally it makes sense.

Moses knew that his people depended on him to build a strong framework after the oppressive but clearly defined years of slavery. To survive in that harsh landscape they needed new ceremonies, at once mystical, to satisfy their souls, and practical, to keep their bodies free of disease.

At least once a year there would be a complete cleansing, when all cooking utensils would be 'kashered'. The Hebrew 'kasher' means to make fit; in this case by sterilizing all the utensils in very hot water.

No leaven – that repository of potential digestive unease: 'On the first month, in the fourteenth day of the month, ye shall have the Passover where unleavened bread shall be eaten.' As if to compensate for all the strict dietary rules, on the anniversary of your freedom every year you will have a feast – and remember.

'Of course, Passover is big business now,' said Jacques. 'Oil and butter and wine have to have a special 'Kosher for Passover' label on them approved by the rabbis – which costs money. Each year the Union of Orthodox Jewish Congregations of America publishes a book of Passover products listing "kosher-for-Pesah food". There are even "searching sets" with a candle, a spoon, a feather and a bag for sale.'

1985 was the first year that Baron Rothschild made wine for Passover.

'It is still young,' said Jacques. 'But better than the usual Seder muck.'

TWO

There were twelve at the Seder: children and friends and cousins; Franca, Jacques' Italian sister-in-law; Nicole, the daughter of fourteen generations of rabbis, who had not celebrated the Seder since childhood; and Mrs Morgenstern, eighty-five, half-blind, wearing an old silver and black embroidered silk dress, and singing to herself in Spanish during the meal.

The table was set in a big room overlooking a terraced hillside of cherry blossoms, pale now against the rose and turquoise dusk. Below, the lights of Nice were just starting to appear. Susie laid out the Seder plate: a hard-boiled egg, a roasted lamb bone, some lettuce, bitter herbs, and a mixture of dates, spices and apples called haroset – to represent the mortar that the Jews used for the pyramid bricks.

Jacques explained to us that they had done their best to ensure not a

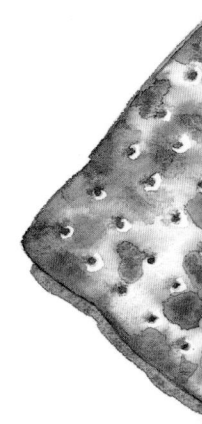

scrap of leavening was left in the house. If some remained, it was turned, with this blessing, into dust.

'In other words,' said Susie, in her strong New Jersey English, 'there is no need to be fanatical.'

Jacques broke the matzo, dipped the herbs in salt and the lettuce in haroset. He began to sing in a rich bass, the Hebrew words buzzing through his beard.

'How does this night differ from all other nights? On all other nights we eat bread and matzo. Why on this night do we eat only matzo?'

'We were slaves to Pharoah in Egypt, and Moses was sent to free our people from bondage ...' The questions roll out, the same every year, as are the answers.

'That would have been enough, that He took us out of Israel, but God did more ...That would have been enough ...'

The meal began with two rectangular patties each, one made from the white of leeks creamed with matzo and herbs, the other with spinach, to sprinkle with sugar or salt. 'They are supposed to resemble the Tablets of the Law,' said Susie. 'I came back from the market with all my fifteen rag bags full of spinach to make them – you know what happens to spinach – it cooked down to *nothing*.'

Susie's mother was famous in all of New Jersey's Jewish tapestry stores. She used to go from shop to shop asking for samples to make rag shopping bags. Susie makes hers from tired table linen, napkins, her children's old clothes. 'I look at them and they are my life,' she said. 'The Nice shopowners say, "Here she comes, Madame Morgenstern et ses sacs."'

The next dish was fresh mackerel in a rosy sauce of Provençal tomatoes and Nice's famous Alziari olive oil, flecked with flat Italian parsley, then chicken soup that had been simmering all morning, with little matzo dumplings – knaedles – floating in it.

'The aesthetic of knaedles,' Susie told us, 'is that they be light and fluffy.'

'You should have separated the eggs to lighten the dumplings as we do in Venice,' said Franca.

'We like them solid like cement. Of course, this chicken soup is the basis of everything – the Jewish penicillin.'

'Yes, we have soup too, in Venice. But stuffed goose neck for the main dish instead, with aubergines alla Veneziana.'

Susie brought out the source of the smell perfuming the house, a boned roast of lamb, rolled with prunes and raisins, pine kernels, garlic and herbs, and bronzed with olive oil and a squeeze of lemon juice. Crisp potato and leek cakes came with it, and a purée of young courgettes. These were old Mrs Morgenstern's Sephardic recipes, with the strong Mediterranean emphasis on vegetables and herbs.

A long, long stretch of prayers and snatches of the Haggadah, all in Hebrew. Susie kept repeating, 'Faster, Jacques, faster', just as she and her three sisters used to say to her father. 'That is always the way of you Americans,' Jacques said. 'Fast food, fast prayers.'

He poured a cup of wine for Elijah. Nicole's twins ran to open the door so he could enter, and a warm, damp breeze blew in, smelling of the ocean. Jacques put a record on, a scratchy recording of an old Spanish children's song with an endless number of verses and Mrs Morgenstern woke up for the finale and sang along in Hebraic Spanish, swaying to the tune:

> Then came God
> And smote the Angel of Death
> Who slew the slaughterer
> Who killed the ox
> Who drank the water
> That quenched the fire
> That burned the stick
> That beat the cat
> That ate the little goat
> That father bought with two gold coins.

'This is the bread of affliction which our father ate in the land of Egypt. Let all who are hungry come and eat. Let all who are in need come and celebrate Pesah with us. Now we are here. Next year we may be in the Land of Israel. Now we are slaves. Next year may we be free men.'

RECIPES

Passover in Nice was really two feasts: the first Seder on Friday night and the second on Saturday. Most of the cooking was finished by Friday, however, as no cooking is supposed to be done on the Sabbath (although Susie cheated a bit).

The first night showed the vegetable heritage of Jacques' Sephardic ancestors in Turkey; the second night reflected Susie's Russian-American Ashkenazic family (where frying and strong seasoning is not at all typical): gefilte fish or chopped chicken livers instead of the mackerel, a plain roast chicken instead of lamb.

FRIED SPINACH LEAVES WITH MATZO
(makes 8–10 patties)

These spinach patties with the Leek 'Dinim' are meant to look like Moses' Tablets of the Law – two little rectangles, side by side on each plate. I serve them in my non-Jewish household in a puddle of fresh tomato sauce – tomatoes peeled, seeded and cooked down quickly with onions, garlic and olive oil, freshly torn basil leaves stirred in at the end. Very pretty against the dark green of the spinach and the gold of the fried leeks.

1 lb/500 g fresh spinach leaves
3–4 matzos, soaked in water until very soft
1–2 eggs, beaten
½ tsp salt, lots of black pepper (or to taste)
½ tsp ground mace
olive oil for frying

(1) Wash the spinach very well under water and chop finely. Squeeze out the matzo and knead together for several minutes with the spinach and spices until it sticks together, adding more egg if necessary to make it stick. It should be very soft. Form patties about 2 in × 3 in/5 cm × 8 cm and ¾ in/2 cm thick. Chill for at least an hour to firm up.

(2) Heat olive oil over medium heat and fry the patties on both sides. They should be just browning on the outside but still bright green within. Serve warm or at room temperature.

LEEK 'DINIM'

Leek and matzo patties (makes 8–10 patties)
Save the green parts of the leeks to make Potatoes 'Elmondigas'.

2¼ lb/1 kg leeks
2–3 matzos, crushed
1 egg, beaten
½ tsp salt, lots of ground black pepper (or to taste)
olive oil for frying

Discard the roots and jagged tough leaves of the leeks, trim the green leaves and reserve. Finely chop the whites and cook in 2–4 tbsp of olive oil over medium heat until they are soft and golden and have given off any excess moisture. Mix them with the matzo, egg and seasonings, form into the same size as the spinach patties and chill well. Fry in olive oil over medium heat until golden brown and crisp.

MACKEREL IN TOMATOES AND PARSLEY

A recipe from Susie's Sephardic mother-in-law; the red sauce to symbolize the Red Sea. It should be said that the tomatoes Susie used were the glorious, fleshy Provençal ones with a blush of pink in their skins (nothing like the watery, woody excuse for tomatoes we see in Britain) and the oil used to cook them a deep golden extra-virgin olive oil from Alziari in Vieux Nice.

A deep nickel sauté pan was lined with olive oil and 'about a ton' of freshly chopped parsley cooked in it until it just changed colour. Fourteen seeded, peeled and puréed tomatoes were immediately poured in with a tsp of salt, 2 of sugar, 15–20 coarsely crushed peppercorns, and the juice of 2 lemons. This was cooked down for about half an hour and the beheaded, cleaned mackerel slipped in afterwards and barely simmered for about 10–12 minutes, until the flesh flaked to a fork.

The fish was served in a deep brown earthenware dish, with more lemon if desired. A grey mullet or other fleshy white fish could be used instead of mackerel.

CHICKEN SOUP WITH FLUFFY HERBED DUMPLINGS

(Serves 8)

Chicken soup, as Susie told me, is the basis of everything, 'the Jewish penicillin'. This one is a deep gold, thickened with almonds, and is inspired by an old Polish Ashkenazic recipe. I add fresh tarragon to the dumplings – for the delicious aroma and the flecks of green.

1 small free-range* chicken (preferably a boiler),
cut in pieces, with its giblets
2 halved, peeled turnips
2 halved carrots
2 halved celery stalks with leaves
1 big onion, stuck with 6 cloves
2 trimmed leeks
6 tbsp ground almonds
salt and black pepper to taste
4 carrots, peeled and cut in long chunks

Dumplings
2 eggs, separated
3 fl oz/90 ml water
1½ tbsp olive oil (or chicken fat)
4 oz/125 g matzo meal
¾ tsp salt, lots of black pepper
handful of fresh tarragon or chives, finely chopped

(1) Cover the chicken and giblets with 10 pt/6 l cold water and bring to a slow boil, skimming often until not much scum rises to the surface. Add all except the dumpling ingredients and the almonds and bring back to a boil. Reduce heat, partially cover pot and simmer for 2 hours. Allow to cool to room temperature, shred meat into a bowl, discard bones, turnips and cloves, and purée vegetables with almonds (omit the vegetable purée and almonds for a more delicate soup). Chill stock until fat can be easily lifted off.

(2) An hour before needed, return stock to the pot with purée, carrots and chicken meat. Taste for salt, and bring back to a gentle simmer. Whisk together the egg yolks, water, oil, salt, pepper and herbs and stir into the matzo meal. Leave to absorb liquids. Twenty minutes before needed, beat the egg whites stiff and fold into the yolk mixture. If it does not seem firm enough to hold its shape, dredge in some more flour. Divide into 8 large or 16 small portions and drop by spoonfuls into the simmering soup. Cover and cook 15 minutes. Serve each person a dumpling or two and scatter more herbs over the soup.

*I have specified free-range only because it is important that the chicken be full of flavour, and so many battery hens are not. Boiling fowl are hard to find in some places, but the flavour is again that much better.

SHOULDER OF LAMB WITH GARLIC, DRIED FRUIT AND PINE NUTS

Have the butcher bone the shoulder for you if possible – it is not difficult to do, simply tedious. Crush 4 cloves of garlic with 2 tbsp olive oil, the juice of half a lemon and plenty of salt and pepper. Spread it over the inner surface of the meat, add a handful of pine nuts, chopped prunes and raisins, and roll tightly. Tie with string in 4–6 places. Rub more olive oil, salt, pepper and lemon juice into the skin and leave to marinate for at least 3 hours – or overnight in the refrigerator.

Before cooking, place the roast in a pan not much bigger than itself, rub it again with olive oil and lemon and scatter another generous handful of pine nuts and chopped dried fruit around it. Put it in an oven preheated to 450°F/230°C/gas mark 7, turning the heat down to 375°F/190°C/gas mark 5 after 15 minutes – and roast it for about 12–15 minutes to the pound/500 g (or slightly longer if you do not like pink lamb). After 20 minutes, start basting with the juices, adding more lemon juice to the pan if the dried fruit starts to burn.

Lift the roast out onto a serving dish and let rest for 20–30 minutes, then slice thickly, pour over the pan juices and scatter with the fruit and nuts.

A glorious dish – served with courgettes cooked slowly in olive oil with lots of garlic until no more liquid is given off, then puréed, seasoned, and stirred with chopped flat-leaf parsley.

POTATOES 'ELMONDIGAS'
Potato croquettes (serves 8)

'Elmondigas' refers to the Latin American Spanish generic term for anything fried. The potatoes should be about twice the size of a walnut for the maximum amount of crunchy crust.

1 lb/500 g potatoes, peeled
reserved leek greens from Leek 'Dinim'
1 egg, beaten
salt and plenty of black pepper
1/4 tsp nutmeg
matzo meal
olive oil for deep-frying

Boil together the potatoes and leek greens with a tsp of salt. When tender, squeeze in a cloth to remove as much liquid as possible, then mash or purée with a little egg (saving some for frying), nutmeg, and lots of salt and pepper. Chill until firm. Shape into little cylinders, roll in reserved egg and then in matzo meal and fry in hot oil until deep golden brown on all sides. Serve warm.

RAVICOS
Spinach stalks in garlic, lemon and olive oil

In the sprawling vegetable markets of the south of France it is possible to find young spinach, the leaves still attached to stalks and roots. The coarser roots are trimmed off and the leaves kept for other recipes. The stalks are cooked separately – boiled until tender in water with olive oil, 2 cloves of garlic and lots of lemon. They are drained, dressed with more olive oil (extra-virgin this time), lemon juice and shredded garlic, and served cold or hot.

A note about 'koshering' – a process of extracting every sign of blood from meat. I have not given any details of the process in my recipe methods, assuming that Jewish cooks will add their own.

UNDER THE VEIL

—

A Feast of Alms on the
Northwest Frontier

'Why are you here?' asked an old moneychanger when I landed in Islamabad. I told him I had come to celebrate Idh-ul-Fitre with friends.

'You cannot,' he said bluntly. 'To celebrate Idh you must have fasted. Idh is for the faithful.'

'I *have* fasted,' I said. Which was true enough; the food on the plane had been too repellent to eat. I left the question of faith to a higher judge.

Ramadan, ninth month of the Muslim year, the holy month of denial when the Koran was revealed to Mohammed, is the Muslim time of fasting. Between dawn and dusk for thirty days the faithful all over the world are forbidden to touch their lips to either food or drink.

Peshawar, ancient and legendary city of the fierce Pathan people, Kipling's land, is machine-gun distance from the Khyber Pass and Afghanistan. The people there take Ramadan (or Ramzhan, as they call it) very seriously. The most religious break their fast in the evening; simply, with dates, a pinch of salt and a sip of milk or water.

Men faint in the streets of Peshawar during Ramadan. At work they suffer from headaches and dehydration. Women faint too, and suffer, but you don't see them – they are locked away in the purdah of their own homes. This is one of the strictest, most old-fashioned cities in Pakistan. The women that venture out are shy and muffled figures, swathed in full-length burkhas or white cotton chaddor veils that reveal only their eyes. When they faint, they lie on the ground like small tents whose ridgepoles have been jerked away.

The rewards for fasting, the most important pillar of Islam after prayer, are great. Zakat (charity) and Haj (pilgrimage) are behind it. It is said that for any good you might do, rewards will be given by angels – for fasting, by Allah himself.

The more immediate earthly reward for the Ramadan fast is a three-day feast – Idh-ul-Fitre, the Feast of Alms – when families return to their homes and celebrate. The eldest must offer gifts to the youngest, the rich to the poor, the host to his guest.

Idh begins when someone sights the new moon. He must be brave enough to swear it on the Koran, and to face disgrace if he is challenged. Sightings vary north to south, east to west, and the village Pathans around Peshawar are proud of the fact that their Idh, whether thanks to Allah or to man, almost always precedes that of Islamabad.

ONE

It was a hot Ramadan, unusually so for early May: 38°C by 9.00 a.m., then 40, 42, 44. The heat was another presence, the villain of the story, who crept up on you and pressed a heavy hand down on your shoulder,

made your heart beat in your ears and your eyes sting with sweat.

You could still see the ruins of the recently bombed arms depot at Islamabad airport when I flew out, although the smoke was only metaphorical now. There were no tourists at all. Pakistan was hot, but not with package tours: the plane, a little Fokker that bucked and shied its way like a half-broken colt through thunderous weather patterns over the Salt Hills into Peshawar, was full of international news journalists shaking hands and giving each other the VIP whammy.

'Anchor man, ABC-TV.'

'BBC News.'

'Political correspondent, *Financial Times*.'

'*Paris Match.*'

They looked at me. The Russians were starting their withdrawal from Afghanistan in about ten minutes and these guys were going to be right there when the big story broke. I felt slightly embarrassed to admit that I was there to research a book on food.

I tried to look like someone with ulterior motives.

Making the call from Peshawar airport to my future hosts, Pathans of the Mohammadzai tribe, family of a London acquaintance, was not easy. Two hours of dialling and hanging up while other people went off to hotels and the airport got emptier and the sky darkened outside. Finally I was alone with a dead telephone and two curious security guards. Women on their own are always a curiosity in Pakistan.

'Dust storm,' said one of the guards.

'Tomorrow maybe holiday. Airport close. No sleep here,' said the other, and then made a call for me, which got through.

I asked my friend's sister on the phone if I could save her the trouble of picking me up, maybe make my way to her in a horse-drawn tongah and see a few sights in the city.

'No,' she said abruptly. 'You cannot go to the Old Town.'

In a street they call Storyteller's, in the heart of the Old City of Peshawar, where Mochi Lara Bazaar runs towards the central square, Chowk Yaadgar, they were blowing things up.

The Pathan shopkeepers said it was Afghan refugees making trouble. The Afghan refugees said it was anti-government Pathans giving them a bad name, or Mujahideen, or Russian spies. The Mujahideen leaders took the credit when it suited. The Russians said nothing: they were not officially present.

While I was saying goodbye to Yasmine, a nut-brown man dressed like Gandhi picked up my suitcase, lifted it quickly onto his head and disappeared at a trot out of the airport.

The man turned out to be the night watchman, an old soldier who had fought in the Khyber Pass with a Scottish regiment. Or perhaps he said against; he was almost toothless. We talked of the sticky Idh sweetmeats that he loved: pinwheel jelabis dripping in syrup, barfi fudges of sweetened condensed milk with rosewater; dishes of manchay or shawi – vermicelli fried crisp in ghee, then simmered in cream and sugar and spice and scattered with shaved almonds and dried fruit; and of remembered Idh feasts: rich curries and great beaten metal platters of rice pilau, and ice-cream made of snow from the Hindu Kush.

Then my host turned up in his jeep and took me away.

TWO

Ahmed was a handsome, sullen young man with a withered hand, who had recently returned from a visit to his sister in England. He was separated from his wife. His mother and sister said she was mentally disturbed. They looked after his little boy.

Ahmed's mother and his older sister Yasmine were dark, heavy-browed and deeply religious. Yasmine told me that she was twenty-four, but I knew from her sister that she was thirty-three, the spinster of the family. She kept insisting on the similarities between Islam and Christianity.

'We too believe that Mary was a virgin,' she would say, and several times, 'Did you know that a Muslim man is perfectly allowed by our religion to marry a Christian woman?'

She told me that the Pathans valued pale skin just as much as English people did.

'My mother is very worried about Ahmed's son, Jani, because he is so dark, not like us. But that is his wife's blood.'

The four teenage cousins staying for Ramadan seemed to spring from another, lighter-footed species; slim and whippy as young willows, with gazelle eyes and quick, shy smiles.

'Your cousins are as beautiful as film stars,' I said to Yasmine. She looked shocked.

'In this country, only prostitutes are film stars,' said her brother. 'And we Pathans do not like people who are flattering too much.'

We broke fast at sundown the first evening, secure in a fortress of a house behind two flanks of wire-topped walls and two gardens like medieval moats patrolled by savage guard dogs. Yasmine brought jugs of iced fresh mango squash to dampen the dust in our throats.

'Not too much,' she said. 'It will make you sick after fasting.' But I was too concerned with trying to sneak a water-purification tablet into my glass to drink a lot.

We ate sitting cross-legged outside on the rope beds Pathans call cuts (in Urdu, 'charpoy'): crisp and spicy chickpea fritters dipped in cool coriander and green-chilli chutney, with yeasty naan breads to scoop up chicken stew, and firm white peaches, small as plums but very sweet. The sounds were the click-buzz of two-inch cockroaches bouncing off a swinging lightbulb and the cosy scratching and clucking of chickens.

The older women prayed between courses while the young girls washed up.

After dinner Ahmed drove us into the centre of Peshawar to see the Idh lights and bustle. Villagers had come to the city to do holiday shopping and the roads were a Dodgem ring with camels and painted Afghan buses instead of bumper cars.

While Ahmed went to buy us bottled drinks at a roadside stand, the women sat in the car behind the purdah of tinted glass. But I rolled my window down a little, disobediently.

First they thought it might be Idh tomorrow, and they would have to return immediately to their village to welcome family and members of their tribe. We loaded suitcases, cooking pots, spices, tin trunks of clean bedding into a big jeep. We waited, and drank green cardamom tea and watched television. When no word came from the village elders of a moon sighting, my hosts decided it would not be Idh tomorrow, so we unloaded everything again and went to bed.

For a while the fan overhead stirred air that was as sticky as overcooked dal, then slowly whirred itself to a halt.

The temperature stealthily rose until blood pounded in my ears louder than the Swiss cuckoo clock on the wall. Even the cockroaches stopped rustling. Everything was still and waiting. The hot villain of the story stood on my chest, heavier than the Fat Man in a circus.

Sirens at 2.30 a.m. pulled me out of a sleep that was like a coma, and the eerie wails from the mosques as the muezzin called the faithful to prayer lulled me back into heat-drugged delirium.

At 3.45 there was a sharp tapping on the window.

'Auntie, auntie!' said one of Yasmine's young cousins (the 'auntie' not familial but a symbol of respect). 'They saw the moon! Today is Idh! Please pack quickly!'

Yasmine had said that I must observe purdah during Idh. I threw all the clothes and books and notebooks back into the suitcase I had unpacked two hours earlier, and then struggled to pull the loose, pyjama-style shalwar kamiz over my sweat-drenched skin. Wrapping a chaddor around my head and upper body I went out into the night, feeling very dashing and mysterious; like a female version of Rudolph Valentino in *The Sheik*, but hotter.

THREE

The early morning was a long sweltering tunnel lit by the flares of the Afghan refugees' bonfires. Some shadowy forms still slept, but most people were leaving Peshawar for the villages, travelling home in whatever transport they could afford. I saw flocks of chaddor-covered women in grain carts yoked to wet-look buffalo; families of five piled on single motor scooters; three men on a bicycle; four tall, bearded men, with cartridge belts and Kalashnikovs over their shoulders.

'Mujahideen,' said Hussein, our driver. 'Going home to their families for the holiday.'

We passed them all. The only sound audible through the dreamy hum of the jeep's air-conditioned cocoon was our horn parting the flow of people so they streamed away in a silent film to left and right. The only lights were the twinkling bulbs that covered shops selling piles of Idh sweetmeats. The shops were open all night and doing a thriving business now that Ramadan was over.

Near dawn, the dull silver-cutlery gleam off smooth water lit a group of Afghan tribeswomen crossing a river by ferry to their camp of mud huts opposite.

'There was a bomb there yesterday,' said Yasmine. 'And Hussein says our village may be bombed, so we must keep the children inside.'

My hosts' battle-scarred house, a huge, white-washed monster scarred by bullet marks as if from smallpox, rose behind the mud and tin shacks of their village like the prow of a thirties liner above sampans. There were armed guards on the gate. Inside the walls were grounds with oxen, chickens, sunflowers and hibiscus, five thin, motherless puppies, a bus painted with village scenes, some farm machinery. This was the men's compound. Beyond it in an even more secure courtyard there was a great slow bustling of women.

An old woman appeared, with the face of an unwrapped but well-preserved mummy. Her glasses were tied around her balding scalp with a piece of string and her hands were full of corn husks to start the fire. Yasmine scolded her for not having the tea ready.

'We must be quick,' she said. 'Our farmers will come soon to pay their respects to my older brother, and their wives to my mother, who is the eldest. She keeps the old tradition of offering her people food at Idh, to show her respect for their work. You will see. Many will come.'

An ancient man with a white beard shuffled into the garden. He had made us all garlands of scented jasmine and hibiscus. Yasmine and her mother thanked him brusquely and carried on doing whatever mysterious things they were doing. No one wore the garlands except me. They hung over the backs of the chairs for days, the petals gradually turning brown and dropping.

By mid-morning the dusty kitchen area was filled with old servants, village women, and farmers' wives from miles away. Young cousins appeared, the palms of their hands specially hennaed for the holiday.

A lady of ninety-three with a few dyed orange hairs scattered over her head did a dance and rubbed her stomach to show the fun I could have at *her* village. She gave me an 'Idhi' – an Idh gift – of one rupee.

Each visitor was embraced by the women of the family as an old friend, regardless of social status.

'We are one tribe,' Yasmine explained. 'Like the fingers of a hand, not all the same length, but equal.'

One of the women squatted by the fire, tied an end of her long headscarf to the leg of a charpoy in a lovely economic gesture, and sifted flour through the pink chiffon to make parathas for me.

Male servants walked in and out carrying trays of fresh tea and sweets to the men's quarters. Buffalo meat to enrich the rice pilau later simmered in a big pot. The youngest boy played with a live dragonfly

that his older cousin had tied to a string.

Modestly covered in my chaddor, and with the children acting as chaperones, I was allowed to step outside the women's courtyard (still a good 250 yards from the men's circle of charpoys), where another cook, Gul, was preparing rice pilau for the fifty or more visitors. First he partly cooked the rice in lots of salted water, draining it through a wide bamboo sieve onto the dry earth. Then he scooped the rice into a round-bottomed terrine big enough to stew one of the smallest boys, and added a pan of onions that had been sliced, dried in the sun and fried in ghee. He stirred in cinnamon bark, cumin seeds, whole cloves, and some of the buffalo broth, packed the buffalo meat on top and poured over lots of melted ghee. Finally he sealed the terrine with a paste of flour and water, and set it on a low fire to cook.

He kept glancing at me as if he could not understand my interest, occasionally offering me spices to identify on his outstretched palm.

Gul's oven was a long log, burning at one end, pushed against the main wall of the compound; his thermostat a handful of corn husks added to the fire when he needed more intense heat.

He had cooked for the family since he was seven, learning the craft from his father and grandfather, who worked there before him. He told of Afghan dishes cooked for feasts, of rice pilaus made for two hundred with almonds and dates and candied peel of bitter orange; and of his own family meals: sweet river fish shaped like aeroplanes caught near his village, dry-cooked in chunks like chicken tikka, or grilled over an open fire with a masala paste and slices of citrus.

Suddenly one of the children tapped my shoulder.

'Yasmine says you are getting too hot. You must come back inside.'

Two of Yasmine's cousins, stunning young men with gold skins, pale, flashing eyes and exuberant black moustaches, came to pay their respects to her mother. We shared a plateful of crisply fried beef and green chilli 'chappli' kebabs, brought warm from the market beyond the walls. The cousins said that a bomb had killed thirty last night near the Afghan border when the youngest was crossing. He was a medical student from the politically active Kabul University.

'It is not so dangerous living *in* Kabul,' he laughed. 'Just leaving it!'

I asked him how the Russians' departure would affect Pakistan and the Afghan refugees there. He was wary of my questions, and waited for Yasmine's nod before replying.

'Afghans, Pathans: we are the same. We speak the same, share religion, food, history. But we are a poor country; three million extra people are costing too much. And you Europeans took all the richest refugees. We Pakistanis, especially in the NWFP, we got only the poor.'

The two cousins began to tell me the history of the Pathan people. They spoke of their descent from Alexander the Great as if the event had occurred last week, or yesterday.

'Just look at all the people here who have fair skin, red hair and blue eyes, if you want proof,' they said. 'If you need proof.'

I tried to remember any Greeks with red hair and blue eyes.

They said casually that Muslim men were allowed to marry Christian women. They told me of a dashing Pathan chieftain in the 1920s who had ridden down out of the mountains and kidnapped a British colonel's wife right out of her bedroom in the middle of the compound. She was held to ransom and finally returned to her husband.

'But she was not dishonoured,' they said proudly.

I remembered that this was the country where a married woman who registers a case of rape must produce four Muslim male adults of good repute as witnesses. If she cannot prove the rape, she can be prosecuted

for adultery, while the rapist goes free for lack of evidence. The penalty for a woman's adultery is stoning to death.

It is clear that sexual desire can never be a joking matter here.

That night we ate under a cobalt sky and Van Gogh stars.

The white pock-marked fort loomed up three storeys, the long, tiled verandah looked onto a courtyard of walnut and bitter-orange trees and stunted bushes of fleshy-petalled roses. There were two handsome men in crisp white lawn robes, beautiful girls and barefoot servants, and the scent of jasmine.

Around me, the swish and slice of Pathan conversation. Understanding not one word, I looked to the food. We ate wild mustard greens like the fretwork leaves of salad burnet, fried in ghee and green chillies and browned garlic, with freshly baked Pathan maize bread used as a ladle (we ate with our hands): the epitome of village cooking, two dishes that have passed from all but the most primitive of Lahore and Karachi menus. Yasmine passed a creamy stew of chicken and the pig-tailed squash that they call 'toreh' and we know as ajija, and a plate of fried spiced aubergine slices in firm curd scattered with toasted cumin. 'Summer food,' she said. The biggest platter was heaped with the rice pilau made by Gul, full of chunks of buffalo. When everyone had stopped eating, Khushal turned to me.

'Would you like some faluda from the market?'

'Faluda?'

'You will like it – ice-cream we Pathans make from cardamom and rice-flour vermicelli and condensed milk and snow.' He sent one of the young boys out, who returned minutes later with a tray of little bowls.

At midnight the women lay down to sleep on rows of charpoys along the verandah. Electric fans whined overhead. On the white plaster wall next to me was a cluster of lime-green gekkos, flat and symmetrical as an Escher print. I spread myself with Jungle Formula repellent and dreamed of giant mosquitoes.

FOUR

For the three days of Idh, relatives and old servants came and went. I read, and roamed around the edges of this cosy circle, trying to find something between meals and sleeping that would take my mind off the heat. I played with the children and talked to the teenage girls about school. Bread was baked twice

daily in a clay tandoor oven, a soda bread at noon and a primitive maize flour version, called Gawar Dodey, in the evening. When any of the servants let me help with the cooking, Yasmine scolded them, and told me to go and sit on the verandah where it was cooler. Everyone else sat in the shade around the kitchen.

Every night Yasmine bolted the door that connected Ahmed's bedroom with our verandah – whether locking him in or us out I never dared ask. All the other male relatives went home to their families in the evening.

Yasmine and her mother shuffled back and forth between kitchen and verandah as if burdened by the weight of insurmountable tasks, but only the young nieces and the servant, Gulraishe, appeared to do any really energetic work. Gulraishe never seemed to stop, watering plants, washing floors with a handful of twigs, cooking meals, kneading dough twice a day to make bread from flour she weighed in hand-held scales with a stone at one end.

I said to Yasmine that Gulraishe must get very tired. She shook her head. 'These thin peasant women do not feel the heat as we do.'

There was no telephone. Often there were electricity cuts, and the fans stopped stirring up the red dust that covered every surface. There was one lavatory for all of us, with a toilet you flushed with buckets of water, not a place for contemplating Life. A shower nozzle had one temperature that depended entirely on the heat outside.

Five times a day there were prayers, but they seemed very relaxed, to be easily interrupted by children's games and questions. The men prayed elsewhere. A bell rang from their quarters at lunch and dinner, when Yasmine's brothers would leave their male guests on the other side of the wall and come to share our meals. The times shifted, but both meals were interchangeable; always substantial, in spite of the heat and our lack of exercise.

There might be aubergine pakoras, or a scrambled egg curry with fresh coriander; perhaps with spiced lamb or buffalo. There was pilau left from the men's daily banquet, okra stewed with tomatoes and green chillies – not too hot, the Pathans like their food milder than the rest of the subcontinent; sliced cucumber or tomatoes sprinkled with vinegar and coarse salt. There was always fresh-baked bread, just as there were always fresh parathas for breakfast. Several times there were little bowls of faluda from the bazaar.

In the evening, Hussein, who was foreman and occasional baby-sitter as well as driver, strolled through to lock the gates, carrying a holster and pistol on one shoulder, Ahmed's younger son on the other.

Within the walls there was peace and boredom stirred only by the women's gossip. Beyond there was constant noise – hoots and honks from early until late. Every day, desperate to know what was happening in this outside world, I would creep up the stairs to the frying-pan heat of the flat roof and peer over the parapet to the streets below.

Everywhere there were men in white and blue shalwar kamiz, laughing, enjoying the fair, pounding spice and snuff, scratching hot portions of their anatomy. Men in shops covered in rainbow flags and twinkling lights. Men selling fresh pomegranate juice, ice-cream, snacks, pyramids of revolting sweets. 'GURRUM GURRUM KEBAB' ('Hot Hot Kebab'), vendors cried. And 'RASHA KANA VALE KANA OKHRA KANA GURRUM GURRUM SAMOSA' ('Come here, take it, eat it, hot hot samosa').

Further out I could see the white, low buildings of the mosque where the men went to pray, and the knobbly-kneed outlines of naked, skinny little boys as they leapt onto inner-tubes in a slowly unwinding river.

One day I told Yasmine that I wanted to talk to cooks in the bazaar.

'Impossible!' she said. 'It would bring disgrace.'

'I could do with a bit of disgrace – and some exercise.'

She shook her head firmly. 'Not you. Disgrace on *us*. But my brother might let the driver take you out in the jeep after dark.'

I didn't blame her really. She had told me in an unguarded moment how she trained in law in Peshawar's Women's College, did tremendously well – was even offered a job with a firm in Lahore. Then her mother said she could not continue because people said she was doing bad things with her professors. So she said she would study in Karachi instead. But her mother said that temptation stalked the halls of residence and women there had no morals.

Her brother offered the money for a correspondence course learning nursery techniques, a more suitable job for a woman, even one who at thirty-three was unlikely to find a husband.

She had shrugged off my sympathy impatiently. 'What are lawyers anyway – a pack of snarling jackals,' she concluded, not entirely convincing even herself.

And here I was, a wayward young woman able to travel the world on my own, with my own income, my own home, complaining of two weeks of being cooped up.

That night I noticed a big bruise coming up on my arm from a collision with a green bug the size of a sparrow.

FIVE

The day after the Idh holiday, the last buses left the village. Youngest cousins, nieces and nephews and old servants were given clothes and money and went back to their homes in Islamabad, Peshawar, some across the border to Afghanistan. Finally I was allowed out with Yasmine's older brother Khushal and his children to see the country

and the family's farms.

'You are honoured,' said Yasmine. 'Even our mother does not ride in the front with my brother as you do.'

We drove out through lush orchards and crops laced together by old British irrigation channels. Men and women harvested sugar beet together in one field, the women working with heads uncovered.

'So some women work in the fields without burkhas or chaddors?'

'Only if they are very poor,' said Khushal curtly. 'Purdah is a sign of prosperity, not poverty. It means that your wife does not have to work, a sign of status.'

At a mud-walled village surrounded by sunflower fields, men ran to fetch charpoys for Khushal and his eldest sons. Khushal told me that some politicians wanted him to educate his village people at least to primary level.

'But *then* what will happen? They will come to me to find them jobs in an office – and how can I do that? And then they will not want to clean my house, nor even their own.' He looked around. 'Two years ago we had to level this village when they caused us too much trouble.'

He didn't say what kind of trouble, but hooded his eyes and shook his head when I asked. I walked through the village gate with his daughters and youngest son.

Women came to shake hands and showed me into a six-foot-square room, spotless as a mud room ever could be. There were three charpoys with flowered pillows and woven rugs. The walls had been limed white, the dirt floor swept. Rifles leaned against two big padlocked aluminium trunks. A chandelier of folded coloured cigarette papers hung overhead, and there was an old hand-tinted photograph of some fierce-moustached ancestor on the wall. There was

nothing else. Into the room crowded fine-featured women and their
shy, mostly naked children. One graceful girl fanned me steadily with a
grass fan she had made.

'Tell them I come from England,' I said to Khushal's son.

'They won't understand England.'

'Well, a country far away then.'

'They don't know about countries,' he replied. 'I will say a distant
village.'

I asked him what they said to that.

'They say they are sorry they have no electricity for a fan.'

Under a tree outside I could see a buffalo drinking from a pool
where two small, scabby children splashed. A girl dipped a jug into the
water and brought it to me mixed with fresh melon squash.

There were squawks and feathers flying from behind a mud wall. A
woman cooked me some fresh parathas. A little later there was rice and
a bowl of tomatoes, ghee and chewy, tasty chicken.

'In our country,' said Khushal's son, 'Chicken and rice are feast
dishes, food we offer to honoured guests. It is the same with you?'

I appreciated the eleven-year-old's courtliness as he carefully
translated back and forth for me while I ate. The women watched us,
giggled and fanned, saying the odd thing that Khushal's son didn't
repeat. He looked embarrassed.

'I am really too old to be here with the women,' he said shyly.

As I left, the village elder brought me his favourite ox to photograph.
He thanked me graciously, but with more than a hint of complacence,
like a man with a beautiful wife who is used to the envy of others.

I had eaten as much as was humanly possible in the 44°C heat.
Khushal broke the news that there was to be lunch at another farmer's.
I felt slightly hysterical at the thought. It was not yet 10.00 a.m.

The pattern of the next farm was the same on a smaller scale: mud
walls, shy, beautiful women and children. This time there was a wild

monkey tied to a tree and lunch could have served twenty.

At 10.30 the children started to bring the dishes and lay them on the table before me: wild mustard greens stirred with chillies and garlic; cold, salted lassi, a yoghurt drink that I gulped gratefully, having heard that it was an antidote to dysentery, hepatitis, almost everything catchable on the subcontinent.

'I think it is not good to drink too much,' said Khushal's son, who ate nothing. 'Sometimes the buffalo in these villages have ...what do you call the fever?'

'Tuberculosis?' I said.

'Tuberculosis, yes.'

There were little creamy pakoras of beaten onions and potatoes, crisp on the outside; the lightest of pilaus, mixed with crunchy, deep-fried chickpeas and plump raisins; stewed chicken and okra, fresh naan bread, just baked; spicy mutton and potatoes. Maybe buffalo too. Perspiration dripped from my forehead into my eyes.

The women watched, fanned, refilled my plate, oblivious to protests. 'You don't like our food?' they asked sadly.

The temperature crept up until I was panting with the food and the heat. I drank cup after cup of tea.

In two hours I had done all the things Westerners are advised against. The list swam before me: lovingly handled sweets, meat, bread, unboiled water, unpasteurized milk, unpeeled fruit and salad vegetables – a whole ream of 'uns'. I never suffered any consequences, but hours, days later was still full, and still awed by the hospitality. I wondered what these people could have done to deserve having their village levelled.

At dusk that night there was an old episode of *I Love Lucy* on the new Sony television. Ahmed adjusted the set to get Lucy's hair the right shade of persimmon, then strapped on a holster and gun to go out with Hussein for their nightly inspection of the orchards.

I ran up to the roof to watch them go: two tall men with pistols strapped to their immaculate white pyjamas, driving off in a Toyota jeep full of machine guns to protect their apricots.

They slowed to pass Gulraishe, work finished with us for another day, padding barefoot back to her family with a basket of our leftovers on her head. In the distance a small figure cantered his water buffalo home along the curling river, and above, like the Pakistani flag made real, a sickle Idh moon cradled a single star.

SIX

The story should have ended there. I thought of a poem I'd read somewhere:

> Noodles this evening
> Pulao at noon
> Sweet yellow rice
> For you, little moon.
> O, thread of silver
> Night's precious boon
> Rising within us
> Little Idh moon.

It would have made a good ending, suitably romantic: East meets West.

What happened instead was this: the next day, Yasmine told me her family was not returning to Peshawar as planned, although they had already postponed their departure for three days. Every morning there had been the vague reply, 'Perhaps tomorrow.'

No fans had worked for twenty-four hours. The villain of the story had his claws around my head and he was squeezing tight. He was in league with the boring side of me that liked clean sheets and air-conditioning and gin and tonics on hot nights. I needed to get back to the city and out of the claustrophobic atmosphere of the women's quarters.

'Is there a bus I could take from here to Peshawar?'

'You cannot take a bus,' Yasmine said. 'It would bring disgrace on the family. You must learn submission if you want to live here.' She swept angrily into the house.

I packed my bags and walked from the women's compound into the men's. Before I had gone ten feet, Ahmed appeared. He was furious. I was more furious. We exchanged bitter words about each other's cultures. Finally he told me to get into the back of his car and he drove me to a hotel in town. We shook hands stiffly, at my insistence, and I thought of the sayings he had quoted once about Pathan pride:

'If you dishonour a Pathan he will hate you forever.'

'If you try to force a Pathan into Heaven, he will fight you, but you can lead him politely to Hell.'

That day Yasmine wrote to her sister in London to say that I had tried to climb into Ahmed's bedroom one night and they had been forced to send me away.

RECIPES

Breaking the Fast

This is how jaded appetites were revived on hot evenings, an alchemy that still works on cool nights in England.

PAKORA

Deep-fried vegetable and chickpea-flour fritters

Chickpea or gram flour, deliciously nutty-tasting but prone to damp, is the one constant in a pakora; vegetables and method are variable. In a poor village pakora may contain mostly flour, with onions, garlic, salt and a little roasted cumin mixed into thick paste balls and fried. Richer homes make a thinner batter and dip slices of vegetables – cauliflower, aubergine, potato – into it.

Serve pakora with a bowl of good sharp homemade chutney, and some plain yoghurt whisked with very finely chopped onion.

ONION AND GARLIC PAKORA

(enough for 6 as a starter)

6 oz/180 g chickpea flour
2 tsp cumin seeds, dry-fried 3 minutes, ground
1¼ tsp salt
4 tsp vegetable oil plus extra for deep-frying
about 8 tbsp warm water
3–4 green chillies, seeded and finely chopped
4 garlic cloves, peeled and crushed
2 onions, finely chopped

(1) Sift together flour, cumin and salt and rub in the oil until the mixture forms fine crumbs. Whisk with warm water – enough to form a smooth thick batter. Cover and leave in a warm place 30 minutes.
(2) Over a medium flame, heat 1 in/2.5 cm of oil until a chunk of stale bread turns brown in 60 seconds. Stir remaining ingredients into the batter and drop by tsp into the oil. Cook a few pakora at a time, 1 minute each side. Lift out and drain on kitchen paper. Just before serving, heat the oil again and refry the pakora for another 30–45 seconds before serving to give them extra crunch.

CAULIFLOWER AND AUBERGINE (EGGPLANT) PAKORA

(Serves 8 as a starter)

1 small cauliflower
4 small aubergines/eggplants
6 oz/180 g chickpea/gram flour
2 tsp coriander seeds, toasted, roughly crushed
¼ tsp cayenne
2 tsp salt plus extra for aubergines
4 tsp vegetable oil plus extra for deep-frying
about 4½ fl oz/125 ml warm water

(1) Cut aubergines crosswise in ½ in/1 cm slices. Salt in layers in a colander and weight. Break the cauliflower into 1 in/2.5 cm flowerets. Follow method given in previous recipe for making pakora batter – this one should be thinner.
(2) Rinse the aubergine and pat dry. Heat the oil as before. Dip the pieces of vegetable in batter, then drop in the hot oil a few at a time, turning over when they are golden. Do not worry about browning them too much – you should refry them as before to crisp them just before serving.

CHUTNI GASNEETCH

Fresh coriander and green-chilli chutney

Pickles and chutneys in northwestern Pakistan are made with vinegar rather than the mustard oil prevalent in the Punjab, and as with all Pathan food they are seldom spicy hot. The following is a superb, fresh-tasting chutney to eat with any rich foods. Pathans across the Khyber Pass might add a spoonful each of raisins and crushed walnuts.

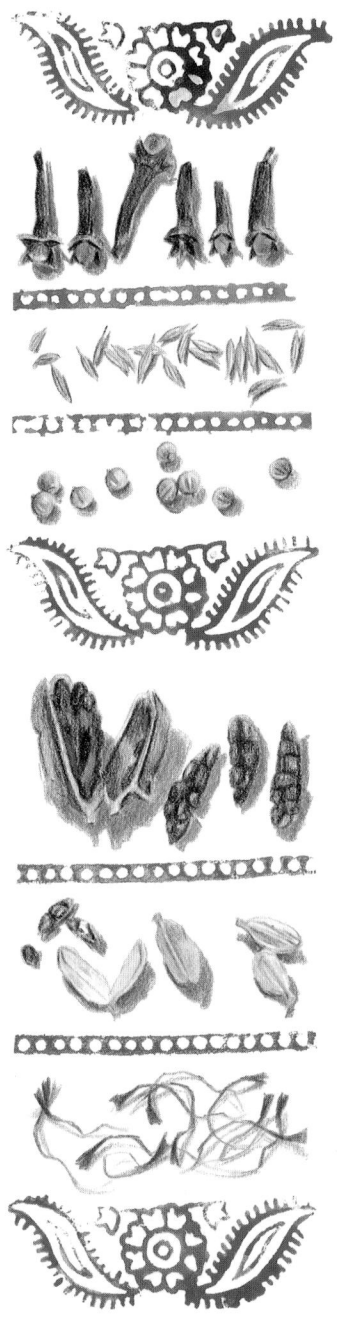

> *about 3 oz/90 g fresh coriander or mint leaves*
> *1 green chilli, seeded*
> *1 tsp cumin seeds, dry-fried until fragrant, and ground*
> *¼–½ tsp salt*
> *1 tsp sugar*
> *3 or more tbsp vinegar or fresh lemon juice*
> *½ small onion, very finely chopped*
> *1 tbsp yoghurt (optional)*

Pound or roughly purée together the mint or coriander, chillies, cumin, salt and sugar. Stir in enough vinegar or lemon juice to make a sauce the consistency of thin cream. Leave for several hours and stir in the onion (and yoghurt, for a creamier chutney) just before serving.

MANCHAY

Crisp vermicelli pudding with cream and dried fruit

After evening prayers during Ramadan many Muslim men go to banquets at friends' houses, or stroll the market streets, eating so much to compensate for their daily fast that they gain rather than lose weight during the fasting month.

   Later I had an extraordinary Ramadan dish called manchay, of vermicelli fried golden in ghee and served with cream, dried fruits and slivered toasted almonds; a magnificent dish reminiscent of Persian nights. But sweet enough, as M.F.K. Fisher once wrote, 'to make every tooth in my head quiver like a stricken doe'.

In a Pathan Kitchen

The open-air Pathan kitchen I got to know grew out of the garden wall of the house like some organic sculpture by Henry Moore. At one time the ground had been half paved in an attempt to keep down the fine, pinky-white dust. As all the cooking preparations from sifting flour to preparing vegetables and washing up took place on loosely woven straw mats placed on the ground, everything – people, dishes, food – quickly took on the same agreeable pale pink shade.

The bread oven was baked pale pink clay; the stove was a foot-high pale pink clay ledge with a gap for the fuel.

Paratha were cooked on a tawa, a shallow, slightly scooped iron dish set over the fierce heat of corn cobs burning in the clay stove. During Idh, the round, flat breads were sometimes served with an Afghan version of clotted cream.

The following recipes are typical of Pathan daily food. Twice a day we would sit down to eat from a low table laid with four or five dishes – one bread, two or three vegetable 'curries', one or two meat, fish or chicken dishes. Where a specific Pathan or Dari (Persian/Afghan) name was given for the dish, I have written it; otherwise I have simply used English.

PARATHA

Enriched fried bread

Very rich, with layers like puff pastry, and delicious with chutney and plain yoghurt.

8 oz/250 g strong plain flour
½ tsp salt
about 6 fl oz/180 ml warm water
2 oz/60 g melted ghee

(1) Sieve the flour with salt. Make a well in the centre and pour in the water a little at a time, working it in roughly, just until the dough will form a soft ball. On a lightly floured board knead the dough, pushing away with the heels of your hands, folding it over and repeating until it is smooth and flexible (about 5–7 minutes). Cover with a damp cloth and leave 10 minutes.

(2) On a lightly floured surface roll the dough out about ¼ in/0.5 cm thick, brush well with melted ghee, dust lightly with flour and fold in three like a napkin, ghee inside. Cover with a damp cloth and leave 10 minutes. Repeat this process three times.

(3) Before cooking, divide the dough into eight balls and roll each to less than ¼ in/0.5 cm. Heat a non-stick pan over medium heat and fry the parathas 30 seconds the first side and 20–30 seconds the second, then 20 seconds on the first side.

SAAG

Spinach or wild mustard greens stir-fried with chillies and garlic (serves 4–6)

Saag is a hold-all term for seasonal greens. I had the same dish cooked with two different kinds of leaf: one a cultivated turnip leaf, one a wild creeping form of mustard that had leaves like Granny's crewel work. In Karachi some fashionable fast-food restaurants now serve just the 'rustic' combination of saag and rotis.

6 tbsp ghee
4 garlic cloves, finely chopped
3 green chillies, seeded and finely chopped
1 tsp salt
½ tsp cumin seeds, dry-fried and ground
3 ripe tomatoes, chopped, peeled (or 1 tin, drained)
1½ lb/750 g fresh spinach, trimmed, washed and finely chopped

Heat the ghee over a medium hot flame in a frying pan. Cook the garlic and chillies in it until the garlic is softened and just starting to brown. Add salt, cumin and tomatoes and continue cooking until most of the tomato liquid has evaporated. Add the spinach and stir-fry until all its liquid as well has evaporated.

RIVER FISH IN SOUR ORANGE MASALA

(serves 4)

Gul told me one day of stopping by the river 'that flows from Kabul', to eat at the fish stall there. They took a meaty fish he said was shaped like an aeroplane, boned and cut it in chunks and spread it with a masala like the one used for chicken tikka, then skewered the chunks and barbecued them over hot coals. But his favourite fish he cooked himself, spreading on it a masala made from the sour oranges that are so plentiful, and frying the whole fish crisp in hot mustard oil, squeezing more sour orange on after.

2 tbsp coriander seeds, 1 tbsp cumin seeds
1½ tsp salt
2 tsp cayenne pepper
1 small onion, chopped
juice of 2 sour (Seville) oranges (or 1 sweet orange
and 2 lemons) plus another orange to squeeze over
8 tbsp Greek yoghurt (ordinary yoghurt does not have the
same creamy quality as the Pakistani style)
4 whole trout or similar river fish, cleaned
3 tbsp chickpea or ordinary flour (if frying)
mustard oil (if frying)

(1) In a dry frying pan over medium heat toast the cumin and coriander for 3–4 minutes until fragrant. Grind them to a powder in a mortar with the salt and purée in a blender with the cayenne, onion, juice and yoghurt. Make three diagonal slashes on each side of the fish and rub the yoghurt mixture inside and out. Leave to marinate for an hour.

(2) Cook until brown outside and flaky within – over a barbecue preferably, or 7 minutes each side under a grill. Or the fish may be dredged in flour and pan-fried crisply about 5–7 minutes each side.

BORJEE

Scrambled egg curry with fresh coriander (serves 6)

The quantities of finely chopped onions, mild chillies and coriander make the texture of this dish so completely different from any other scrambled eggs that it is barely recognizable as such. With parathas and a plate of spicy saag, it is lovely simple food for a hot summer evening.

6 large eggs
2 tbsp water
1/2 tsp salt
3 tbsp ghee
1 small onion, finely chopped
2–3 fresh green chillies, seeded and finely chopped
1/2 tsp ground cumin
1/2 tsp ground coriander
pinch of turmeric
3 tomatoes, seeded, peeled and crushed (or tinned)
handful fresh coriander leaves, coarsely chopped

Beat eggs, and water and salt lightly. Melt ghee in a frying pan so that a drop of water in it spits. Add the onions and chillies and stir until the onions are soft. Stir in spices for a minute or two and add tomatoes. Cook the tomatoes down until all the liquid has evaporated, reduce heat to very low and add the eggs, stirring constantly until they form a soft mass. Serve immediately, sprinkled with fresh coriander.

A Feast on the Frontier

What distinguished the three days of Idh feasting, apart from regular boxes of sweetmeats brought warm from the bazaar, were the great pilaus* of rice. The most exotic was a golden mixture of saffron, candied orange peel, and shredded dates – Moghul court cooking indeed; the presence of saffron indicated the wealth and hospitality of my hosts.

   *Pilaus may be reheated, but are better if served immediately after cooking. The rice, however, will stay warm in its heavy covered casserole for about twenty-five minutes.

CHAPPLI KEBABS

Ground lamb or beef and green-chilli patties (serves 6 as a snack)

The kebabs of Afghanistan and Pakistan's northwest frontier are famous – every bazaar has a pavement stall grilling skewers of meat and poultry. These spicy meat patties, called 'chappli' after the leather sandals worn by the Pathans, are perhaps most famous in Peshawar and its surrounding villages.

2 tsp coriander seeds
1½ tsp cumin seeds
¾ lb/350 g ground beef (or lamb)
9 oz/250 g spring/green onions, finely chopped
3 oz/90 g maize flour (I use Quaker Mexican masa harina –
but fine cornmeal is not bad)
½ sweet red pepper, finely chopped
2 tomatoes, seeded and finely chopped
1–2 tsp salt
3 green chillies, seeded and finely chopped
vegetable oil for deep frying

Dry-fry the coriander and cumin for 3 minutes and grind to a powder. Mix with all the remaining ingredients and shape into flat ovals (sandal soles) about 2½ in/6.5 cm by 1½ in/4 cm by ½ in/1 cm thick. Heat the vegetable oil over medium heat and fry the kebabs, browning on both sides.

RAITAS
Yoghurt salads

Served in the hot summer months, made with thick, creamy local yoghurt – use Greek set yoghurt as a reasonable substitute. If you have a barbecue going, it is good to grill instead of frying the sliced aubergine for the added smoky flavour.

AUBERGINES IN YOGHURT
(Serves 4 as a side salad)

1½ lb/750 g aubergines, cut in ½ in/1 cm slices and salted
vegetable oil for frying
18 fl oz/500 ml Greek yoghurt
1 tsp ground cumin
1 small onion, finely chopped
1–2 garlic cloves, finely chopped
½ tsp salt (or to taste)
8–10 fresh mint leaves, chopped (plus extra for decoration)
garam masala or chauk* (optional)

Rinse and pat dry the aubergines and fry in the oil until no longer opaque – they absorb quite a lot. Lay them in overlapping rows in a serving dish. Whisk together all the other ingredients apart from the garam masala, adding a little water if necessary to make the yoghurt slightly thinner. Pour this over the aubergines and leave for at least an hour. Before serving, sprinkle over some garam masala or chauk and top with mint leaves.

Garam masala – spice mixture that can be sprinkled over most Pakistani cooked foods to add extra flavour (try it instead of salt). The time given below after each spice is how long they should be dry-fried before grinding. This quantity should fill a small spice jar, and will keep for several months. 1½ in/3.5 cm crumbled cinnamon stick, 1 tsp cloves (7 minutes) 1½ tsp black cardamom seeds, 1½ tsp black peppercorns (5 minutes) 3 tsp coriander seeds, 1½ tsp cumin seeds, 3 tsp nutmeg (3–4 minutes).

Chauk – flavouring for raitas. Brown onions and seeds in ghee until mustard seeds start to pop, then pour over raita. Use 2–3 tbsp ghee, 1 finely chopped onion, ½ tsp mustard seed, ½ tsp cumin seed.

PATHAN RICE

A great joy for anyone cooking basmati rice is the enticing roasted cashew-nut aroma that fills the air.

Gul and Gulraishe used two distinct methods to prepare their pilaus. Until reading Helen Saberi's book *Afghan Food and Cookery* I didn't realize that these two cooks represented two schools of Afghan/Pathan rice preparation.

The important things to remember when cooking basmati rice are:

(1) After removing any foreign particles, rice must be rinsed in cold water until water runs clear. This removes starch on the grains which would make the rice sticky.

(2) After rinsing, rice must be soaked in cold water to make the long grains flexible so they will not break during cooking.

(3) Use a heavy casserole or saucepan with a close-fitting lid and put a towel between the lid and the casserole for the final cooking if necessary to ensure a close fit.

(4) Handle the rice gently from start to finish – the long grains are very delicate.

PILAU

Rice with lamb, raisins and crisp chickpeas (serves 8–10)

A traditional pilau. Buffalo meat was used to make it in the village, but lamb seems a good substitute. Obviously the Pathans would not have used tinned chickpeas, but they are far quicker and the flavour is just as good as dried.

> *1 1/2 lb/750 g basmati rice, picked over*
> *6 tbsp ghee*
> *3 finely chopped onions*
> *large pinch of saffron*
> *2–3 lb/1–1.5 kg boned lamb, fat cut off*
> *salt, pepper*
> *seeds from 4 black cardamom (or 1/2 tsp green)*
> *1 tin chickpeas, drained (or 14 oz/400 g cooked)*
> *vegetable oil for deep-frying*
> *3 large carrots, peeled and cut in julienne strips*
> *6 oz/180 g seedless raisins*
> *2 tsp cumin seeds*
> *1 tsp cayenne powder*
> *1 1/2 tsp ground cinnamon*

(1) Wash the rice under running water until the water runs clear. Cover in twice its volume of water and leave to soak for at least 30 minutes.

(2) Melt the ghee in a large pan and cook the onions in it until soft and golden. Lift out with a slotted spoon and purée with the saffron. Add the meat to the pan and brown well. Add the salt, pepper and cardamom seeds and enough water just to cover the meat. Cook over low heat until the meat is tender to a fork.

(3) While the meat is cooking, prepared the vegetables. Deep-fry the chickpeas in about 1 in/2.5 cm hot oil until they are brown. Lift out and drain on kitchen paper. Heat a tbsp of ghee in a frying pan and cook the carrots and raisins in it until the carrots are lightly browned and the raisins puffed.

(4) Preheat the oven to 300°F/150°C/gas mark 2. Bring 4 pt/2.25 l water to the boil with a tsp of salt and cook the drained rice in it for 3 minutes, then drain the rice and return to the pot with the meat piled underneath.

(5) Add the meat broth to the puréed onions to make about 12 fl oz/360 ml liquid, stir in the spices and vegetables, reserving about a third, and pour the liquid over the rice. Cover tightly and finish cooking in the oven for another 45 minutes. Turn out onto a large serving platter with the meat in the centre and scatter with reserved vegetables.

NORINJ PILAU

Saffron and candied orange rice (serves 8–10)

A gorgeous, exotically flavoured dish made with the sour oranges so common in Pakistani gardens. If you cannot find sour (Seville) oranges, use the zest from two small sweet oranges and one lemon.

1½ lb/750 g basmati rice, picked over for stones
6 tbsp ghee
1 large free-range chicken (with giblets, neck,
wing tips etc.) cut in 3–4 in/8–10 cm pieces
3 onions, chopped
seeds from 8 cardamom pods
2 in/5 cm crumbled cinnamon stick
1½ tsp salt, lots of black pepper
4 oz/125 g sugar
4 oz/125 g shelled unsalted peanuts
zest of 2 large sour oranges (or substitute)
cut in julienne strips
4 oz/125 g shredded date flesh
big pinch of saffron

(1) Rinse the rice under cold water until the water runs clear. Put the rice in a bowl, cover with double the volume of water and leave to soak, draining after 30 minutes.

(2) While it is soaking, melt the ghee over a medium-high heat and brown the chicken pieces on all sides. Lift out with a slotted spoon, add the onions and cook until golden, then return the chicken and giblets to the pot with the cardamom, cinnamon, salt and pepper, cover with 2½ pt of water and simmer until the meat is tender (about 30 minutes). Lift out the big pieces of chicken and set aside. Shred any meat that is left on the back and wings and set aside. Discard the cinnamon stick and purée the broth and onions.

(3) Bring 8 fl oz/225 ml water to a rapid boil with the sugar and bubble until it forms a thin syrup. Stir in the peanuts and orange peel and boil 5 minutes. Lift out fruit with a slotted spoon. Add saffron to the pot and continue cooking a further minute or two. Remove from heat.

(4) Preheat oven to 300°F/150°C/gas mark 2. Measure out the syrup and add enough of the onion broth to make double the volume of rice (about 3¼ pt/1.8 l), adding extra water if necessary. Bring to a boil in a large, heavy, lidded casserole. Add the drained rice, three quarters of the peel, nuts and dates and any shredded meat. When the liquid returns to the boil, stir once and cover the pan tightly. Reduce heat to a simmer and cook for 10 minutes, or until all the liquid is absorbed.

(5) Pile the chicken pieces on top of the rice and cover again tightly. Put in the oven for a further 20–30 minutes. Arrange on a big serving platter with the chicken in the middle – and scatter the reserved fruit and nuts over the top.

PATHAN ICE-CREAM

I never managed the knack of making the rice vermicelli ice-cream called faluda – perhaps you need Afghan snow. This ripe mango kulfi is more common.

3½ pt/2 l whole milk
4 tbsp sugar
2 green cardamom pods
flesh of 2 ripe mangoes, puréed, 1 sliced mango

In a large saucepan, bring the milk, sugar and cardamom to a boil, stirring constantly. Lower the heat and simmer, stirring every 5 minutes, until the milk is thick and reduced by about two-thirds. Allow to cool and beat in the mango purée. Freeze until firm and serve with slices of fresh mango.

NABI'S DREAM

A Wedding in Kashmir

The Vale of Kashmir is the jewel in the navel of the lesser Himalayas – if 18,000-foot mountains can ever be considered lesser. Its view of those iced peaks is as close to the lost horizons of Shangri-La as James Hilton could have imagined.

During the Independence struggles between India and Pakistan in 1947, when the Maharajah of Kashmir was dithering over which way to toss his jewel, a Pathan irregular force from Pakistan burst into the Vale and marched on the state capital, Srinagar. The Maharajah panicked, acceded to India, Indian troops recovered the border, and the valley was sliced in two. So it has remained: one-third in Pakistan, two-thirds (the best bit) in India, with Indian troops patrolling the border.

Kashmir's body, the state of Jammu and Kashmir, lies today in India, but her face points west to Pakistan and Central Asia. Her most famous son, Jawaharlal Nehru, first prime minister of India, may have been a Hindu, but in the Vale itself 94 per cent of the people are Muslim. They cheer for Pakistan in international cricket matches; many still practise purdah; their marriages are arranged, in strict Muslim fashion, by their parents; their language, even their food, is more Afghan than Indian.

During times of celebration Kashmiris hold elaborate feasts prepared by men called wazas, who have inherited the skill from their fathers, and who are distinct from other chefs in that they cook for special occasions alone.

Over a thousand wazas travel from party to party in the Vale, with their own spices, recipes, pots, assistants, setting up kitchens next to striped wedding tents and houseboats. Their food is lavish, a flashback for once to Persian opulence rather than Afghan frugality, and they are paid well for their skills: during the wedding season in October a good cook can earn as much as 10,000 rupees (about £600) a month. The cost of these wedding feasts may be more than a whole houseboat family on the Kashmir Lakes earns in three years.

ONE

From the verandah of my houseboat you could see eagles swooping around Akbar's sixteenth-century hill fort of Hari Parbat. From that hill you could see the peaks of Gulmarg, and from Gulmarg, on a clear day, the distant white smudge of K2 was just visible: it is the second-highest mountain in the world, and high enough for me.

Every morning at sunrise a kingfisher the size of a quail's egg dived for fish off my balcony rail into the reeds of Nagin Lake, and just before dusk the sun dropped

almost audibly from the sky, leaving a pink-rimmed silhouette around the carved houseboats across the lake (which featured in the BBC television series *Jewel in the Crown*) and the roofs of their next-door neighbours, a leper colony (which did not).

Gulam Mohammed Major's house, a bleached pine 'dhunga' boat in the shadow of the one I rented from him, was not named *Maharajah's Delight*, or *Jewel of the Lake*, or *Buckingham Palace*, as were the rented houseboats, nor had it prints of 'Highland Cattle in the Glens' as my boat had – just sleeping quilts and pillows, and a video in one corner.

Gulam Nabi, the boat boy, and his father lived in the front room with Nabi's two sisters, his mother, and his little brother, John. Mr Mohammed Major, in the back, could listen to the English World Service and dream his colonial dreams in peace. He used to work for an old English lady, a major's widow (hence his name) at the hill station of Gulmarg, and when she died she left him the money to buy his first houseboat. Mr Major was very old – ninety, even ninety-five – and had outlived nearly everything except his fondness for money.

Nabi, nineteen, but looking a rakish forty, thought that Mr Major pretended to have no money but was really very rich. 'Old is gold,' said Nabi, in his impeccable Sylvester Stallone English.

Mustaq, Nabi's eldest brother, was engaged to a girl whose family owned two houseboats – a good catch for a boy whose family had nothing. He was a golden boy of twenty-three, a water-skier, a charmer of clients, a loving son, his father's favourite. But he died suddenly of a brain tumour in the spring, and his fiancée needed a new husband to save her from dishonour. So began Nabi's dream.

TWO

One afternoon Nabi told me his plans for the future. He was saving to marry his dead brother's fiancée, 'Because our book says we must look after our brother's family', but first he must pay the school fees for his little brother and find husbands for his sisters. 'There must be week-long wazwans for hundreds of relatives, and the wazas, maybe twenty of them to cook for so many, must be paid thousands of rupees. Are weddings so expensive in your country, Miss?'

THREE

'Someday I will buy my family a house,' Nabi said another day, his arm looped through my boat's balcony. 'You see how we are – all in one room. And in winter here on the water is very cold and damp. Even with the winter wives. Even with extra mats on the floor.'

They make the mats by drying lake grasses. Their winter wives, called 'kahngris', are coal-burning firepots that hang from a thong under their woollen ponchos, the exteriors of the pots insulated with tree bark. Some Western doctors believe that they can cause stomach cancer in the wearers. They certainly cause dreadful burns when spilled.

Kashmiris call their winter the Time of Three Sisters: Forty Days' Death, Twenty, and Ten. The last Sister is the cruellest because everyone is weak. Irises, symbols of money, are planted on the graves of those who don't survive.

In winter, when thick snow prevents Nabi walking his usual half mile to get bread from the baker, Mima and her sister make socheh – chapattis rolled with sugar or ghee.

'Because for those you do not need the baker's tandoor oven,' said Mima. 'Only flour and water and a pan.'

Mima and her sister and mother cooked for the fifteen to twenty guests on Mr Major's houseboats in an open-air hut reached by stepping through the window of their boat. They had three bottled gas stoves, wooden floorboards through whose gaps you could see the lake, and one tap bringing water. 'Not from the lake like dirty houseboats. We have a tank. This is costing money.' It often freezes solid in winter.

Birds flew in to pick up any crumbs – friendly bulbuls with punk top-knots, and canny crows and mynah birds, who would steal the fresh curd if the top was left off the jar. Drinking cups hung in a wire basket from the ceiling, spices were locked in the cupboard. There was one basket of wild onions, one of tiny pink garlic heads from Mima's garden by the side of the kitchen, and another of the famous sweet Kashmiri red chillies that could be seen drying on valley roofs in the autumn.

Several mornings a week a man came by shikara with fresh vegetables, bought from the floating market near Srinagar. An acre of farmers paddled and haggled there, trading kilos of kohlrabi for kilos of cauliflowers, or for lily pads culled from the lakes for cattle fodder: shikara after shikara full of different greens, lumped communally under the umbrella word 'haak', that reappeared cooked in mustard oil, garlic and chillies, on every daily menu.

Everything floated in Kashmir, including the farms. Built on platforms of dried lake weed and mud, they could be towed conveniently from place to place, resulting in the occasional disconcerting sight of a row of runner beans sliding away silently – as if the earth had suddenly tilted on its axis.

FOUR

One morning Nabi knocked on my door. 'Miss, Miss, come with me to meet the baker, and the waza at Hazratbal who will cook when I marry. He makes dishes today for a tomorrow engagement.'

We passed the school where Nabi studied English, Urdu and Hindi.

'Very pretty girl I was liking at school. But she lives in a house and goes to college now, so she must marry a rich man. No Life Without Wife, my father says. No Knowledge Without College. No one is listening to the boat people because they think we have no education. We have no one to speak for us. So I pay for my little brother to go to good school.'

Hazratbal seemed to have a disproportionate number of bakers for such a small town. 'But when they are showing the very holy hair from Mohammed's beard here in October,' Nabi said, 'you cannot walk for people here.'

Nabi's favourite baker sold the same goods as all the others: roht, a sweet, Persian-style bread rolled like a coiled snake; doughnut-shaped tsachvaru, crusted with sesame seeds; and round chaute, with its parallel row of fingerprints and faint essence of cinnamon.

The baker stood in a deep hole dug in the dirt floor and slapped bread against the clay tandoor oven. Tandoors are cooler towards the top away from the coals, but the pale scald marks on the baker's arms were still visible where he had burnt himself over the years.

Dried grass and plastic sheeting were stuffed into the windows of the waza's kitchen where the glass had fallen out, or never was to begin with, and the surface of the lumpy dirt floor was covered with cooking utensils, ashes from old fires, and logs as long as men on the burning ends of which pots balanced precariously. Piles of straw pulled in or out of the fire served as thermostats.

The waza brought out a spotless padlocked pine box, 2½-feet square, and incongruously clean against the squalor of the floor. Inside it was divided into twelve cubicles filled with spices. There were two kinds of cardamom – the little green fragrant one, and the large, black and hairy pods that have an earthy, musky flavour; dried ginger, red chillies, turmeric, coriander and cumin seed, cinnamon, pepper, dried mint, whole cloves, and kohlrabi greens reduced to a pulp in oil, then dried. In a separate canister was a purée of onions that had first been sliced, then dried in the sun and pounded with garlic.

Gulam Mohammed Waza shut his box of magic tricks with a flourish. 'Today we make only ten or twelve dishes. For a wedding, a big wazwan, we can make twenty, even thirty.'

One of the waza's assistants crouched mashing tomatoes to a seedless paste for a dish of homemade curd cheese simmered with tomatoes and spices. Another pounded red chillies. A third patiently stirred a huge pot in which unrecognizable portions of a sheep's anatomy drifted up and down lethargically. A whole ribcage simmered in a broth that looked like the water of a communal bath after the last person has left, but tasted deliciously of spice. The ribs would be cut up later and deep-fried, the broth, 'yakhni', would form the base for subtle kormas.

The waza pounded a vast granite mortar of meat to a pulp, for the pièce de résistance of all wazwans: pingpong-ball-sized 'gustaba' and 'riste' meatballs that are simmered in cardamom-flavoured curds or chilli sauce.

'For a wazwan you will have some meat with bones and some meat without bones,' said the waza. 'But without bones, this is very hard to do. You must pound and pound until the meat is smooth like a Kashmiri shawl.'

Gustaba and riste are the kind of dishes whose worth a foreigner must accept on faith – like monkey's brains or raw

snake's liver. Pandit Nehru called them the cashmere of Kashmiri cuisine; to me, after the waza had pounded away all trace of sinew (a test of his skill), the famous meatballs had the texture of pork luncheon meat, although the sauces were subtle and creamy.

On the way home I asked Nabi when he would marry.

'In the autumn, when the tourists have gone. That is when most Kashmiris marry. The wazas are very busy then, very rich. Not like at Ramadan when we are fasting. Then wazas are getting quite thin. When the lotus leaves are going dry and we are going to shoot ducks by the lake at Hazratbal, then I will marry. But perhaps not this year. You like duck, Miss?'

'Does Mima have a good recipe for duck?'

'Oh yes, Miss. Mima very clever girl like you.

It was a mistake mentioning the duck. Mr Major heard of my interest. A whole one appeared, covered in a sticky beige gravy that clove my tongue to the roof of my mouth like a day-old peanut butter sandwich: the disinterred corpse of Raj cuisine.

Mr Major watched closely while I ate. 'Tastes good,' he said, proudly. 'English people liking ducks. Tomorrow we cook you nice boiled meats. And special tapioca pudding. Some English peoples call it maggots in batter.' I shuddered.

Mima came in to see how I had liked the duck.

'Is this a Kashmiri recipe for duck or an English one of Mr Major's?' I asked. She looked puzzled.

'Bawtuk mints duck,' she explained. 'Duck mints bawtuk.'

'And this is how you usually cook bawtuk here in Kashmir?'

'Kashmiri mints bawtuk,' said Mr Major, helpfully.

Mima added, 'English mints duck.'

'Same thing: duck-bawtuk, bawtuk-duck.'

I said, 'Ah yes,' feebly, and gave up. Mima and Mr Major seemed relieved.

Later Nabi told me that when they cooked wild duck for themselves, Mima plucked it and hung it to dry, then jointed it, browned it in mustard oil, and simmered it with kohlrabi greens, chillies and lots of garlic, and a splash of vinegar.

'Not little garlic from Mima's garden, Miss – big garlic from market.'

'But that sounds delicious, not what she cooked for me.'

'On no, Miss – that was Mr Major's recipe just for you.'

FIVE

Near Hazratbal we had seen the tents of the people who drove their sheep and goats down from the hills to be slaughtered for the biggest feasts. They were a wild-looking bunch, men and women with the faces of predatory birds, and the same uncanny way of unblinkingly rotating their heads almost full-circle.

I wanted to see Pahalgam – the gam (village) of these shepherds (pahal) – so I took a taxi on the first clear day.

We drove through Srinagar, east towards Ladakh past the military garrisons. Mustaq the eighteen-year-old driver, shouted 'Tonga-wahs' at the other vehicles as they lurched towards us on our side of the road.

Near Pampur there were miles of dry dust fields that would be purple seas of saffron crocuses in the autumn, then miles of silvery rice paddies where pickers ate their breakfasts under the shade of white mulberry trees.

At the Spring of Bawan, the visitors' book dated back to 1827. A man with a hatchet face plucked at my sleeve.

'I priest,' he said, baring too many teeth in a poor imitation of a smile. 'You give money for holy fish. Cost plenty money. Very holy fish.'

The goggle-eyed carp in question opened and closed their mouths as if struck dumb in the middle of a particularly vacuous discussion.

At Pahalgam the pony-trekking men had seen my taxi coming, and a tidal wave of about four hundred galloped towards us on their short-legged and long-suffering mounts, the riders whacking each other quite remorselessly about the heads to be first at the car. Fortunately, Mustaq had been there before and plunged confidently straight through without slowing, like Moses parting the Red Sea, leaving the seething mass to engulf the next arrival.

We stopped in a narrow river gorge with glittering peaks almost claustrophobically close, at the beginning of a Hindu pilgrimage route to the holy Amarnath caves 25 miles and several thousand feet above.

Well up the side of one of the mountains, past grazing ponies and sprays of wild dog rose, three ragged, hunched old men with villainous expressions struggled to sow maize on a near-vertical field. At thirty-five, Abdul Khalik Eerena was the eldest; the other two were his sons. Abdul invited me to sit under his walnut tree for tea.

'You honeymooner?' he grinned.

I shook my head. 'Writer.'

'Oh sorry, but many honeymooners here. You like walnuts? These very good. Make good chaute.'

He showed how his wife toasted the kernels to remove the skins, then pounded the nuts to a paste with salt, finely chopped wild onions, vinegar and yoghurt.

'Not too wet. Very good with rice and dal and chicken for Big Idh. Very special. You come back Pahalgam for honeymoon we kill some chickens have big feast, make chaute for you.'

Despite my protests, he walked halfway down the mountain to see me on my way, then climbed briskly back on his sturdy sherpa's legs. By the time I reached the bottom, he was once more at work with his sons, three ants toiling across a cliff that soon vanished into cloud.

SIX

Nabi was very excited when I got back. 'So you want to go in shikara with my sister and mother to meet my wife?'

Haleema was a tall, beautiful girl who walked like a cream-fed cat, a princess among fiancées, with wrap-round green eyes and golden skin.

One of Haleema's sisters breast-fed her two-year-old daughter to stop her crying. Haleema cuddled another pretty rosy-cheeked five-year-old, clearly suffering from rickets. Next to a giant ghetto-blaster in one corner sat the grandmother, a toothless old woman of forty in striped football socks, lighting her hubbly-bubbly from a burning kahngri, and drawing contentedly on it.

I was offered 'English' tea but opted for the fragrant green Kashmiri kava, brewed in a tall samovar with milk, sugar, slivered almonds and whole cardamoms, served with plates of cakes and poppy-seed biscuits and tsachwaru bread smeared generously with butter.

Haleema's sister, her eyes naughty, said, 'Kashmiri weddings costing very much. They are so expensive in England?' I gave Haleema a little money for her wedding which she passed immediately to her mother.

SEVEN

On a bright June day with a breeze from the Himalayas that sent waves scudding over yesterday's puddles, Nabi and I took a moto-rickshaw into Srinagar. A sign on the road read: IF YOU ARE MARRIED, DIVORCE YOUR SPEED.

'Old Town is where everything happens, Miss. When India and Pakistan play cricket, we cheer Pakistan because they are Muslim boys like us. Many times there is fighting here: between Sunnis and Shias, between Muslim and Hindu boys. Then the army comes.'

This time there was nothing more dangerous in the Old Town than a small boys' cricket match with bricks as wickets.

We walked past the SUFFERING MOSES shop to the wooden mosque of Shah Hamadan in the centre of the Old Town. It was carved in the fourteenth century, evidently by the Kashmiri equivalents of Hansel and Gretel. There was a stern sign: WOMAN AND NON MUSLIMS NOT ALLOWED BEYOND HERE. But the amiable priests allowed me to tiptoe barefoot beyond the sign and peer at an Early Gingerbread interior.

In the shadow of the mosque, a man sat below a mound of punctured blood-red balloons. 'Drying cockscombs,' said Nabi. 'These the wazas will crush to make the red food colouring for my wedding masalas.'

A girl walked by covered from head to ankle in a black silk burkha. 'Beautiful girl, Miss – see how she is covered from our eyes. When I

marry, I will make Haleema wear one to stop men looking.'

'Mima says she won't let you do that to her friend, Nabi.'

'Yes. But she says I must pick her nice boy to marry.'

'She wants to see him first.'

We took a shikara back to Nagin, and stopped to buy honey from Nabi's friend, Haseena Khan. Her cottage, straight from a Devon postcard of fifty years ago, was blooming with delphiniums, hollyhocks and beehives.

The honey was packed in old brandy bottles. You could have lotus, almond, five-blossom, a smoky jasmine version, or a strong, dark saffron one that tasted of steamy encounters with Latin men.

'Up in the hills I have another three hundred hives. The people cook wild rhubarb and mulberries with honey there; or quinces, and chill them until stiff as a pudding. Or they dry wild apples – our own Tret and Malmu – in the sun and eat them in winter boiled with amaranth flour and honey. Very good, very nice.'

'Mick Jagger was here two years ago to buy my Royal Jelly. You know Mick Jagger? You like Haleema?'

EIGHT

I asked Nabi to tell me again the plans for his wedding.

'This is how it will be, Miss: relatives putting henna on my little finger the first night, and singing our Kashmiri music. Then next day wazwan – not too much – maybe 150 people. After dinner we serve tea and sing whole night.'

I had heard this Kashmiri music at an engagement party weeks before. It was a nagging, eerie sound. No instruments, just groups of women inside a vast striped tent keening a sobbing duet of question and answer in alternate chorus with others outside. The bride-to-be sat with eyes downcast, strung like a sacrificial victim with coins and ornaments and a necklace of gift money.

'On third day starts real wedding, the big dhunga decorated with carpets and lights and flowers, the wazas cooking for 300 at lunch – good things. Many animals killed, hearts and kidneys and livers grilled on fire – and after lunch I must go to read Koran by my brother's grave. Then the dhunga to Haleema, and all the way will be fireworks and more fireworks and dancing on boat.'

A man comes to take Nabi to the priest. Three times the priest asks, 'Are you agreed to marry with this girl?' And three times Nabi answers yes, and signs a paper, with witnesses. The priest reads it to all the people, saying, 'So that they will know what they have done.'

For the big wazwan a carpet is rolled from room to room down the boat. Around each big plate of rice four men eat.

'Wazas coming in and out with new dishes. First the dry: roasted chicken, red from the cockscombs, and skewers of kebabs like you have had, and ribs of sheep and goats cooked in spiced curds and crisp-fried in oil. Then the wet: ruangan tsaman and gustaba and riste and rogan josh with peppers and saffron, and palag korma in spinach sauce. Then Haleema is coming back to our boat but sleeping separate with others.'

'Fourth day very early I must buy dried fruits for strength in night. And this night I sleep with Haleema all night.'

'The parties go on for many days, Miss. But this is my dream: to save money for a proper honeymoon – like you people who come here. And we can live in a house on the land, not always in one room, never alone. This is not a good life.'

I looked around at the turquoise lake and thought of breakfasts of fresh curds and lotus honey and cherries bought from a shikara, taken with eagles and kingfishers. But Nabi shrugged.

'What do we have? Nothing. At least with a store a man might earn money even in winter.'

NINE

In late July a letter arrived in England, dictated by Nabi, but written, as usual, in the hand of his friend the tailor.

Dear and Dearest Madam,

Hope this letter will find you in good mood and good health. I did received your letter enclosed with photographs and was besides with lots of joy and happiness. And I would like to bring you also in good mood, bringing a very good message in your notice that my engagement with Haleema is to be held after Big Idh in first week of August.

I hope you will not forget one and will keep me always in mind fresh and fresh. Perhaps I don't think I can forget you even after my death.

Rest I am giving you salaam and good wishes from my family.
Sincerely yours, GN Major

In August I heard that President Zia of Pakistan had been killed. There was rioting in Srinagar's Old Town. All tourists, including those on the houseboats, were being asked to leave Kashmir.

I thought of Nabi's dream and wished him well.

RECIPES

Breads

Most Kashmiri food is actually closer to Afghan cooking than to Indian. With the exception of chapattis, Kashmiri breads are the leavened, tandoor oven loaves of

Afghanistan and Persia: chewy, dense, with a crisp crust, sometimes a hint of cinnamon, the tops sprinkled with toasted seeds.

The base for Kashmiri breads is a very finely ground wholemeal flour with no trace of bran. Aata – Indian chapatti flour – is as close as I have found to the same quality in the West. The usual leavening is a mixture called 'khameer' of 2:1:1 live yoghurt, flour and sugar, which is left overnight in a warm place. Yoghurt can be unreliable in producing the same leavening results every time, but even a commercial yeast mixture left overnight to ferment improves the taste and texture of bread.

Terracotta flooring tiles preheated in a hot oven provide a little of the heat-retentive qualities and earthy aroma of the baker's tandoor.

TSAUTE
Breakfast and lunch bread

May be made in two ways: in the morning, roll it out in an oval 8 in × 5½ in/20 cm × 14 cm, about ¼ in/0.5 cm to ½ in/1 cm thick. Wet your fingers and press them deeply down the centre of each bread to form 4–6 parallel rows of six holes, leaving the outer rim free and higher than the centre. (This makes the centre crunchy and the edges soft and chewy for energetic breakfasts.) Brush the top with beaten egg yolk and bake as advised in recipe.

For a smaller afternoon version – better for scooping up sauces – roll the dough out into 5 in/12.5 cm circles and make the same holes as before. Brush the top with yolk and sprinkle with lots of sesame seeds.

Leavening
1 oz/30 g fresh yeast
2 oz/60 g strong plain bread flour (or chapatti flour)
8 tbsp warm water
1 tbsp sugar

14 oz/400 g strong plain bread flour (or chapatti flour)
½ tsp cinnamon
pinch of salt
approximately 4 fl oz/100 ml warm water
1 egg yolk, beaten
sesame, poppy seeds, etc.

(1) The night before you want the bread, mix together the leavening ingredients, cover with plastic film and leave in a warm place.

(2) The next day, sieve together the flour, salt and cinnamon in a large warmed bowl. Roughly mix in the leavening and slowly add water, working it in until the flour will form a soft ball. Turn the dough out onto a well-floured board – you need quite a lot of flour because the dough is so soft – and knead for 7–10 minutes, pressing down with the heels of your hands, turning it and folding it over. (Alternatively, you can do all this in a food processor, finishing up with 2–3 minutes' hand kneading.) When the dough is smooth and pliable and no longer has any sticky surfaces, put it in a large well-floured bowl, cover with plastic film and leave for 1–2 hours in a warm, draught-free place.

(3) Thirty minutes before you are ready to bake the dough, preheat the oven to 475°F/240°C/gas mark 9 and put in a baking stone or a heavy metal baking sheet.

(4) Form the dough into whatever shape bread you like (as per recipes – this recipe makes 4 large or 8 small, or 6 'doughnuts'. Doughnut shape requires another hour's rising after it has been shaped), brush with egg and bake for 10 minutes, then lower heat to 425°F/220°C/gas mark 7 for a further 10 minutes until golden brown.

TSACHWARU
Doughnut-shaped tea bread

These are the bagels of Kashmir. Using the same dough as for tsaute, divide it into eight little sausages and roll into doughnuts 2¾ in/7 cm × 1 in/2.5 cm. Brush the tops with beaten yolk, sprinkle liberally with sesame seeds and bake for 20–25 minutes until golden. Serve, split, with butter and jam or homemade clotted cream and sweet cardamom tea.

Yoghurt/Curd

A firm curd, usually made from rich buffalo milk, the fat in it essential to the creamy texture of Kashmiri dishes, especially those with a Persian/Moghul slant. I use Greek yoghurt.

CHAUTE
Walnut chutney

Walnuts grow wild in Kashmir, and a version of this appears on every table. Enough for eight people at dinner.

2½ oz/75 g walnut pieces
pinch of salt (or to taste)
½ tsp sugar
½–¾ tsp chilli powder/cayenne
½ small onion, very finely chopped
2 tbsp white wine vinegar
2 tbsp yoghurt

Toast the walnuts slightly in a frying pan until they begin to give off their aroma, then roughly purée with remaining ingredients. Will keep for up to 48 hours in a sealed jar in the refrigerator. Serve with rice and spicy foods.

Knol-kohl/kohlrabi

The humble kohlrabi, scorned by most Europeans except the Germans, made its way to Kashmir and by 1895 had shrugged off its Western origins enough for a Walter Lawrence, writing in *The Valley of Kashmir*, to describe it as the national vegetable.

The leaves are cooked like spinach in light summer dishes with lotus roots, lake fish, ground lamb, curd cheese; with red chillies and mustard oil. In colder months, the roots are cut in chunks and simmered in a rich, sweet sauce with kidney beans. Like other vegetables that do not survive the mountain frosts – tomatoes, marrow, chillies, onions – it is sliced and sun-dried in late summer/early autumn for winter storage, later to be eaten with oil, salt and pepper, or pickled with sweetened vinegar and roasted spice. It is one of the most nutritious vegetables, rich in protein, calcium and vitamin C, with a sweet, nutty taste if eaten when no bigger than a tennis ball.

NADR/NEDR
Lotus (root)

The great belled leaves of lotus plants rise well above the water of Kashmiri lakes, their wax-perfect pink flowers opening in the summer. They look anything but edible, yet the Kashmiris find a use for almost every part. Women and children paddle their shikaras through watery fields of lotus, shearing off leaves and stems for cattle fodder. The rhizomes, those scruffy brown link-sausage shapes that taste faintly of artichoke hearts, are used in chunks with meat as 'Nadrtmaaz', in thin sliced fritters known as 'Nadr moinj', with curd and greens, and sun-dried for winter use.

Lotus roots need to be peeled and cleaned well before cooking, as lake mud works itself deep inside. Drop the cut pieces in acidulated water to prevent them browning while you prepare dishes.

NADR CHURM
Deep-fried lotus root chips (for 6 as a snack)

vegetable oil for deep-frying
1 lotus root (about 14 oz/425 g),
peeled and sliced in ¼ in/0.5 cm rounds
1 cup rice (or other fine) flour, sifted with 1½ tsp cayenne,
1 tsp ground cumin, 1 tsp salt and 1 tsp ground turmeric

Heat the oil until it smokes, toss the slices of root in the flour and fry a few at a time until pale golden. Drain on kitchen paper, heat the oil to smoking again and fry the pieces for another minute until brown. Serve immediately. Good with fresh coriander chutney.

NADR HAAK/SAAG KAMAL KAKRI
Lotus roots stewed with greens and fresh curd (serves 4)

'Kamal' means lots, 'kakri' good and 'saag' spinach (or mustard greens or kohlrabi or...it is an umbrella term). It was served as one of the many dishes at a June engagement.

5–6 tbsp vegetable oil
½ tsp ground turmeric
½ tsp cayenne
½ tsp paprika
4 garlic cloves, crushed
½ lb/250 g fresh lotus root, peeled and cleaned
1 pt/570 ml Greek yoghurt, whisked smooth
1 tsp coarse salt
1 lb/500 g fresh spinach (or spring/collard greens)
pinch bicarbonate of soda
6 tbsp yakhni or strong meat broth (optional)

(1) Cut the lotus root in ¼ in/0.5 cm slices, and quarter them. Holding the greens tightly in one hand, slice them crosswise at ¼ in/0.5 cm intervals.
(2) Heat the oil in a heavy saucepan, large enough to hold all the ingredients. When medium hot, stir in the turmeric, cayenne, paprika and garlic and cook until the garlic softens. Add the lotus root and brown, stirring constantly. Lift out with a slotted spoon.

(3) Pour the yoghurt and salt into the remaining oil and stir constantly (to prevent it separating) until reduced to a thick sauce. Return lotus root to the pan with the spinach, soda and yakhni (or water). Stir until the spinach wilts, lower the heat and simmer, uncovered, until most of the liquid has been absorbed – about 25 minutes. Serve with grilled meat and basmati rice.

TSOONGT
Apples

Red and white October-ripening Anbru or Amri was once the most popular – for its beauty and sweetness, the power of its fragrance. Now it is rarer, and where it grew are orchards of Delicious and American. The best native when it can be found is the little sour-sweet Trel. It used to be collected at night for cider. Rotten windfalls, like medlars, taste of chocolate. Apples are eaten in the winter stewed with lotus honey.

TSOONGT PUDDING

Boil down 2 pt/1.25 l of whole milk with 3 green cardamom pods. When reduced by half, add two apples, peeled, cored and diced, and several spoonfuls of sugar. Continue to cook until thick and custardy, stirring often to allow the steam to escape. Purée, pour into little earthenware saucers (or a silver bowl) and chill well. Absolutely delicious with toasted almonds.

In The Waza's Kitchen

The most important part of the waza's kitchen was his invaluable padlocked spice box, but the most dramatic were the several log fires burning in the middle of the floor, a sort of one-log, two-log, three-log method of heat regulation. An Aga operates on the same principle.

The Feast

As opulent as the preparation and final result of the wazwan may appear, the underlying thread is one of good sense – the basic canny nature of the Kashmiris reasserting itself through the cream of Moghul tradition.

Seven or eight sheep may be sacrificed to the feast to feed the 300–500 guests over several days, but every part is used. The spiced water that simmers the ribcages – which are deep-fried as tabak maaz – becomes yakhni, the stock for two kinds of korma, and is mixed with creamy curd for the gustaba. The baskets of scarlet chilli peppers and tomatoes that are pounded to a paste are used to flavour many of the dishes. The whey extracted from the milk when making curd cheese enriches the meat stock. Even the tail and tripe are eaten (Kashmiris have no prejudice against organ meats), although the tripe is elevated to princely status by cooking it with saffron. Particularly robust eaters may drink a heart-stopping mixture of beaten curd and yakhni.

YAKHNI
Aromatic lamb broth/stock (to make about 1 ½ pt/800 ml)

TABAK MAAZ
Barbecued (or deep-fried) breast of lamb
(to serve 6 as a starter)

Yakhni, the highly scented stock that results from gently simmering the breast of lamb, is the base of the pyramid for many of the sauces to follow. If you are planning to cook any of the other feast dishes, try to buy the breast bones with plenty of meat still attached. Allowing 3–4 ribs per person, but keeping the piece whole, trim off the fleshiest part of the meat and set aside for gustaba or riste.

It is worth making the broth the day before it is needed (as the waza did) so that any excess fat can be lifted off easily when cool. Unused broth can be frozen for later use.

Tabak maaz makes a delicious, not too heavy beginning to a meal whose richer centre might be the creamy gustaba and spicy riste.

about 2 lb/1 kg whole breast of lamb with bone
(weighed without extra meat) plus 1 lb/500 g lamb bones
1 unpeeled onion, quartered
2 whole garlic cloves, slightly crushed
2 black and 6 green cardamom
1 tsp coarse salt
8 whole cloves
1 3 in/8 cm cinnamon stick
½ tsp ground ginger
3 pt/1.7 l cold water (you can use the whey from making
tsaman cheese for part of this)
2 tsp homemade garam masala (page 111)

(1) In a large, heavy saucepan, bring all ingredients except the breast of lamb to a boil over medium heat. Slip the whole breast into the liquid and lower the heat to a gentle simmer. Skim off any scum that rises to the surface over the next five minutes, half-cover and simmer for 2½ hours. At the end of the first hour, remove the breast of lamb and reserve. Strain the finished broth through muslin, discard solids and refrigerate or freeze until needed.

(2) When you are ready to serve the breast of lamb, you can cook it in one of two ways.

The best way: Rub it well with lots of mustard oil or melted ghee, sprinkle with garam masala and barbecue until golden. Brush with more melted ghee, and serve with coarse salt, the breast sliced in pieces.

Alternatively: In a heavy saucepan, heat 2 in/5 cm of vegetable oil or lard until smoking. Slice the breast of lamb between the bones and deep-fry until brown in the oil. Sprinkle with garam masala and coarse salt before serving.

Note: The wazas also treat pieces of chicken in the same way, simmering them in a spiced broth, then spreading the tender meat with a paste of Kashmiri red chillies · and garam masala, and barbecuing them as for tabak maaz. Try using the paste recommended for riste (page 132).

SIKH KEBAB
Grilled or barbecued ground lamb (to make 8–12 sausages)

Like giant skewered sausages in appearance ('sikh' means 'skewer'). Like them, too, in tasting better fresh from a smoky barbecue than an electric grill. Squeeze on fresh lemon or lime juice while they are still hot. Or wrap them in a blanket of tandoor bread in memory of their Afghan/Turkish heritage.

2 garlic cloves, chopped
1 small onion, chopped
1½ tsp salt
1 tsp ground cumin
seeds from 4 green cardamom pods, crushed
¾ tsp black pepper
1½ tsp cayenne
3 tbsp chopped fresh coriander
2 tbsp besan/chickpea flour
1½ lb/750 g best lamb, minced twice

In a blender, reduce everything except the lamb to a purée. Add to the lamb and knead very thoroughly until well blended and smooth. Leave uncovered in a cool place for 1–2 hours. Divide the mixture into 8–12 long sausages and press firmly onto skewers. Grill until well-browned (about 15–20 minutes) not too close to the heat.

GUSTABA AND RISTE
Giant meatballs in two sauces
(to serve 6 as a main course with other dishes)

These are the cashmere-smooth meatballs that made Pandit Nehru nostalgic for his Kashmiri home. Two dishes really, but they are easily cooked together, and make a more spectacular presentation – the creamy gustaba on one side, chilli-red riste on the other. Wazas, depending on their skill and inclination, may pound the meat for 6–7 hours. Triple grinding or mincing in a food processor saves time.

Meatballs
2 lb/1 kg lamb, minced twice
1 tsp salt
1½ tsp ground coriander
2 tbsp full-fat yoghurt
1 tsp ground ginger
1 tsp dried mint

Gustaba sauce
2 tbsp ghee and 2 tbsp vegetable oil
1 onion, finely chopped
1 pt/500 ml Greek yoghurt
1 tsp salt
1 tsp ground white pepper
4 whole cloves
3 green and 1 black cardamom
1 in/2.5 cm stick cinnamon
12 fl oz/350 ml yakhni (or good strong lamb stock)

Riste sauce
1 tbsp ground paprika
½–1 tsp ground chilli/cayenne
½ tsp ground ginger
½ tsp ground cumin
½ tsp ground turmeric
2 tbsp vegetable oil

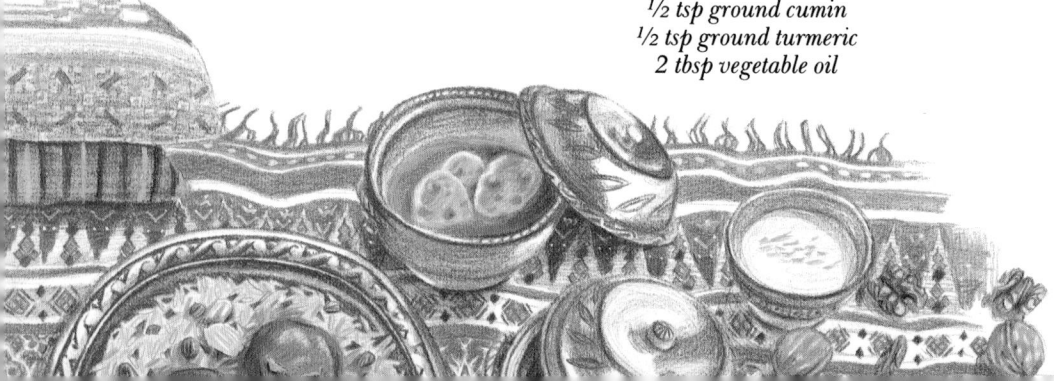

> *2 tbsp ghee*
> *4 cloves*
> *seeds from 3 green cardamom, crushed*
> *18 fl oz/500 ml yakhni (or strong lamb stock)*

(1) Knead all the ingredients for the meatballs until well blended, then purée in a food processor for 1–2 minutes until the meat feels pasty between your fingers rather than sinewy. If any particularly tenacious bits of gristle or sinew remain, discard them. Divide mixture into 12 balls.

(2) To make the gustaba sauce, melt ghee and oil over medium heat in a heavy saucepan big enough to hold all the ingredients, including 6 meatballs. Stir-fry onions until soft (about 7 minutes), lift out with a slotted spoon and purée with the yoghurt, salt and pepper.

(3) Fry whole cloves, cardamom and cinnamon over medium heat in remaining oil for 1 minute – until you start to smell them – and pour in the yoghurt mixture, stirring constantly until it has reduced to a thick sauce with oil just beginning to show around the edges. Pour in the yakhni, and the meatballs in a single layer.

(4) Continue cooking, stirring often and rolling the meat around in the sauce, for 1½ hours, or until the sauce is the consistency of thick cream. Do not allow to boil hard – it should just roll over. If necessary, put a heat-dispersing mat underneath.

(5) For the riste, whisk together paprika, cayenne, cumin, ginger and turmeric with 2 tbsp water. Melt ghee and oil over medium heat in a heavy saucepan. Add all the spices and fry until the mixture is thick.

(6) Pour in the yakhni and the remaining 6 meatballs, in one layer as before. Lower the heat and continue as for gustaba, stirring occasionally until the sauce is thick.

(7) To serve, first skim off the excess fat – a nod to Western tastes; it would never be done in Kashmir, where the shimmer of melted ghee is considered an indication of bounty. Pile basmati rice (an almondy, raisiny pilau, if you are feeling energetic) down the middle of a large plate. Pour the creamy gustaba and its sauce down one side and the riste down the other. Scatter a dusting of finely chopped fresh mint or coriander over the top.

KAVA

Kashmiri spiced tea (serves 8)

It is the custom in Kashmir first to offer guests a cup of sugared tea, and then another salted or with a pinch of soda. Although the sugared tea is usually green and flavoured with cardamoms alone, for very special occasions a rich blend of spices and nuts may be added. The Kashmiris like their tea either salty or very sweet; as I don't, I prefer to add sugar to taste.

> *2½ pt/1.5 l cold water*
> *6 tbsp milk*
> *4–6 tbsp tea leaves (not green or scented)*
> *5 green cardamom pods*
> *2–3 tbsp flaked almonds, some crushed*
> *2–3 tbsp shelled pistachios, roughly crushed*
> *2–3 threads saffron*

Bring milk and water to the boil, add tea and cardamom, reduce heat and simmer for 3 minutes. Strain and simmer liquid with the nuts for another 2. Pour the tea into a pot, add saffron and leave to brew for 3–5 minutes before serving.

RUANGAN TSAMAN

Slices of homemade curd cheese in spicy sauce (serves 4–6)

In Hazratbal the shops that were not bakeshops were selling samovars, cooking pots and intricately carved pine churns to whisk yoghurt into refreshing liquid 'lassi' for breakfast, or to cream it for thick sauces. Nearby at Alshtaan was a man who made pure cows' milk curd cheese. 'Some cheese too hard and some too soft,' said Nabi's father. 'So I must go to Alshtaan to get the best.'

I never discovered what this man used to set his cheese – there was a rumour that he used soda – but in most homes it is done with lime or lemon juice. Making fresh curd cheese is the simplest of processes: the only trick in setting it is to be sparing with the lemon juice. You want as little as possible to keep the curd light.

4 pt/2.25 l whole fat milk
3–5 tbsp fresh lemon or lime juice
6 tbsp mustard oil (or other light vegetable oil)
1 medium onion, peeled and finely chopped
4 garlic cloves, peeled and crushed
1 tsp coarse salt
½ tsp ground ginger
3 whole cloves
seeds of 3 green cardamom pods, crushed
1 tsp turmeric, ¼ tsp cayenne, 1 tsp paprika whisked
to a paste with 2 tbsp cold water
2 lb/1 kg tomatoes, peeled and seeded

(1) Make the cheese: heat milk in a heavy pan until it starts to rise to the boil. Reduce heat, pour in 3 tbsp lemon juice and stir gently for a few seconds. The milk should curdle, i.e., separate into greeny whey and lumps of white curd. Not a pleasant sight, but it gets better. If curds do not form, add more juice until they do. Pour the curds and whey into a pudding bag or several thicknesses of cheesecloth and leave to drain for an hour (you can use the whey in breads and soups). Wring out any excess liquid and place under a weight for another hour.
(2) Slice the block of cheese into ¼–½ in/0.5–1 cm slices. In a heavy saucepan, heat the oil over a medium-high heat and brown the cheese on both sides – this stops it disintegrating later. Lift out with a slotted spoon and drain.
(3) Cook the onion until golden (about 7 minutes) in the remaining oil over medium heat, add the garlic, salt, ginger, cloves and cardamom seeds and stir for 5 minutes. Pour in the cayenne/paprika paste and simmer until the oil begins to show around the edges. Mash the tomatoes slightly and stir into the spices. When they have reduced a little and thickened, slip in the cheese slices and cook for 20 minutes, adding spoonfuls of water if the sauce starts to dry out.

TSAMAN HAAK

Curd cheese simmered with greens

A green and white version of the preceding recipe. Make the cheese as before and simmer it with spinach or kohlrabi greens, using the same sauce as for nadr haak – yoghurt, garlic, onion, etc. – but adding ½ tsp ground ginger and the crushed seeds of 3 green cardamoms to the sauce, and substituting tsaman for the lotus roots.

• Serve both these dishes with a sprinkling of toasted cumin seeds.

1789 ~ 1989

BASTILLE DAYS

———

The Bicentennial of the
French Revolution

REVOLUTION

ONE

On the evening of 20 January 1793, Louis XVI, devoted father and designer of locks, dined more modestly than usual: chicken with vegetables, two glasses of wine, water, cherries steeped in eau de vie, a few sweet biscuits. Perhaps he had lost his usually robust appetite at the thought that the next day he would lose his head as well.

The aristocracy and the literary élite in the Bastille were still eating well, although not well enough for the Marquis de Latude, who complained to the prison governors of chickens prepared with insufficient bacon. So many of the Bastille prisoners had brought their own chefs with them that it was considered too expensive for ordinary men.

At the height of the Terror, the deputy Jean-Baptiste Louis Joseph Billecoq, counsel to parliament and secretary-general of the Jacobite Club, and one of the many involved in creating the phoenix of the New Republic out of the ashes of the Ancien Régime, left his post in the National Assembly (where he had helped to draw up the revolutionary

Declaration of 1789), kissed his wife goodbye, and went to prison, perhaps to his death.

He was in his late twenties, a man of the haute bourgeoisie of Paris, with poet's eyes as yet untouched by the guillotine.

His wife brought food to the prison every day. Every day his friends and companions took the tumbril ride to the guillotine, entertaining the restaurant clientele watching them pass in the Rue St Honoré, and possibly amusing Prosecutor Le Bon as well, who delighted in dining while executions he had brought about took place.

Inside the prison, M. Billecoq wrote not of death but of the great spirit of camaraderie, and of his good fortune in having the opportunity 'to see how people outside our little society live; and to experience new tastes, new food'.

Here is how he passed part of his eight months in prison:

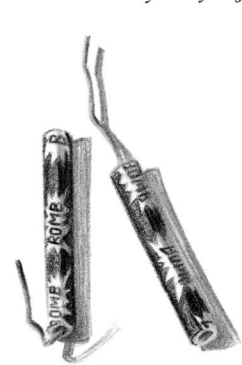

I got up at six in the morning, a little before my cohabitants, and after a short prayer often silent (and too often only silent, at that perilous time of my life when God was my only refuge), I spent a little while reading. When everyone in the cell was ready, we would all sit down to eat. To this end, a table was laid on which each man and woman placed the food that had been sent by his or her family or had been ordered from outside. This meal was one of the warmest and best times. Stories, philosophy, jokes — even about the seasoning and preparation of the food. The meal finished, Renault, or Beudon, or me, who were the youngest and most vigorous, would wash and arrange the cell. But each one made his own bed, with the exception of one or two.

Released from prison, rescued, just days before his own execution, by the death of Robespierre, he lived until 1829, when he died at the age of sixty-four, but not before seeing his daughter Anne married in 1824 to the son of Louis Beguin, a lawyer and fellow deputy with whom Billecoq sat in the National Assembly.

A picture of Jean-Baptiste's great-grandson taken with Olga of Russia stands on the piano of Xavier Beguin Billecoq, who, in the summer of 1989, to celebrate the 200th anniversary of the Reign of Terror, organized a competition for the best Revolutionary Feast offered by any restaurant that year.

Café Procope won: opened in 1686 as a Paris coffee house, and once haunted by every major revolutionary figure, its 1989 menu included 'Tête de Veau Dr. Guillotine'.

The Café Flo offered an entrée of 'Potage à la Reine' followed by a dessert of 'Poupelains à la Bourgeoise'.

The Hôtel de France in Beaune served up:

LA PECHE DU CITOYEN

SIX GASTEROPODES REPUBLICAINS

GIGOT ROTI SANS CULOTTE

The Hostellerie de Térèsme in Crépy en Valois offered a tumbril of cheeses, 'La Charlotte Corday', and 'La Coupe Guillotine' to finish.

TWO

In the offices of the Maison de la France, M. Xavier Beguin Billecoq, an excitable handsome little man with the poet's eyes of his ancestors and the English tweediness of a true French bourgeois, 'Responsable du Patrimonie et du Bicentennaire de la Révolution Française', spread out a collection of yellowing paper covered in beautiful sepia copperplate.

'These are family tonics for illnesses and recipes that Anne Billecoq's daughter Marie collected together at the end of the last century. Pauline, the cook, saved the recipes.'

The recipes and notes dated from the early eighteenth to the mid-nineteenth century. He held up an old playing card of the period on which someone had scribbled a recipe 'to be taken against the Plague'; a pale blue sheet with an eighteenth-century round-head pin stuck through it and a mixture for eau de Cologne using bergamot and tincture of amber; and medicinal advice from 1764, to be used against the epidemic carried by dogs in that year.

He told me that he had a picture of a M. Hippolyte Billecoq dancing in Vienna with the Duchess of York while she was pregnant with the future Queen Victoria.

'Hippolyte spoke well of her nimble polonaise,' he said.

In parting he gave me photostat portraits of his revolutionary relatives, and an extract from the 'Marseillaise des Bons Vivants': '*A table, citoyens! Vidons tous les flacons.*'

THREE

On the night of 13 July 1989, world leaders accompanied the select from France's upper echelons to the new Bastille Opera, not to storm it, but to attend its gala opening. The lower echelons were in the streets enjoying the biggest Bastille Day bash the French have ever had.

The Bastille station was closed because of the gala, so the crowds of us on the Métro were forced to leave at the Place de la République, where a free rock concert had attracted so many people that movement was restricted to an eel-like wriggle.

I saw a friend in an outdoor café clinging to his table as a drowning

man to a log, but was helpless to do any more than wave across the sea of bodies and be swept down Boulevard Voltaire towards the Bastille. All around me fireworks cracked and banged until I twitched like a shellshocked veteran of the Western Front.

In the exquisitely beautiful Grand Véfour restaurant, centre of a circle of food-loving conspirators in 1789, the 'bon ton', and the not so bon but definitely well-heeled were eating a highly bred eighteenth-century menu recreated by the chef for the bicentenary: 'Les oeufs de caille en coque brisée' (180 francs), Homard Thermidor (350 francs), Dodine de pigeon de Bresse à la fleur de thym (260 francs), and a soufflé au chocolat made with old, old rum (95 francs).

The rabble haunted pavement braziers down the boulevards. Men with olive skin and beady black eyes grilled merguez sausages and forked them into baguettes smeared with mustard. Price: 15 francs. Heavy pans flipped crêpes – to be eaten crisply hot with a squeeze of lemon and a sprinkling of sugar; and people passed cheap bottles of vin de table to strangers and friends.

In six Paris arrondissements the traditional Bastille Day open-air dances went on all night, and at a street party off the Rue de Sèvres a louche brass band dressed as sailors played breathy blue jazz while I danced a 4.00 a.m. tango with a boy from Algiers.

On the night of the fourteenth, a little man called Goude with a flair for self-promotion unparalleled since Bonaparte put together a ten-million-pound parade down the Champs Élysées. It featured a steam train from Russia rolling through enough white confetti 'snow' to cover the Siberian Steppes, the Royal Scots Dragoons and the Queen's Own Hussars, carrying colours won at Waterloo, marching ahead of fire engines drenching British dancers in rain, two elephants, a moving ice rink with skating bears, and the opera singer Jessye Norman standing on stilts under a tricolour tent dress and singing the *Marseillaise*.

By 1.30 a.m. it was all over. Empty wooden stands faced in toward the Place de la Concorde where a fortunate few had watched the parade while the Paris mob queued forty deep down the boulevard. The rich miss all the fun. A wind blew Arctic storms of white confetti back up the Champs Élysées to the Arc de Triomphe. And I walked back with a friend through streets of tired people trying to find any place at all to have one last drink before bed.

'All the bars close at 2.00 a.m. here,' said my friend. 'And the posh restaurants who have always dealt with posh clients would not dream of doing anything for the Revolution.'

We finally had a coffee in a pseudo-English pub on the Boulevard St Germain.

Paris – La Semaine Folle, July 1989: it was the best of times, or, depending on your personal prejudice (and history), it was the worst.

RECIPES

June, July and August 1794 was the worst period of the Reign of Terror, and a bad time to be in the restaurant business in Paris.

After 1792, food shortages and resulting rationing caused an almost complete disappearance of eggs, butter, oil, salt, soap and candles. Eggs still existed, but one needed money. The police were lucky. After one denunciation of the grand pâtissier Dubois in 1794, 3,000 fresh eggs were found in his cellars. The pâtissier soon had his turn underground.

Many of the people who had patronized the cafés of Paris were in prison; Antoine Beauvilliers, France's first restaurant owner of Michelin level, served eighteen months. His silver service, faïence and starched white linen, worlds removed from the style of lowly caterers of the past, had attracted a clientele so quasi-aristocratic that they were part of the gaudy Beauvilliers' downfall (although he survived to write a famous cookery book).

In Beauvilliers' absence the restaurant continued under new management – Naudet, president of the revolutionary tribunal – and a less pleasant clientele, who enjoyed asking for 'fresh and nicely bloody meat'.

At a time known more for its famine from bad harvests than for its feasts, it is hard to imagine that the art of cooking thrived. Yet it did.

A Madame Mérigot wrote and published a cookery book during the Revolution, *La Cuisinière Républicaine*, appropriately (considering the grave grain shortages) devoted to potato recipes.

Even in prison the Parisians did not forget their stomachs. Grimod de la Reynière (restaurant critic and witty chronicler of gastronomy) wrote of the condemned:

The victims in the prisons are still interested in food, and through the prison hatch pass some of the most exquisite dishes – especially for those who are eating their last meal and find it difficult to forget the fact. In the bottom of the dungeons one finds these condemned ones making deals with restaurateurs, signing away one valuable after another while making particular conditions about the quality of the next season's young vegetables ...The little puddings and meringues that arrive attest to the skill of our pâtissiers, as well as to the preoccupation of Parisians, free or imprisoned.

During the Revolution, austerity (or the appearance of austerity) prevailed. Famous dishes had Royalist names changed to something more egalitarian. The Twelfth Night brioche previously known as 'Gâteau des Rois' (Kings' Cake) incurred revolutionary wrath – it was thought to have monarchist tendencies. Canny pastry-cooks altered its name to Liberty Cake and traced a Phrygian cap on the surface.

But as noble heads fell, unemployed chefs began to open their own businesses, or went to work for new republican masters who had tired of frugality. De la Reynière said, 'Of all the arts, the culinary one has made the most progress over the last ten years. The famous cooks once concentrated in the houses of financiers and grand seigneurs keep excellent boutiques today.'

In the coffee houses, gardens and arcades of the Palais Royal little fast-food operations had long been running, serving exotically perfumed ice-cream and 'Bouchées à la Reine' (now hastily renamed vol-au-vents). From 1781, when the Duc d'Orléans, strapped for cash, began building the galleries to be rented out to restaurant owners and others, and all through the Revolution, the Palais Royal was the centre of fashionable Paris and French gastronomy.

Beauvilliers' restaurant was here; Véry's; the Café de Chartres, later to become the Grand Véfour, which served many of the great gourmets (and the future revolutionaries) of the time.

In 1785 the Almanach du Palais Royal recommended the Café de Chartres to travellers – 'A numerous and good group of people get together here in this vast local to read the English and German papers.' Another broadsheet put it slightly differently – 'it is the rendezvous of all the thieves, pimps and villains that fill the capital, not to mention the countless lively flowers who lodge on the gallery mezzanine.'

A good place to brew coffee and revolution then. And in the little Palais Royal Café de Foy, on 13 July 1789, Camille Desmoulins stuck a chestnut leaf from the palace garden into his hat as a cockade, shouted 'Aux armes, citoyens' and led the storming of the Bastille.

Dishes of the Day

The following recipes come from Anne Billecoq's collection. Where they seem clear, I have translated them fairly directly – putting in any clarifying details that seem necessary. Where there was more room for error I have worked the recipes into a form more easily understandable.

PURÉE DE MARRONS OU NOISETTES
Chestnut or hazelnut purée

(The recipe suggested that one would serve beef rissoles on top of these savoury purées, but they are absolutely delicious with any kind of roast meats – especially game. If you wish to use fewer nuts, or can't be bothered peeling them all, use 3:1 puréed potatoes – cooked in bouillon – to nuts.)

Skin the nuts well, cover them in good beef bouillon/broth and cook until very tender (about 45 minutes). Purée them with a few spoonfuls of butter, and enough broth to make a not too stiff cream, seasoning well with salt, ground black pepper and a little sugar. Serve with slices of bread fried in butter or oil.

• To remove skins from chestnuts: make a crosswise cut through both outer and inner skin, trying not to pierce the nut itself, three quarters of the way around each nut. Boil for 5–10 minutes and peel the skins off while still warm. Hazelnuts: crack off the outer shell and toast the nuts lightly, then rub off the inner skins.

GARBURE AUX MARRONS
Chestnut soup

(A garbure is a broth or soup served with breads spread with various savoury ingredients – in this instance, chestnuts.)

Remove skins from chestnuts. Put them in a big pot with several chunks of fatty pork or bacon, some pieces of meaty bones (if you have them), 2–3 carrots cut in chunks, an unpeeled onion stuck with cloves, 2 bay leaves and a few celery stalks with their leaves, roughly chopped. Cover in water and simmer for one hour. Crush the chestnuts coarsely and strain the broth. In a heatproof earthenware casserole, put first a 'bed' of bread, then one of chestnuts. Continue with bread, then nuts, seasoning each layer well with salt and black pepper, and barely cover with the strained broth. Heat through on the stove or in the oven.

• (You may add strips of ham to the layers, or slices of leftover Christmas turkey, even dried apples or pears, and slip the casserole under a hot grill before serving so that the final layer of bread is nicely toasted.)

SAUMON AU COURT BOUILLON
Salmon poached in herbed broth

(Wild salmon was not an uncommon fish of the time. Found in most of France's rivers, it was forbidden for commoners to fish for it – until the abolition of privileges during the Revolution, that is, when 'droit de pêche' and 'droit de chasse' were abolished.)

Cut your salmon into thick steaks. In a pan big enough to hold them all in one layer, put some melted lard, a clove of garlic, an onion, a big anchovy or two and a few sprigs of parsley, all finely chopped. Lay the salmon steaks on top, spreading olive oil or butter over each one, and season well with freshly ground black pepper. Add two bay leaves stuck with two cloves and moisten with a mixture of red wine and bouillon (see above – and note the use of red wine rather than white!). The liquid should come about halfway up the steaks. Simmer (do not boil), covered, for about 15 minutes – or until the fish flakes easily. Lift the fish out, salt the bouillon and reduce it over high heat. Serve it poured over bread fried crisply in olive oil, with the fish on the side.

● *A court bouillon for fish*: ½ pt/300 ml wine to 1½ pt/800 ml water simmered for about 30 minutes with the trimmings of the fish, a couple of carrots and a leek cut in large pieces, an unpeeled onion studded with a few cloves, a bouquet garni, a slice of lemon, and a spoonful of whole peppercorns, the resulting bouillon strained before use.

CANARD À LA MÉNAGÈRE
'Housewife's duck' (serves 4)
(I tried this on the stove – as the recipe said – several times before coming to the conclusion that it works better, and is less fatty, in the oven. The quantities are those used by Jane Grigson in a similar recipe of the period that she published under the name 'Bourgeoise'.)

1 large duck
1½ lb/750 g very small white turnips, trimmed
2 tbsp bacon fat or lard, 1 tbsp butter
3 tbsp flour
1 pt/570 ml stock/broth
a bouquet garni of thyme, parsley, bay
1 large peeled onion pierced with 6 cloves
salt and pepper
a little vinegar or lemon juice

(1) Preheat oven to 375°F/190°C/gas mark 5. Melt the fat in a heavy frying pan and brown the duck very well on all sides, so that the fat from it runs. Place the duck, onion and bouquet garni in a baking dish big enough to hold the turnips as well.
(2) Brown the turnips in the fat and lift out with a slotted spoon. Pour off all but about 2 tbsp of the remaining fat (save it to cook other vegetables), cook the flour in it until it turns a pale gold, and slowly stir in the stock. Pour this over the duck and cover loosely. Put in the oven for 1½ hours, or until tender to a fork. After an hour, add the turnips.
(3) The original recipe says to remove the lid and finish the browning, adding a splash of vinegar and lemon juice at the last minute – to cut the fattiness of the duck, I expect. Grigson's advice is the one I now follow: pour off the gravy at the end of the 1 ½ hours, and chill it so the fat can be lifted off easily. Keep one eye on the duck in the oven. Season and reduce the sauce over high heat if necessary, adding the splash of vinegar, and pour it over the duck.

GÂTEAU DE ST ANDRÉ
Meringue-coated cake

A very pretty lemony cake topped with a hat of crisp meringue. The original recipe did not give precise details, specifying only that the cake should be flavoured with lemon zest, split in two and spread with 'confiture juste', and topped with a meringue of two egg whites.

6 oz/180 g butter, softened
8 oz/250 g caster sugar
8 oz/250 g plain white flour, sifted with a pinch of salt
4 eggs, separated
grated zest of 1 lemon

Topping
2 egg whites
3½ oz/100 g caster/fine white sugar
apricot confiture/jam

(1) Preheat the oven to 325°F/160°C/gas mark 3. Butter two 9 in/23 cm round spring bottom cake tins and line with rounds of buttered greaseproof paper. Beat the butter to a cream and add ⅔ of the sugar, beating until very light. Whisk in the egg yolks one at a time. Stir in the lemon zest, and then the flour in several batches.
(2) Beat the egg whites until stiff in a large bowl and then beat in the remaining sugar until the mixture is shiny. Stir ¼ of the egg whites into the flour mixture to lighten it, then gently fold this mixture into the egg whites. Spoon half the mixture into each pan and bake for 1–1¼ hours until the cake pulls away from the pan. Turn out onto a rack and spread each half generously with apricot jam when cool.
(3) To make the meringue topping, first preheat the oven to 285°F/140°C/gas mark 1. Butter a baking sheet, sprinkle it with flour and mark a circle on it the same size as the cakes. Beat the egg whites in a very clean bowl until stiff, then dredge over half of the sugar, beating until the mixture is smooth and glossy. Dredge over the remaining sugar and gently fold it in with a large metal spoon. Spread the meringue over the surface of the circle you have marked and bake for 1 hour, or until just firm. Turn out on a rack to cool and then assemble the cake layers with the meringue on top.

RATAFIA D'ORANGE
Fresh orange liqueur

A delicious festive drink for Christmas or New Year.

1 bottle plain eau de vie (or Polish pure spirits,
or gin, if either is more readily available)
2 whole oranges, cut in chunks
1 lb/500 g sugar
6 cloves

Put all ingredients together in two bottles and infuse for 6–8 weeks, stirring often. Strain through muslin before using.

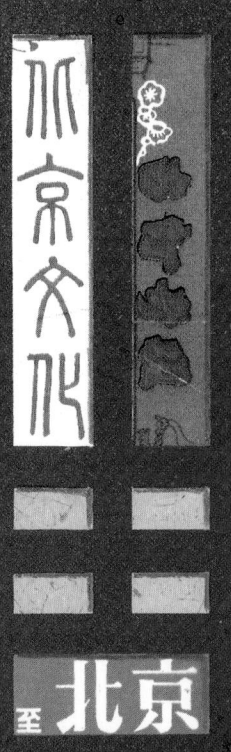

MOON RABBITS AND SQUIRREL FISH

———

Mid-autumn Moon Festival in China

During the time of the great Chinese dynasties it was an imperial ritual to worship the autumn full moon. People made offerings of moon-shaped cakes and sat in a circle to share them. The round moon: symbol of completeness, a reminder to travellers of loved ones at home.

The Mid-autumn or Moon Festival occurs on the fifteenth day of the eighth lunar month, when the moon is said to be at its fullest and brightest of the year.

In the autumn of 1988 I went to China with a group of friends. One of them, Dr Wang, had left China fifty-six years before and never returned. I had wanted to go to China since childhood in British Columbia, where China was not the Far East, but the Far West, and the Chinese were called the Yellow Peril by people my mother said didn't know any better. My father's business partners, two beautiful and completely westernized Chinese sisters, had welcomed us into their family, as was the custom in Chinese business relationships.

Their mother had escaped from China with a few precious belongings: red lacquer chests smelling of sandalwood, bamboo-framed watercolours of what looked like a land of misty mountains and magic floating pagodas and cormorant fishermen, and, best of all, a round wicker basket with six blue figured cups and a matching teapot fitting snugly into the padded cotton lining. The family used to take it with them to keep tea hot on long winter's train journeys.

I had just seen the movie *Doctor Zhivago*. Russia was the closest country to China on my atlas. I pictured the Chinese train steaming straight as a ruled line across those paper-white snowy steppes, with black wolves in the distance like inkspots. I knew that someday I would go there too.

ONE

At 5.00 a.m. on the day before the Moon Festival the hotel in Shanghai gave us mooncakes in our breakfast boxes. We were on our way to the airport to catch the 7.00 plane to Guilin.

The hotel porter said that the Moon Festival was the time when people shared as big a banquet as they could afford. In the north they would spend a morning making Jiaozi dumplings together, which were part of almost every festive meal. Lots of mooncakes and other

moon-shaped food – chicken cooked in pumpkins, fresh pomegranates, winter melon soup, meatballs – would be eaten as well.

'And everyone all over the country tries to return to their family.'

'So the airport will be quite busy then?'

'Busy, yes.'

'How busy?'

He looked at me pityingly. 'Quite busy.'

The entire population of eastern China was attempting to return to their families in western China on the 7.00 a.m. flight to Guilin.

The Chinese travellers seemed to know something that the Westerners did not. They pushed ahead of us, not hard, but steadily – with the full weight of the Orient behind them. More and more kept arriving, but the guards on the gate let no one through. The waiting room started to fill vertically as well as horizontally. Chinese fathers put children on their shoulders. One man balanced a large iced cake on his head. An old woman in Mao blue gripped a bonsai tree on her shoulder. Seven o'clock came and went. There were enough people to fill five, then ten planes.

Suddenly we found ourselves being squeezed towards the gate. A German group nearly started a fistfight with two Swiss travellers. An Israeli woman burst into tears. The Westerners became more and more irate and red-faced. The Chinese remained absolutely calm and implacable and pressed forward regardless.

At 11.30 we were popped out of the first room into the waiting room on the other side. It was huge and empty.

At 12.30 a China Airlines employee passed through, handing out packets of sweet biscuits. Ten minutes later we were told to collect lunchboxes. Then there was an announcement saying our plane was about to leave. We rushed to the door. It was a false alarm. We walked back to our seats, occupied now by more Chinese. Our lunchboxes had been cleared away. The plane left at 3.30.

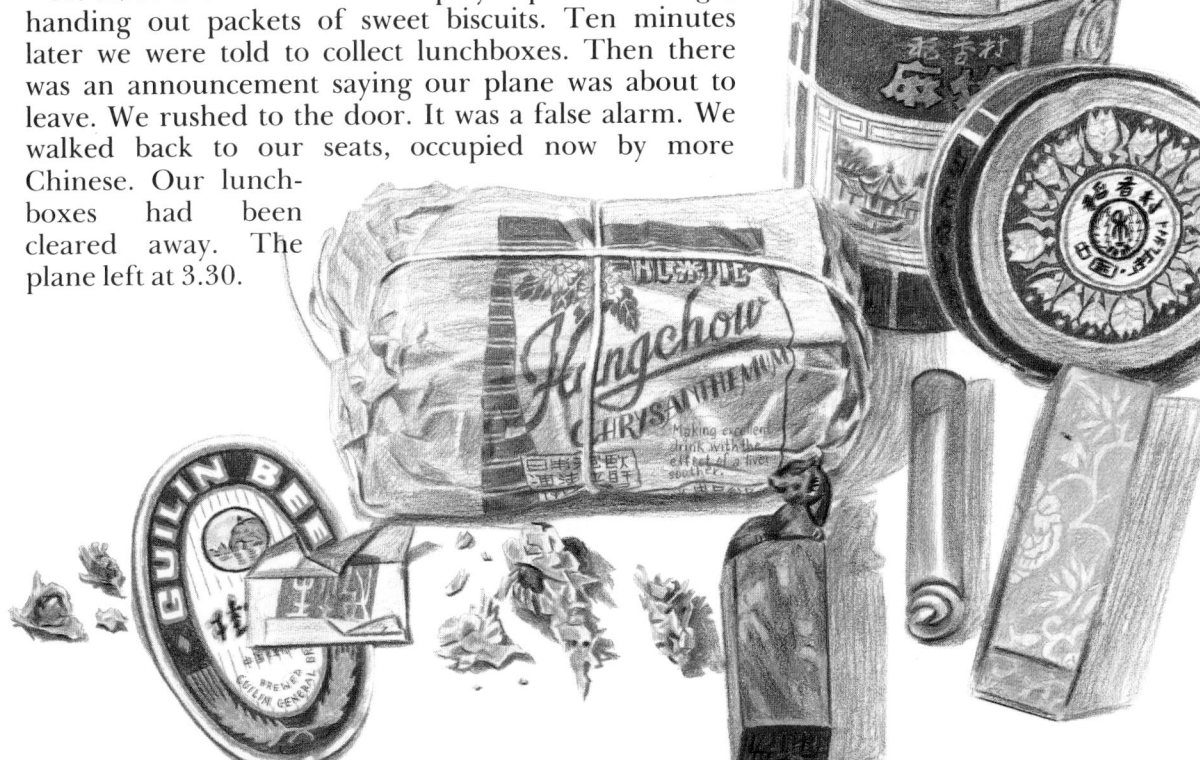

As we flew in over Guilin I recognized it instantly. The modern buildings were wrong, of course, but the cone-shaped mountains, the curling river, the green patchwork rice fields and black brushstrokes of cormorant fishermen were just as they had been in those bamboo-framed paintings.

'The Moon Festival: From sunset and the rising of the moon, till midnight, everyone walks about with his relatives and friends in the streets, public places and gardens, and on the terraces of the houses, to watch for the appearance of a hare, which according to these people, is on that night to be seen in the moon. In the preceding days, they send to each other tarts and cakes, called yua-pim – that is, cakes of the moon; they are round and flat, and made to resemble her. On the surface of them is placed the figure of a hare made of nuts, almonds, pineapples, kernels, sugar, and other ingredients. They eat these cakes by moonlight – the wealthy to the sound of melodious music, and the poor to the din of drums, gongs, and other noisy instruments.'

The previous paragraph was written in 1843. It is from a book printed in London called *Peter Parley's Tales About China* and is a reasonably accurate description, with the exception of the melodious music, of what took place in Guilin a hundred and fifty years later.

Mooncakes, first made in the shops of Chang'an (Xi'an) in the Tang dynasty, have changed slightly since Parley's time; they are moulded now with images of the Moon Rabbit and the Moon Palace, or with Chinese characters indicating their fillings: bean paste, lotus-seed paste, different fruits, seeds and nuts, egg yolk, chicken, cassia or date paste. Their common ingredients are dough, oil, sugar and maltose. Most of them are unrelentingly nasty. Imagine a sweet mincemeat pie flavoured with liver pâté and a little aftershave, and stuffed with a hard-boiled egg, and there you have a mooncake.

Each city has its own recipe. In Guilin the most popular shop was run by an old man with one eye, who folded boxes while his tiny grandson sat on a bamboo seat arranging display packs. They couldn't sell cakes fast enough for the crowds.

The mooncake shop was between a chemist with shelves of dried snakes, deer antlers and pickled lizards, and a restaurant that advertised its menu with jugs of live snakes and a pile of recently slain pangolin. A pangolin is a sort of scaly anteater that looks and tastes like an old armadillo handbag. It was difficult to know which to try first – the chemist or the restaurant.

After dinner we walked down through a street market lit by acetylene flares to the Lantern Festival in Elephant Trunk Park (named for the strangely shaped hill in the Li River that is said to resemble an elephant drinking). People are buying short stacks of live frogs strung one on top of the other with knotted straw. A civet cat, snarling and spitting, is weighed still in its cage. Bowls of frothing eels. Dead monkeys. A whole skinned and boiled terrier stretched on a platter. Badgers with their back tendons cut so they will not thrash about. The conviction grows that the Chinese will eat anything.

Approaching the park we run the gauntlet of souvenir stalls. 'Jus' lookin'. Jus' lookin',' the stallholders call.

Ahead of us a school of plastic goldfish lit from within reflect an orange glow onto the faces of the children carrying them. In Elephant Trunk Park there are paper lanterns strung from the trees, and crowds gathered round life-size mechanically animated scenes from a famous Chinese fable, 'The Monkey King'. The mechanical figures are all slightly shabby, as if they had been made in a more colourful decade and never repaired.

There are Dodgems, fast-food stalls, the unremitting crackle of cheap fireworks. Then slowly the curve of a huge silver bubble appears above the hill, expanding and floating up into the sky like soap being blown through a plastic ring. A great sigh from the crowd. The moon has arrived.

Along the breakwater there are fireflies, and moonlight reflected in the Li River where it snakes its way east silhouettes the figures of chastely courting couples.

Dr Wang's family came from a village near our last stop, in Guangzhou. All their property had been confiscated during the revolution, and he

was very bitter. Now the Chinese government was offering to let him buy his old home back.

'Huh,' he said. 'They just want me to pay for repairs to building that all their bloody people wrecked.'

'It would be interesting to return, though – to meet relatives you have not seen since childhood?'

'We will see. They all expect big presents, you know, because they think I must be rich coming from West. And I would have to pay for a big banquet for all my relatives. Very worrying. My brother went back five years ago, ate so much he had heart attack.'

'Surely you can eat as little as you want.'

'Very difficult situation,' he said, shaking his head, and I imagined a complicated system of Chinese diplomacy and face-saving. 'Best cooks in all China come from my province.'

In the end, Dr Wang decided that his village would be too much of a health risk. We had a huge banquet in one of Guangzhou's oldest restaurants instead. For eight people it cost about £3 a head.

The train to Hong Kong lacked the charm of those in the interior. From Nanjing to Changzhou the soft class cars had brass plant stands on every table, and white lace antimacassars embroidered with images of the Nanjing Bridge. We were brought blue and white figured cups of tea with china lids to stop the liquid splashing. When I looked out the window to see the long straight line of the train extending ahead of us, another train passed going in the opposite direction, in its windows the reflection of six people and six matching blue and white cups.

In China they call the Mid-autumn Festival the Day of Reunion.

RECIPES

Pictures from a Moving Train

In China it is rare for diners to pass a plate of food around the table; chopsticks, as an extension of the hand, serving this end in an equally if not more democratic fashion. With the dishes on the table, the law of survival of the nimblest applies, whereas if a dish is passed around the table, it is inevitably the last person to receive the dish who is left with the poorest choice of morsels. Some may prefer this method, particularly in the case of dishes such as camel's hump, fish lips or bear's paws, but never the gourmet.

Food and Drink in China, *Gong Dan, Beijing 1986*

15 September – Xi'an in central China

In the shadow of the old mosque northwest of Xi'an's fourteenth-century bell tower an old man steams cobs of sweet corn in a wok on the street. His plump

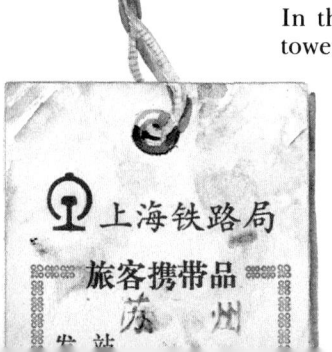

grandson, face full of baked sweet potato hot off an oil-drum brazier, sits on a portable plastic potty next to him.

Xi'an's large population of Hui Muslims (dating from the time when Xi'an was the end – or the beginning – of the Silk Route) is evident: kebab stands line the streets every night. The kebabs, of ground lamb mixed with sesame oil, hot chillies and garlic chives worked into tiny pieces, are threaded, very practically, onto bicycle spokes.

Tall wooden houses in the old Muslim quarter have cafés selling, among other things, a delicious, savoury Chinese version of an Eccles cake. A piece of dough is laid out in a long, flat strip on an oiled surface and spread with spicy chilli and mustard sauce and spoons of ground pork or lamb mixed with lots of chopped spring onions. This is rolled up like a walnut whip, flattened, and fried until golden.

At the Dameengun commune outside Xi'an there is a stout pumpkin plant with orange blossoms on it curling up the side of a farmhouse, and a pretty courtyard where someone has put flower cuttings in a row of beer bottles. In the kitchen is a shrine to the ancestors. The grandmother says that they use the pumpkin for soups and stir-fries, or steam chicken in it, as they would do with winter melons, for festive occasions. She is looking forward to her birthday party when her children will cook for her – long noodles for a long life.

SPICY CHICKEN IN PUMPKIN
(serves 4–6)

The Chinese title of this dish means 'A Long Life to Everyone'. The pumpkin, if not steamed for too long, makes a delightful edible serving dish. For banquets it would be carved with decorative patterns or auspicious words. The Chinese peppercorns are a spicy northern Szechuan addition – Chinese sausage may be chopped and steamed in the pumpkin with the chicken for a southern touch.

3–4 lb/1.5-2 kg whole fresh pumpkin
1 chicken of 2–3 lb/1.5-2 kg
1 tbsp mashed red bean curd (optional)
2 green onions, finely sliced crosswise
1 in/2.5 cm thumb of ginger, peeled and finely chopped or grated
1/2 tsp salt
1 tbsp sugar
2 tbsp Shaohsing wine or medium-dry sherry
1 1/2 tbsp soy sauce
2 oz/60 g uncooked rice
1 tbsp Chinese peppercorns
2–3 tbsp peanut or other vegetable oil

(1) Cut a lid out of the handle end of the pumpkin and scoop out the seeds and pulp – the seeds can be roasted in a little oil and salt in the oven for a tasty snack. Stand the pumpkin in a heatproof bowl.

(2) Chop the chicken in chopstick-manageable pieces, mix with the marinade ingredients and leave in a cool place for 20 minutes or so. In the meantime, dry-roast the rice and peppercorns in a frying pan until the rice is golden and the pepper fragrant. Grind the rice and pepper to a powder.

(3) Toss the marinated chicken in this spiced rice and stir-fry for a couple of minutes in hot oil. Spoon everything into the pumpkin, cover with the lid and steam the pumpkin in a bain-marie or wok for about 40 minutes – just until the pumpkin is tender to a fork but not collapsed. Serve the pumpkin whole with steamed rice, and scoop out a bit of the orange flesh with every spoonful of spicy chicken.

16 September – a free market near the Terracotta Warriors

Rows of people squatting selling moon-shaped fruit – pomegranates, green apples, persimmons. Clay ovens built into the street, whole cooked ox tongues going 'blah' on plates.

We walk back to the hotel through a long pavement traffic jam dedicated to food. Mongolian hotpots with families gathered round, noodle soups, dumplings, steamed breads. A man with a set of teeth that look as if they don't belong to him throws a handful of noodles into his smoking wok with some shredded garlic, ginger, bean sprouts, green onion stalks, while his assistant fries a flat little omelette, chops it into long strips with a cleaver, and scatters it over the cooked noodles. The cook slams the plates down on his crude pavement table and gestures to us to help ourselves from the chopsticks in a tin in the middle. The secret to street eating anywhere – pick the cook with the cleanest fingernails.

XI'AN NOODLES
(serves 4 with other dishes)

Buy some of the needle-thin dried noodles that are sold in bags of little curled nests, and pre-cook them as described on the packet.

You will need as well:

3 eggs
6 tbsp light vegetable oil
4 slivered garlic cloves
1 shredded 'thumb' of fresh peeled ginger
8 spring onions cut in 2 in/5 cm lengths
a couple of handfuls of fresh beansprouts
a handful of shredded cabbage
2–4 tbsp soy sauce
2 tsp sugar
4 tbsp homemade stock or broth
2 tbsp sesame oil

(1) Beat the eggs lightly with a tbsp of cold water, pour into a very hot oiled pan and fry quickly on both sides. Slide it onto a plate and slice it into long strips about 1 in/2.5 cm wide.

(2) Heat the light oil until it smokes in a wok. Stir-fry the garlic, ginger and onions just until the garlic starts to colour, then stir in everything except the egg strips and the sesame oil. After a minute, remove from the heat, toss in the sesame oil (and more soy sauce, if necessary), and top with the egg strips. Serve immediately straight from the wok.

18 September – in search of Old Nanjing

It is clearly the lotus root season – their linked-sausage shapes much in evidence. The market along the old canal northeast of the Wengcheng Gate has steamers full of dumplings and sesame bread, and a stall offering twenty different shapes of beancurd.

For breakfast, a two-girl production team make foot-long multi-strand crullers of pastry called 'you tiao', to eat with rice porridge or soybean milk. One girl expertly tosses dough up and down in the now familiar skipping-rope action used to make all noodles until she has a handful. She throws them into a wok of bubbling oil and her partner quickly winds them with two long chopsticks to give a barley-sugar twist, lifting the cooked pastry out to be snipped in half.

A man staggers by, dragging a whole tree as long as a house, his load only slightly lightened by the three small wheels at one end. A small boy is having his hair cut in pudding bowl shape at a low stool in the street. Next to him a woman cuts a chicken's throat and bleeds it into the gutter. A grandmother empties her chamber pot six inches to the right. We step out into the road to avoid a pavement pool game.

Nanjing pressed and salted duck

Salted ducks and geese looking like the flattened victims of a road accident hang in windows all over Nanjing. These are the city's speciality – a prize raised in the city suburbs.

The raw poultry (cleaned, washed, and well dried) is cut open from under the wings. About 5 oz/150 g of coarse salt and the same quantity of Chinese peppercorns are roasted in a pan until the salt turns golden and the peppercorn becomes fragrant, then coarsely ground and rubbed all over the goose or duck. The poultry is then put in a glazed earthenware bowl and weighted heavily. It is kept in a cool, dry place, turned every two days and rubbed with more salt and pepper.

After 7–10 days (or longer, in the case of a large goose) the poultry is washed and dried, covered in rice wine, spring onions and ginger and steamed for an hour until tender.

At a memorable feast in the fifty-year-old Jiangsu restaurant, three of these glorious ducks were chopped into pieces and brushed with a glaze of sesame oil just before serving. With them came thirteen or fourteen other dishes, including a platter of deep-fried rice birds the size of sparrows (to be eaten whole, like uccelletti), and a luscious stew of fat little river eels like overgrown elvers, braised in smoking hot oil with Chinese wine, sugar, ginger and red chillies.

19 September — by train to Changzhou

On the quayside of the Grand Canal, which is grander in size than content, we stumble on what my ancient guidebook describes as 'excellent opportunities to observe timeless canal life'. A long row of whitewashed houses open onto a cobbled path along the canal. Two old women play mahjong at a dolls'-sized table. A man peels live eels, stripping their skins back as one would a banana peel. There is a noodle factory with sheets of noodle dough rolling through like bales of fabric, and a musty chemist's shop straight from Aladdin where rows of ceramic blue and white jars flank a wall of wooden drawers. A man cycles by with a live pig in a basket on his bike.

20 September — Wuxi, on the Grand Canal

Hundreds of years ago, a poor monk by the name of Mr Jee went to a humble butcher and begged for some meat. The butcher, being a kind-hearted soul, gave him as much as he could carry. The monk blessed him and said that for his kindness he would show him how to make the best spare ribs in all the wide world.

In the morning, Mr Jee returned. Breaking off a bit of his bamboo fan, he told the butcher to use it to spice his next batch of pork ribs. When the butcher added the scrap of fan to his wok, an intoxicating smell rose up immediately and spread throughout Wuxi.

Soon the delicious aroma had seeped into houses and kitchens all over the town. First one by one, then in small groups, and finally in their hundreds, the citizens of Wuxi pressed into the shop of the humble butcher. His fortune was made, and the fame of Wuxi spareribs has remained constant to this day.

Or so I was told in Wuxi. My only quibble is that there is no mention of the essential bamboo fan in the recipes for spare ribs that I was given.

FRIED AND SPICED RIBS
(serves 4–6 with other dishes)

2 lb/1 kg pork spareribs, chopped in 1 in/2.5 cm pieces
2 tbsp soya sauce
3 tbsp Chinese peppercorns
3 tbsp Shaohsing wine or dry sherry
2 green onions, chopped
1 in/2.5 cm thumb of fresh ginger, peeled and sliced
1 in/2.5 cm cinnamon stick, roughly crushed
¼ tsp five-spice powder
2 tbsp coarse salt
peanut or other vegetable oil for deep-frying

(1) Marinate the ribs for 1 hour in soya sauce, 20 grains of pepper (crushed), wine, onions, ginger, and spices.

(2) Put the ribs and marinade in a heatproof dish and steam for 1½ hours, then heat oil in a wok or heavy pan and deep-fry them until browned.

(3) Over low heat in a dry frying pan, stir the salt and peppercorns until they are fragrant. Crush finely and serve with the ribs.

SWEET AND SOUR RIBS
(serves 4–6 with other dishes)*

2 lb/1 kg pork spareribs, chopped into 1 in/2.5 cm pieces
1 tbsp soya sauce
2 tbsp Shaohsing wine or medium-dry sherry
1 tsp ground pepper
1 tsp cornstarch, mixed to a paste with 2 tbsp water
1 tbsp Chinese vinegar, or wine vinegar
3 tbsp sugar
1 in/2.5 cm thumb fresh ginger, shredded
1 green onion/scallion, finely sliced for garnish
peanut or vegetable oil for deep-frying

(1) Combine the spareribs with 2 tsp soya sauce, salt, wine, pepper and cornstarch and leave to marinate for 1 hour.

(2) Lift the ribs out with a slotted spoon and deep-fry in hot oil until brown. Drain on kitchen paper. Pour off all but 1–2 tbsp oil. Reheat the frying pan and stir in the marinade with the remaining ingredients, cooking until it thickens. Add the ribs and toss until they are well coated. Serve very hot, sprinkled with the green onion.

*These ribs can also be steamed before frying as in the previous recipe, which makes them much more tender.

On the boat from Wuxi to Suzhou we are served platters of crispy soft-shell crab – some the size of pocket watches, others a palm's breadth across – deep-fried whole in batter to be eaten legs and all.

Sweet peppers and luscious black mushrooms are stir-fried with tiny soft-boiled eggs, and there is duck and pork red-braised in sweet Yangzhou-style sauces. Yangzhou cuisine, known as 'jiang nan' (south of the Yangtze River) from the rich 'land of fish and rice' of the Yangtze River valley, takes in the cities of Suzhou, Hangzhou, Shanghai and Nanjing. It is perhaps the least known outside China.

At the back of the boat the cook washes his vegetables and plates in murky green canal water that seethes with a microscopic life of its own.

On the canal bank a hundred geese flow in a thick white wave behind the gooseherd. Shrimp nets; canal barges with babies in unfenced crawl spaces; factories belching soot; medieval scenes of men carrying basketfuls of earth suspended on bamboo poles over their shoulders.

21 September – Suzhou, on the Grand Canal

This garden city is the China I have in my mind's eye; a place of dark fretted woodwork, curling tiled roofs, and humpbacked bridges over stately (if reeking) canals. Views through to inner courtyards where women cook over open fires surrounded by bonsai trees.

Tea in the wooden tea house of the Humble Administrator's Garden is better than the usual watery privet clippings. One woman hands us glasses with leaves in the bottom, another adds hot water. At the rattan tables outside, an old man finishes a cream cake and delicately wipes his beard, then removes his false teeth and rinses them in his tea.

Down a narrow lane that rapidly chokes with people to become a market. Here the distinction between pet and food is blurred: birds in bamboo cages, goldfish, terrapins; then hedgehogs – a mother and two fat babies – clearly destined for the pot, with a head of garlic tied to the cage. Their vendor prods them to show how meaty they are.

Garlic chives tied in graceful bundles on a bamboo tray are arranged as carefully as green brushstrokes; blue speckled eggs piled in a basket threaded with a matching blue ribbon.

The sweet tooth typical of Jiangsu province is sweetest in Suzhou, as well known for its confectionery stores (some of the best mooncakes come from here) as for its old gardens. At the hugely popular Caizhizhai sweetshop one can buy candied strawberries and loquats in season.

Joining a crowd of locals queueing to buy mooncakes, I come away clutching a beautiful box of sesame-seed cakes, a bag of tooth-shattering pine-nut toffee, and another of sugared walnuts. These are shelled, dipped in batter, fried in oil, dropped in hot toffee (just as one would do for toffee bananas) and rolled in toasted sesame seeds.

Toffee walnuts reappear later at the Songhelou restaurant down Guanqian Lu road. Songhelou is so old that it is claimed the Emperor Qianlong ate here centuries ago; not, presumably, in the restaurant's present incarnation, which resembles a Moscow car park.

The interior is more reminiscent of a Shanghai bordello, except that the staff cultivate an air of supreme indifference to their customers. A sign indicates that the Great Wall Chinese Credit Card is accepted.

The standard Chinese feast comprises four cold dishes, six to eight main, two major showstoppers – perhaps a whole fish or a suckling pig – finishing up with soup and rice.

During China's Warring States period, Qu Yuan, a great poet (340–278 BC), wrote *Call Back the Souls*, a tribute to the dead generals and soldiers of Chu, containing a long banquet menu designed, no doubt, to lure the lost souls back.

In the early eighteenth century, the Qing Dynasty scholar Yuan Mei wrote a masterpiece of Chinese cooking theory, *Menus of the Sui Garden*, describing the preparation of many royal delicacies, including a luxurious Manchu-Han banquet made up of six major, six minor, and four accompanying courses, and twenty-four trays of fruit and desserts.

BEGGAR'S CHICKEN

In contrast to the imperial cuisine is this recipe, said to have been invented by a beggar who had stolen a chicken. He killed and gutted his booty, stuffed it with green onion and salt, and covered it in a layer of wet clay to bake under his fire.

Beggar's chicken is still made in Suzhou restaurants, but stuffed instead with a mixture of ground pork, rice wine, ginger and green onions, its skin scored and rubbed with salt and pepper. It is wrapped first in bacon, then in softened lotus leaves, and finally tied with rope, covered in clay and baked in a pinewood fire for 2–3 hours; the end result more for senior party officials than beggars.

SQUIRREL FISH
(serves 4–6 with other dishes)

For the Songhelou restaurant's 'squirrel fish', a whole, meaty white fish is butterflied open, and the fillets criss-crossed with deep cuts in two directions, then marinated, and deep-fried until it looks like some exotic flower. Finally a scalding-hot sweet and sour sauce is poured over, said to make the fish chatter like a squirrel (although mine never has). As the fish has to be deep-fried whole, it is best to have a short, fat fish that fits into the pan.

The fish's head should face the guest of honour – said to be a sign of good luck and respect.

1 meaty white fish (yellow croaker,
red snapper, grey mullet) of about 2–2¼ lb/1–1.1 kg
2 green onions, finely sliced
1½ in/3.5 cm knob of fresh ginger, shredded
2 tbsp Shaohsing wine or medium-dry sherry
½ tsp salt
2 tbsp sesame oil
peanut or other vegetable oil for deep-frying

Batter
(whisked together before frying and kept cold)
2 oz/60 g flour
2 oz/60 g cornflour
1 tsp baking powder
1 egg, beaten
about 6 fl oz/180 ml very cold water

Sauce
4 tbsp sugar
4 tbsp rice or wine vinegar
juice and grated zest of 1 lemon
1 tbsp tomato ketchup
2 tsp cornstarch dissolved in 2 tbsp cold water

Decorations
carved radishes, finely chopped spring onions and
onion curls

(1) Clean the fish and scale it if necessary. Cut off the head (discard, if fish heads are not to your taste) and press firmly down so it butterflies open. Spread the fish open along its back, scoring the flesh (but not cutting through the skin) with diagonal criss-cross cuts. Sprinkle with onion, ginger, wine, salt, and sesame oil and leave to marinate for about 30 minutes.

(2) In a saucepan combine 5 fl oz/150 ml water with sugar, vinegar, the remaining onions, lemon, ginger and ketchup. Bring to a boil, stir in the cornstarch to thicken it (and a few drops of food colouring, if desired) and add the sesame oil.

(3) Pour about 3½ pt/2 l of oil into a deep pan (the oil and the pan must be deep enough to cover the whole fish) and heat over medium until a chunk of stale bread browns in 50 seconds. Dip the fish head in batter, deep-fry until golden and place at one end of a serving plate. Keep warm. Carefully dip the remaining fish in

batter, and slip it into the oil, frying until well browned. Stand well back – the oil will rise up and spit. Lift out and arrange next to its head. Pour the sauce over the fish, scatter with chopped spring onions and radishes and serve at once.

- Chinese cooks use red food colouring to give the batter and the sauce an auspicious colour. It is pretty, but not necessary – the fish looks just as good, if less authentic, without it.

25 September – Moon Festival in Guilin

Roasted peanuts ringed with wedges of roasted egg as a snack on the Li River boat. *Apocalypse Now* jungle scenery. Baby water buffalo.

Teddy, a boy on the boat, tells us that after the Moon Festival feast all the old people sit in the street around the television while the teenagers go out to see the moon and the singing in Elephant Trunk Park.

A par-boiled terrier carried through the hotel to a private dining room. Teddy says that delicacies like these are not wasted on tourists.

27 September – Guangzhou

The famous Qing Pink food market is worse (or better, if you are Chinese) than the one in Guilin. Only the spice street is safe for vegetarians: sacks of peppers from all over China, dried antlers, bears' paws, monkeys, liquorice root, pangolins – and hundreds of different leaves and flowers.

A feast for Dr Wang: at the famous Guangzhou restaurant. The restaurant seats 2,000 and serves 10,000 a day. If you book a week in advance they will organize an imperial banquet of the Ming Dynasty. Ours is less imperial – only fourteen courses, including a whole suckling pig whose skin has been scored, rubbed with sea salt to make it extra crisp, and spread in a red honey glaze – the skin is the only part eaten. Rather like Peking duck, it is used as the outer wrapping for spring onion and Hoi Sin sauce. Then the carcass is removed. 'Chrysanthemum' fish cut in criss-cross slices like a mango and deep-fried. A whole winter melon carved with the name of the restaurant.

Dr Wang: 'In South Chinese banquet you cannot go without winter melon soup – very auspicious.'

'And it gives you a good cleaning out,' says his sister.

WINTER MELON SOUP

Soup cooked in a squash (serves 6–8 with other dishes)

A superb soup of complex flavours, elevated to feast status by the elaborately carved melon tureen. The carving can be anything from simple auspicious words to elaborate pictures of dragons and phoenixes. The same ingredients cooked in a pumpkin (or even on their own) instead of a melon are equally good.

1 Chinese winter melon about 6–7 lb/3–4 kg
6–8 dried shitake or black Chinese mushrooms*
10–12 tinned water chestnuts, sliced
handful of lotus nuts (optional)
¼ lb/125 g good cooked ham, cut in narrow strips

¼ lb/125 g cooked chicken, shredded
2 tbsp dried shrimps or 8 dried scallops,
soaked until tender and sliced
1 in/2.5 cm fresh ginger, peeled and shredded
½ tsp salt (or to taste)
2 tbsp Chinese rice wine or medium-dry sherry
coffee cup of bamboo shoots, shredded (optional)
approx 2½ pt/1.5 l good homemade chicken stock/broth
2 spring/green onions, sliced thinly

(1) Cut the top off the melon to make a lid, keeping the stem on to make a handle, and scoop out and discard pulp and seeds (or roast seeds in a little oil and salt for munching). Enlarge the cavity of the melon by scooping out some of the flesh and chopping it for the soup, making sure you leave about ½ in/1.25 cm of wall so the melon will not collapse during cooking.

(2) Wash the mushrooms, then soak in hot water until tender and slice thickly. Carve and decorate the melon as desired and fill with all ingredients, including reserved melon, and the mushrooms and their water (strained). Put the lid back on. Make a cushion of towel for the melon to sit on in the steamer and steam for 35–45 minutes. Serve hot from melon, scooping out some of the melon flesh from the walls, and scatter the top with spring onion.

This soup is also served in a cup-sized melon so that each person has his own individual soup dish.

*Dried shitake mushrooms should be brown, not black, when dry. If black, they are too old. The top should have a creamy starburst on it where the skin has cracked.

4-JOYS MEATBALLS
(serves 6–8 with other dishes)

Balls, like the full moon, symbolize family reunion in China, so this dish is served for feasts. A traditional poem about the dish, naming the four joys: 'happy rain following a long drought, meeting a bosom friend in a foreign land, the night of wedding in the bridal chamber, and seeing one's name in the imperial honour roll.'

1 carrot
4 in/10 cm lotus root,
peeled and finely chopped
2 eggs
1 tbsp cornflour in 1 tbsp water
9 oz/280 g ground pork
2 tbsp soy sauce
3 tbsp rice wine or medium-dry sherry
½ small onion, finely chopped
1 in/2 cm length ginger, peeled and grated
good pinch of pepper
oil for deep-frying

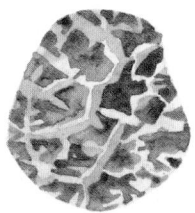

(1) Mix 1 egg with half the cornflour solution and the other with the pork, 1 tbsp soy sauce, 1 tbsp wine, onion, ginger pepper and vegetables, mixing until sticky but firm.

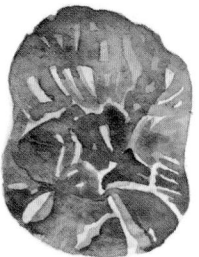

(2) Heat the oil until it begins to bubble. Shape meat into 4 large balls, dip in egg and flour and fry until very brown. Drain on kitchen paper.

(3) Whisk together the remaining soy sauce and wine with 5 tbsp boiling water in a heatproof bowl. Place the meatballs in the bowl and steam on a high flame for 1 hour. Serve the meatballs on a bed of bright green vegetables – perhaps spinach tossed in sesame oil.

Fast Chinese Feasts

At every Chinese banquet there were simple dishes as well as the more elaborate ones. Here are just a few:

ONION BRUSHES

Trim root and bruised leaves off spring/green onions, leaving a piece about 3 in/ 8 cm. Make 4 lengthwise cuts of about 1 in/2.5 cm at each end. Leave in cold water for 30 minutes, or until needed and use to decorate fish, roasts, etc.

BAMBOO SHOOT TREES

Cut bamboo shoots in triangular wedges. Slice 2–3 long grooves on 2 sides and cut into thin slices. Use as spring onions, or to stir-fry with other vegetables (see drawing).

LOTUS ROOT SALAD

Peel and clean lotus root very well. Slice thinly crosswise and dress with shredded ginger, salt, rice vinegar and sesame oil.

STRING BEAN AND RED-CHILLI SALAD

Blanch 8 oz/250 g string beans in boiling water with 3 whole red chillies. Seed and shred the chillies and cut the beans into long, thin strips. Toss together with salt, a spoonful of sugar, some shredded fresh ginger and a little sesame oil.

SPINACH WITH SESAME FLAVOURING

Trim and wash 1 lb/500 g fresh spinach. Cook in boiling water until just wilted. Squeeze out all excess water and slice in long strips. Toss with a tsp of salt and 1½ tbsp sesame oil. Just before serving toss in a tsp of toasted sesame seeds and scatter another tsp over the top.

SPICY CUCUMBERS

Halve a cucumber and scoop out the seeds. Slice very finely crosswise and salt well. Leave to drain for an hour or more. Pat dry. Heat 3 seeded and shredded red chillies in a tbsp peanut oil and pour over the cucumber. Season with sugar, sesame oil, rice vinegar and shredded fresh ginger. Leave overnight and serve as a pickle.

GINGER AND SOY DIP

Steam a jointed chicken or duck for about 1½ hrs in a sealed container containing a bottle of beer, 2 teacups of water or stock, 2 finely chopped spring/green onions, some shredded fresh ginger, 1 tsp salt and some shredded cinnamon bark. Chop and serve with a dipping sauce of 1 in/2.5 cm freshly grated ginger, 3 tbsp soy sauce, 2 tbsp dark rice vinegar and 2 tsp sesame oil.

TRUFFLE DAYS

Harvests in Tuscany, Spain
and Piemonte

We lose the concept of a harvest festival by moving away from our roots (both edible and ancestral) to the city; and with it the harvest feast of boldly flavoured peasant food, food that is close to the earth, inevitably – peasants having sowed, reaped, prepared it.

ONE

In Tuscany I watched the first deep-green olive oil seep through the old wooden presses at a farm near Montepulciano in the rolling golden hills south of Siena; to be poured straight onto slabs of home-baked bread seared over a sweet-smelling chestnut fire.

The bread was rubbed with cloves of raw garlic and sprinkled with coarse sea salt; the fresh peppery oil then added provided all the spice needed.

Anyone who stopped for a visit was offered this instant rough gratification with a glass of the new young purply vino da tavola. For those who stayed there would be beans later, the ones that Tuscans love to eat raw in the spring; dried now, and simmered very slowly until creamy in a mixture of three parts water to one part olive oil. No salt, but a big bunch of sage in the pot for flavour, and more fresh oil rolled over them before serving. More bread, more oil and garlic and salt.

TWO

For thirty years or more in Andalucia, where they still produce the wine that Columbus took with him to America – sack, wine of Jerez, sherry – the aristocracy of the region celebrated the harvest of the grapes, the vendimia, with street parties and ceremonies and parades in their magnificent horse-drawn carriages.

Then Franco died, and in the new liberal Spain a left-wing mayor was elected in Jerez. He put an end to what he felt was the upper class's conspicuous display of wealth.

Andalucia has always been a feudal state of great landowning families, the gap between poor and rich wider than almost anywhere else in Spain. Some of the sherry families still celebrate the vendimia; priests bless the new wine: 'Viva el vino de Jerez – the best and finest, most noble wine in the world'; thousands of doves are released into the sky as the must pours from the press. But the left-wing mayor of Jerez never comes, and his is the more valuable blessing.

Still, wherever there is any sort of fiesta in Spain there will be bullfights in the hot, white afternoons. And when there is a bullfight in Jerez de la Frontera, that evening you can be sure there will be colas de toro – bulls' tails – in the butchers and tapas bars of the town.

A footnote at the bottom of Jerez bullfight poster:

La carne de los toros se encontrará a la venta el día de la
corrida, a partir de las diez de la noche en el Mercado de
Abastos de Madre de Dios.

(The bulls' meat will be sold at the Abastos de Madre de Dios market,
after 10 p.m. on the day of the bullfight.)
A practical people, the Andalucians.

I remember, I remember:
The hazelnut and butterscotch tones of Miguel Valdespino's eighty-
year-old palo cortado, sipped in the old Inocente bodega, where
sunlight dappled vine leaves' shade onto white walls. Talking of the old
family recipe for autumn game cooked with raisiny, woody Solera
1842, and of how Miguel's brother, the chef, used the extraordinary
Valdespino sherry vinegar: a little to spice up lentil or bean stews, a
tablespoon to deglaze the pan after frying, a small glass in a game
marinade to tenderize and bring out the flavour of the meat.
Eating later in the restaurant Tendido 6 (for its position opposite the
sixth section of the bullfight arena in Jerez):

Freshly shucked broad beans simmered with Jabugo ham
and wild garlic shoots
Poached quails' eggs on bread deep-fried in olive oil
Bulls' tails and wild mushrooms stewed in manzanilla
sherry

And a breakfast table set for thirty people in the narrow ancient vestry
of Luis Caballero's Castillo de San Marcos, once a Moorish fortress;
once owned by the Duke of Medina; once a place of pilgrimage after
Santa Maria la Madonna appeared on a twelfth-century turret:

Prickly pears and melons and bowls of pomegranate seeds
Breads spread with burnt orange mantega colorada (pork fat
reduced with paprika and garlic)
Giant pinwheels of deep-fried churros doughnuts to break and
roll in coarse sugar
Baskets of dried apricots, raisins, dates, and dry-roasted
salted almonds and chickpeas, maize and broad beans

Drinking Caballero's salty, bone-dry Manzanilla de Sanlucar while he
spoke of the wine as one would of a lover. 'Keeping the sherry bots
sleeping in luxury in the bodega is very expensive,' he said. 'My brandy
pays for this. Brandy is the rich wife to sherry's expensive mistress.'
In the woods near his home he liked to collect the whippy bitter
green wild asparagus to stir with softly scrambled eggs; or wild
mushrooms to cook with strips of good mountain ham.

A bottle of Lustau's Almacenista amontillado, the label marked 'Viuda de Antonio Borrega ½' like an original lithograph (to signify that it was taken from one of only two casks of this remarkable wine) in the bodega of the widow of Antonio Borrega herself. With it, morning tapas of Pamplona sausage, crumbly old Manchego cheese, jamón (ham) de Serrano, roasted almonds – and garlicky salted bread charred on the fire of the cooper who was repairing Senora Borrega's casks.

'We use only finest American oak casks to store our wine. If one slat breaks we must find another old slat to replace it, otherwise the wine takes on the taste of the wood. With our small stores it would be fatal. More jamón?'

What turns a meal into a feast is as much a question of timing, sometimes, as of ingredients.

THREE

And Piemonte:

There are words whose sound evoke smells, taste, texture. 'Plum' has the round, velvety bloom of that fruit; 'Armagnac' the long warm build-up of fine brandy with its fiery kick at the end; but 'truffle' – somehow that whimsical fluttering noun does not evoke the majestic tuber magnatum from Piemonte, nor hint at its astronomical price.

By 8.30 a.m. on the first morning of the 59th Annual Truffle Fair in Alba, truffle lovers from all over the world added to the usual Saturday

crowds. In the shopping arcade that served as the market – and would do for eight more Saturdays – serious men with funghi faces and checked trilbys stood around in rugby huddles.

Trestle tables had been set up in a big U-shape on which a long row of pinky-beige potatoish lumps sat gracelessly on scraps of paper scribbled with outrageous prices.

A good white truffle can scent a whole room in minutes. Even in the street outside the truffle market the pheasanty aroma was so strong that approaching passersby lifted their noses like old hounds sniffing some equally old and virile cock bird.

At dinner in the restaurant of the Castello Cavour in Grinzane, the maitre d' brought out some fresh truffles.

'About £200 sterling,' he said, pointing into the basket.

'£200 seems a lot for such a small basket!'

'No, no signorina!' He looked shocked. '£200 for that one truffle. For this basketful you would have to sell a small car.'

Considering the price of white truffles in the world today, the air alone in Alba must be worth a small fortune.

I woke up one morning during the truffle festival in a house on the crest of a hill that holds two remarkable Barolo vineyards – Ceretto's Bricca Rocche and Mascarello's Mon Privato – and looked out on a Giotto landscape: corduroy stripe of vineyards sweeping down steeply into a valley whose full depth was hidden by mist and up again to hilltops crenellated by castles and walled villages.

Soft calls from below slurred French and Italian into the slide trombone Piemonte dialect, as the grape harvesters bent in a race against the weather.

Rain, friend of truffle and funghi, was the enemy now.

The trick, I was told at the Cantina Prunotto, is to leave the picking of the grapes as long as possible so they get the sun's maximum benefit, but not so long that they are ruined by early autumn rain.

Millions and millions of lira rest on this gamble. The feeling all over the province is one of a communally bated breath – even more so when there is the possibility that the year might be an outstanding one.

Cuneo locals predicted that 1989 would be one of the century's greatest years for their wine – but good grape years, they say, are bad for truffles. Scarcity and demand pushed the going rate at the opening of the Mercato del Tartufo to several hundred pounds a kilo.

'But hunting truffles for us in the Alba region is not so much a profession,' said Giancarlo Montaldo, a member of Alba's Cavalieri del Tartufo, the Knights of the Truffle, 'as a hobby – a passion even.'

A farmer called Oberto showed me four painfully thin hounds. 'Here my hobby is to run what you might call a truffle-hound university. Dogs

hunt for hunger, so in season they must be kept thin,' he grinned. 'And I am careful with other dogs around – one bitch in heat and you could have truffles the size of chairs that no dog would find.'

After three years of training (a sort of high school in truffle-hunting) a good dog is worth about £1200; after another two (Oxford or Harvard), you could probably double that figure.

White truffles are expensive for a reason. Although they have an altogether more sensuous, provocative aroma than black (imagine a cross between hot ripe nights in a tent and some earthy old parmesan), they are rarer and do not keep as long. Their season is brief, the tubers lose most of their pungent aroma in canning, and attempts to cultivate them commercially have still not been successful. So if the price drops too low, truffle-hunters simply eat their treasures themselves.

The evening opening of the Mostra de Tartufi had about it that indefinable air attached to all Italian events. There were lots of ribbons to be cut by very short, important men, and a loud brass band, slightly out of tune, a long delay, crowds standing around in medieval costumes left over from the previous week's donkey palio, several hitches in the proceedings, a good deal of people rushing back and forth looking anxious, and a general feeling of good will.

Downstairs in the hideous modern building that held the fair a group of truffle-hunters in what appeared to be requisite hunting garb – check trilby, knotted and spotted neckerchief, torch, weatherbeaten jacket with voluminous pockets, curved iron hand-pick – stood about smoking enough cigarettes to blur the edges of the room, and comparing the size and perfume of their prizes.

The next day a parade of oxen carts filled with grapes and wine casks and people in funny costumes wound its way through the city, and on one of the carts a lady sliced hot polenta and spread it with garlicky cheese to hand out to the crowds. You could have a bunch of dolcetto grapes from two pretty girls, or a plastic cup of the new moscato, intoxicatingly sweet and perfumed.

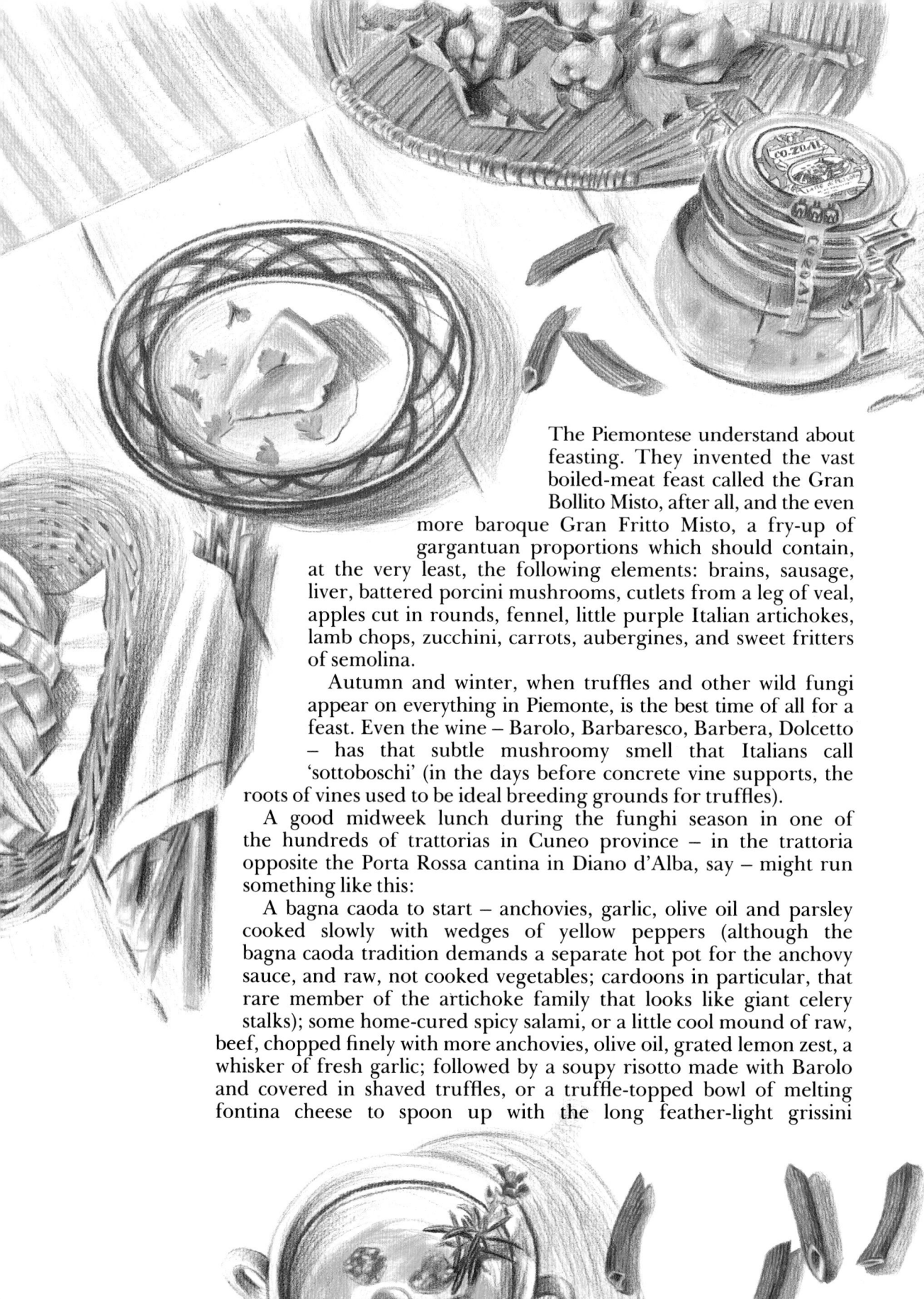

The Piemontese understand about feasting. They invented the vast boiled-meat feast called the Gran Bollito Misto, after all, and the even more baroque Gran Fritto Misto, a fry-up of gargantuan proportions which should contain, at the very least, the following elements: brains, sausage, liver, battered porcini mushrooms, cutlets from a leg of veal, apples cut in rounds, fennel, little purple Italian artichokes, lamb chops, zucchini, carrots, aubergines, and sweet fritters of semolina.

Autumn and winter, when truffles and other wild fungi appear on everything in Piemonte, is the best time of all for a feast. Even the wine – Barolo, Barbaresco, Barbera, Dolcetto – has that subtle mushroomy smell that Italians call 'sottoboschi' (in the days before concrete vine supports, the roots of vines used to be ideal breeding grounds for truffles).

A good midweek lunch during the funghi season in one of the hundreds of trattorias in Cuneo province – in the trattoria opposite the Porta Rossa cantina in Diano d'Alba, say – might run something like this:

A bagna caoda to start – anchovies, garlic, olive oil and parsley cooked slowly with wedges of yellow peppers (although the bagna caoda tradition demands a separate hot pot for the anchovy sauce, and raw, not cooked vegetables; cardoons in particular, that rare member of the artichoke family that looks like giant celery stalks); some home-cured spicy salami, or a little cool mound of raw, beef, chopped finely with more anchovies, olive oil, grated lemon zest, a whisker of fresh garlic; followed by a soupy risotto made with Barolo and covered in shaved truffles, or a truffle-topped bowl of melting fontina cheese to spoon up with the long feather-light grissini breadsticks, some meaty 'fillets' of porcini grilled on an open fire so they are crunchy outside and creamy within, or some saffron-yellow ovoli reali mushrooms bought from a peasant at the back door and dressed with a thread of olive oil, lemon and flat Italian parsley.

Fresh pasta, perhaps with more truffle parings; a terracotta dish of hare stewed in Barolo and wild funghi; an old gritty Murazzano cheese to finish, and a bunch of purple grapes with a dusky bloom to them.

Weighty, rich food then, food to drive your legs up the steep Cuneo hills. Not the most subtle food, but vigorous, intense, full of juice and guts, perfectly in tune with the hard northern setting.

The wonderful local ewes' cheese, called Murazzano when it is within the circle of villages defined by the DOC regulations, and Toma outside it is served as a first course, when it is about two days old and still creamy and fragrant, 'al verde' with a fresh green sauce of parsley, oil and chillies picked up from the Ligurian peasants who used to trade anchovies and salt through the region; or at the end of a meal, golden, dense and sharp after two or three months' ageing under olive oil, worthy of the finest old Barolo.

Murazzano is best in the autumn when the herbs that the ewes have grazed are drier and more concentrated.

'Then they produce less, but better, stronger,' I was told by a cheesemaker called Marisa. She worked at the Murazzano Co-op in the high hills of Alta Langa, south of Alba, and was one of the best dancers in the region – an important consideration in August when a portable wooden dance floor is carried to each of the numerous village festivals.

Murazzano is aged for fifteen days on metal shelves, turned every two days (in times of humidity cheeses are washed in salt water to prevent grey mould), then 1½ months on cloth-covered wooden shelves, and finally bottled in squat glass jars of olive oil – where it will last for months.

Aldo Monchiero and his wife Carla worked a mountain azienda near enough to Murazzano to have DOC cheese. They would prepare country feasts for visitors. These involved their own cheeses, fresh ones served 'al verde', mature cheese with just a teaspoon of its ageing liquor; coppa and salami seasoned by Aldo with dolcetto wine, cinnamon, garlic, cloves (the wine filtered out after two-three days and used as a sauce for pasta); tagliatelle and ravioli made by Carla, bagna caudas, bollito mistos with their own chickens. To finish, 'bunet delle Langhe', chocolate and amaretti grandmother of crème caramel.

Another treat was 'formaggio con latte' – month-old cheese aged for a further month under a mixture of cow and sheep milk and served in its own creamy liquid. It tasted like distilled essence of Piemonte.

Piemonte did not always eat so well. Stay for any length of time around Alba and you will be told how rural families used to eat an evening meal that consisted solely of boiled polenta rubbed against an anchovy hanging from a lamp, the heat of the lamp releasing an illusion of flavour.

One night I went to the celebration dinner of a group devoted to preserving old Piemonte traditions. They held their regular meetings in a mountain trattoria where one of the traditions preserved was the old one of eating and drinking well in good company.

After the usual seven or eight courses that are considered not too out of the ordinary here, a man called Angelo Manzone rose and began to sing in Piemontese. He was about fifty, and had the face of a previously angelic schoolboy who has just realized the fun in lifting money from the church collection box. He sang like a cross between Edith Piaf and Noel Coward and his songs made the whole roomful of people fall about laughing (and me as well, when they were translated into Italian). One of the songs was called 'Cha Cha Cha Glottologico'. At the end of the evening Angelo gave me a tape of his songs inscribed 'Al mio grande amore'.

I felt I could love anyone who could work the word 'glottologico' into a rhyme.

RECIPES

Spain
TORTILLA DE CAMARONES

Fried shrimp pancake (serves 6 as a tapas or snack)

I first had these at the El Faro restaurant in Cadiz, served hot straight from the pan with glasses of chilled manzanilla and a selection of other Spanish tapas but they are a common treat in most of Andalucia's tapas bars.

1 garlic clove, finely chopped
½ lb/250 g fresh raw shrimps, shelled and ground
2 spring/green onions, finely chopped
½ tsp salt
2 oz/60 g flour
4 tbsp fino or manzanilla sherry
olive oil for deep-frying

Mix together the garlic, shrimps, onion, salt, flour and sherry and add enough water (about ¼ pt/150 ml) to make a thick pouring batter. Cover and leave for 1 hour. Heat about ½ in/0.5 cm oil over high heat and drop teaspoons of the shrimp batter into it. Watch out – the moisture in the batter causes them to spit. Cook for 1 minute each side, or until brown and crisp, drain on kitchen paper and serve immediately.

FISH 'EN ADOBO'

Fish marinated in sherry vinegar

A classic Andalusian recipe is to marinate chunks of firm white fish 'en Adobo'. The famous Cadiz cook, Lallo Grosso de Macpherson, recommended a kilo of fish, cut in bite-sized chunks, to one glass of sherry vinegar and one glass of fino sherry (I use Barbadillo's manzanilla instead). Add lots of chopped garlic, salt, paprika and herbs, and refrigerate, covered, for 4–12 hours. Drain, dredge with flour, and fry a few pieces at a time in hot olive oil.

RABOS/COLAS DE TORO

Bull's or oxtail stew (serves 4–6)

A creamy gold sauce with the buttery depths of sherry behind it. The Jerezanos say that sherry is the only wine that 'gives life' to food, so that a dish cooked with it needs no extra spice. In Jerez the stew would appear in little earthenware bowls with fried potatoes on the side. I think it is rich enough to serve just with a salad of bitter autumn greens such as chicory or endive.

3½–4 lb/1.75–2 kg bull's or oxtail, cut in rounds
1 celery stalk with leaves
2 halved carrots
1 onion stuck with 12 cloves
big bouquet of 2 bay leaves, parsley, thyme
salt and pepper
4 garlic cloves, finely chopped
1 onion, finely chopped
2 tbsp olive oil
2 tbsp flour
½ tsp paprika
3½ oz/100 g cured ham (prosciutto), cut in narrow strips
10 fl oz/300 ml fino or manzanilla sherry

(1) Trim all the fat from the tails. Place in a saucepan with carrots, celery, onion and herbs, salt and pepper, and barely cover in water. Bring to a boil, skimming off any scum that rises, cover and reduce heat to very low. Simmer three hours. Keep aside 7 fl oz/200 ml stock and reserve the rest for other dishes (a superb gelatinous base for all soups and stews).

(2) Over medium heat in a saucepan big enough to hold all the ingredients, fry onions, garlic, ham and paprika with the oil until the onions are tender. Sprinkle over flour, stir it until it browns slightly, then slowly stir in the sherry and stock. Add tails and continue cooking very, very gently (the surface should barely shudder), covered, for 1 hour.

(3) Serve in an earthenware dish, brush the tails well with sauce so they glisten, and scatter the top with reserved ham.

You can also add a handful of raisins and pine nuts (saving a few for the top) at step 2 – a nod in the direction of Jerez Moorish origins.

Italy: Beginnings
PEPERONI IN BAGNA CAODA

Sweet peppers in anchovy sauce (serves 8)

Bagna Caoda (which means 'hot bath' in Piemontese) is traditionally served in an earthenware pot with a flame under it to keep it hot, and raw sliced peppers and cardoons to dip in it. The following method is more recent, with peppers cooked under the sauce. In Piemonte they use anchovies preserved in salt rather than oil. If you can find them they have a richer flavour, but need more rinsing to get rid of excess salt.

5–8 garlic cloves, crushed
extra-virgin olive oil (about 6 fl oz/180 ml)
2 tins of anchovies in olive oil
6–8 yellow peppers, cored and quartered

Preheat oven to 350°F/175°C/gas mark 4. Cook the garlic over gentle heat in 3 tbsp of oil until soft and golden. Rinse the anchovies in milk to get rid of excess salt, pat dry, and purée with the garlic, adding enough oil to make a thick sauce. Place the peppers all in one layer in a greased casserole, and pour the sauce first into each pepper, and then all around. Cover and cook for 1½ hours. For the last 10 minutes, put the peppers under a grill so they brown slightly on the edges. Serve with crusty bread to mop up the juices.

The peppers give off a lot of delicious juice. If you have any left over, save it to purée with mashed potatoes, or to drizzle over roast chicken or pork.

TORTA DI CECI

Baked chickpea and parmesan pie (serves 8)

A rustic pie to serve with bitter green winter salads, or instead of potatoes beside a roast or stew. I have substituted tinned chickpeas for the usual dried ones – out of laziness, and because they taste as good.

3 14 oz/400 g tins of chickpeas, drained
4 tbsp good olive oil
1 large onion, finely chopped
a sprig of rosemary, 2–3 sage leaves, finely chopped
2 oz/60 g Parmesan cheese, freshly grated
3 eggs, beaten
salt, pepper
butter

Preheat the oven to 350°F/175°C/gas mark 4. Mash the chickpeas roughly. Heat the oil and soften the onions with the herbs. Add the chickpeas and cook, stirring frequently, for about 10 minutes. Remove from heat and allow to cool a little. Mix in cheese and eggs, season with salt and plenty of black pepper and drizzle the top with a spoonful more oil. Pour into a shallow well-buttered pie plate and bake in the oven for 45 minutes until browning on top. Serve warm.

MURAZZANO IN SALSA VERDE
Cheese in green herb sauce

Young herbal Murazzano ewes' cheese is often served as a first course in wedges under an olive oil and herb sauce. Any mild fresh cheese is good this way (try wedges of fetta served in a bowl under the sauce). Take a clove of garlic, crush it with 2–3 anchovies and a good pinch of dry mustard. Whisk in a peeled, seeded and crushed tomato, a goodish handful of finely chopped parsley, a day-old slice of bread soaked in vinegar and squeezed out, and enough olive oil to make a creamy sauce.

Italy: Some light main courses
(for normal appetites – Piemontese eat them before the main course)

CARNE CRUDA ALBESE
Alba-style raw beef salad (serves 6)

This is the most traditional version of Piemonte's famous raw beef. Young chefs now serve the beef in sheets like Parma ham, thin enough to read through. It is sliced and pounded flat between two pieces of plastic – more elegant, but lacking the vigour of the original.

1¼ lb/600 g very good lean beef
2 anchovies, rinsed of salt and mashed
juice of 2 lemons and grated zest from 1
garlic clove, finely chopped
extra-virgin olive oil, salt, coarsely ground black pepper
Top with
1 small white truffle (if available), or
2 oz/60 g fresh ungrated Parmesan, celery

Chop the meat finely but do not grind it. Just before serving (so that the lemon and oil do not turn the meat from pink to grey) mix it with the anchovies, lemons, garlic, a little oil and salt and pepper to taste. If you are lucky enough to have a truffle, shave that over the top; otherwise, shave over some Parmesan and serve with pieces of celery.

RISOTTO AL BAROLO
Rice in red wine (serves 6)

The dish of someone living with a cellar of Barolo wines under his dining table. From the Belvedere restaurant in La Morra. You can try it with one of the cheaper Piemontese wines – a Dolcetto d'Alba, say – still excellent, if not so lavish. In Alba this would, of course, have shavings of truffle on top. I shave Parmesan instead.

2 oz/60 g butter plus 2 tbsp olive oil
1 onion, finely chopped
1 large sprig of rosemary, finely chopped
1 lb/500 g Arborio rice
15 fl oz/¾ pt/1½ cups Barolo or other red wine*
approx 1 pt 12 fl oz/620 ml/2½ cups good strong homemade broth,
heated to boiling
3 oz/90 g Parmesan, freshly grated (plus extra for topping)
salt and pepper

Melt 1½ oz/45 g butter with olive oil in a saucepan over gentle heat and cook the onion in it with the rosemary until the onion is golden. Add the rice, stir for a couple of minutes until coloured and pour in the wine, stirring constantly. When it has been almost absorbed, cover the rice with a little hot broth and continue stirring until that has been absorbed as well. The broth should just simmer but not boil vigorously. Continue adding a little broth at a time until the rice is cooked through (about 25 minutes) but still very creamy. Remove from heat, stir in the Parmesan, extra butter and seasoning and serve immediately.

*Massimo Martinelli, who makes the delicious Renato Ratti wines, recommended a whole bottle of wine, but then he would.

FONDUTA CON TARTUFI
Creamed fontina cheese with truffles (serves 4)
Small portions, but very, very rich, and as much like the sinewy dinner-party fondue as a soufflé is like a washing-up sponge. In Piemonte it might be poured over zampone sausage, or stirred into fresh pasta. At the extraordinary restaurant La Carmagnole I had a tiny terrine of it layered with truffles and Parmesan and topped with a poached quail's egg. Most often it appears in bowls with a paper-thin topping of shaved truffles. Other good raw mushrooms will do. Serve with one of the deliciously spicy Arneis wines (Ceretto's Blange or Castello di Neive).

1 lb/500 g fontina cheese, cubed
¾ pt/400 ml milk
5 egg yolks, beaten
2 oz/60 g butter, melted
1 small truffle (optional)

Cover the cheese in milk and leave to soak 4–5 hours. Fonduta, like soufflé, is not a patient dish: make it just before serving (it stays creamy about 20 minutes). Over a double boiler, whisk together the melted butter, eggs, cheese and about 6–8 tbsp of the milk that has not been absorbed, stirring constantly until the mixture forms a thick, smooth cream (about 7–10 minutes). Pour into heated bowls, shave the truffle on top, and serve immediately with lots of crusty bread – or a selection of grissini (hazelnut, sesame, etc.).

TARTRÁ (OR BUDINO SALÉ)
Individual Parmesan custards (serves 6)
Tartrá is the old Piemontese word for baked custard. This is a heavenly dish, a very soft and creamy-textured custard, smoky flavoured from the herbs. At the fine regional restaurant La Contea, in Neive, the owner gathers wild herbs to scent the custard, and his wife tops each serving with porcini and surrounds it in a pool of rich tomato sauce scattered with flat parsley, a spicy homemade sausage grilled on the side. I like the flavour of the custard on its own just with mushrooms.

18 fl oz/500 ml milk
large bouquet of fresh sage, green onion, rosemary, 2 bay leaves
4 egg yolks, beaten
2 oz/60 g fresh Parmesan, grated
salt and pepper
butter

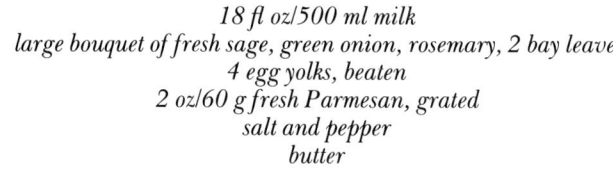

some flat Italian parsley, chopped
2 small porcini, cèpes, or 6 dark field mushrooms, coarsely chopped
Optional
homemade tomato sauce, 6 small grilled sausages
6 small buttered custard dishes

(1) Heat milk just to boiling with the herbs, remove from heat and leave to infuse 30 minutes (this gives a strong herbal taste – less time if you wish).
(2) Preheat oven to 400°F/200°C/gas mark 6 and stand a tray of water (enough to come about one-third up custard dishes) in the centre. Strain the milk into the eggs, add cheese and season lightly. Pour the custard into the dishes and stand the dishes in the tray of hot water. Bake for 15 minutes, or until the custard begins to set, then reduce heat to 325°F/165°C/gas mark 3 and continue cooking 45–50 minutes.
(3) While the custard cooks, fry the mushrooms in a tbsp of butter until all their liquid evaporates and they are dry and well browned. Prepare the sauce and the sausages if using. When the custards are set, cool slightly, run a knife around the edge and turn out onto plates. Top with mushrooms (surround with sauce, if using) and scatter with parsley.

Italy: Main Courses
CONIGLIO CON PEPERONI
Rabbit with sweet peppers (serves 4–6)

During the October truffle festival in Alba the market was full of glorious red and yellow peppers. They make this a colourful dish, full of flavour – very popular in the mountain trattorias of Piemonte. Serve with plain boiled pasta tossed in olive oil, pepper and fresh parsley.

1 large rabbit, about 3 lb/1.5 kg, cut in 2–3 in/5-8 cm pieces
salt and black pepper
flour, a good pinch dry mustard (optional)
olive oil
9 fl oz/250 ml homemade stock/broth
3 fl oz/90 ml red wine vinegar
bay leaf, sprig of rosemary
3 yellow peppers, 2 red, cored and cut in strips lengthwise
6 anchovies, cut in half
3 garlic cloves, shredded

(1) Sprinkle the rabbit pieces with salt and pepper and dredge with flour sifted with mustard. Heat 2 tbsp of oil with the butter in a heavy saucepan and brown the rabbit well on all sides. Drain fat into another pan and pour the stock and vinegar over the rabbit with the bay leaf and rosemary. Cover and simmer very, very gently for 45–55 minutes until the rabbit is tender to a fork.
(2) In the meantime, put the peppers, anchovies and garlic in the pan with the reserved fat – add more oil if necessary: the peppers should stew in it rather than fry. Cook them, covered, over very low heat.
(3) When the rabbit has finished cooking, lift the pieces out with a slotted spoon and keep warm. Add the peppers with their juices to the pan, turn up the heat and reduce the sauce to the consistency of thin cream. Check seasoning. Return the rabbit to the pan to heat through and serve on a big platter surrounded by pasta.

BOLLITO MISTO
Boiled meats with condiments

I was never treated to a full bollito misto, a baroque dish (or series of dishes) like something from another century: whole calves' heads and stuffed pigs' feet, oxtails and chickens and tongues and various veal muscles. Perhaps I did not look robust enough. I did have a simple and much more manageable version – with a good boiled hen and a sliced zampone on the side to spice her up.

Bollitos in Piemonte may come with a green sauce (borrowed from the Ligurian traders who used to pass by on the way from the coast) or with a sweet fruit mustard and a much older honey sauce, 'sausa d'avie'.

FRITTURA DOLCE
Sweet fried bread to serve with bollito (serves 6–8)

Although this is traditionally served with a grand bollito misto or frittura (selection of fried meats), it is just as good with any roasts and stews (like the rabbit in sweet peppers, page 175).

*1³/₄ pt/1 l milk
4 tbsp sugar
4 oz/125 g fine semolina
2 eggs, separated
grated zest of 1 lemon
¹/₂ tsp salt
fine breadcrumbs
oil for deep-frying*

(1) Over medium heat, boil together the milk and sugar until the sugar dissolves. Gradually stir in the semolina, cooking slowly until it pulls away from the sides of the pan. Remove from heat, cool slightly and stir in the egg yolks, zest and salt. Spread about ½ in/1 cm deep in a shallow, greased tray and chill until quite firm.
(2) Cut the cooked semolina into 3 in/8 cm diamonds, dip in egg whites, then in crumbs and fry in hot oil until brown on both sides. Serve hot.

COTECHINO CON PURÉE
Sausage with pesto potato purée

More usual at a country party than the much more elaborate bollito misto was this earthy dish in which a big cotechino sausage was boiled, and its delicious cooking liquor used to purée boiled potatoes. To the potatoes as well might be added a few big dollops of basil, garlic and olive oil pesto – to give it a nice garlicky green flavour.

To cook a cotechino, wrap it in a cloth, cover it with cold water and simmer for about 1½ hrs (or follow the directions your local Italian deli gives you – cotechini vary from one to the next). Make a bed of the garlicky puréed potatoes (they should be very soft but not runny) and slice the sausage in an overlapping circle on top. Drizzle over some more of the liquid and save the rest for cooking beans.

Italy: Endings
BUNET DELLE LANGHE

Chocolate amaretti pudding, to fill a 1¾ pt/1 l pudding mould (serves 8)

This is what happened to the crème caramel when it hit Piemonte – they added almondy amaretti biscuits soaked in Marsala or rum, stirred in chocolate and turned it into something a lot more interesting. This is the classic 'grandmother's pudding' served in the family trattorias of the region. In Piemonte the pudding would be cooked in a fluted mould with a hole in the middle.

Caramel glaze
3 oz/90 g white sugar
3 tbsp water

Pudding
5 medium eggs
2 oz/60 g sugar
2 tbsp pure cocoa powder
grated zest of 1 lemon
2 oz/60 g/large handful amaretti macaroons,
crushed and soaked in 2 tbsp Marsala or rum
16 fl oz/450 ml milk, heated just to boiling

(1) Preheat the oven to 350°F/180°C/gas mark 4 and place a pan with 1 in/2.5 cm water in it (big enough to hold the pudding mould). Make a glaze by boiling the sugar and water over moderate heat, swirling the pan occasionally (you can do this in the mould if you are using a metal one), until it turns golden brown. Immediately pour it into the mould, heated first if it is ceramic, and swirl around to cover it.

(2) Beat the eggs, sugar, cocoa and lemon until light, and whisk in the biscuits with their liquor and the hot milk. Pour into the caramelized mould, place in the pan of hot water and bake for 30–35 minutes, or until set.

(3) Refrigerate pudding for several hours and turn out onto a serving plate. If a lot of caramel has stuck to the mould, heat it (on a heatproof mat, if using a ceramic mould) with a little hot water to loosen it and pour over the pudding.

TIMBALLO DI PERE MARTINE

Spiced pears in pastry (serves 6)

Baked in a bread tin and sliced like a loaf, this spicy tart can be elegant or rustic depending on how the pears react (sometimes they ooze through the crust), but delicious either way. Reserve a few slices of pear to decorate the top and drink with the muscat wine of the region.

Pastry
7½ oz/220 g plain white flour sifted with a pinch of salt
3 egg yolks, beaten
3½ oz/100 g sugar
3½ oz/100 g butter, softened (plus 1 tbsp, melted)

Filling
8 oz/250 g sugar
½ bottle dry red wine
1 cinnamon stick
10 cloves
4 lb/1.8 kg small hard pears, cored, peeled, coarsely chopped

(1) Make a well in the flour and put the pastry ingredients into it, slowly working in with your fingertips. Form into a ball, knead a couple of times, wrap in plastic and chill for at least 1 hour.

(2) Boil together the sugar, wine and spices until the sugar dissolves. Add the pears and simmer for 1 hour. Remove spices and drain any excess liquid (reserve for ice-cream).

(3) Preheat oven to 350°F/180°C/gas mark 4. Line a rectangular loaf tin with greaseproof paper, well buttered on the side that will touch the timballo. Roll out the pastry on a floured board to about ½ in/1 cm thick and trim to a long rectangle that will line the tin on 3 sides and lap over the top. Lay in tin very carefully (the pastry is quite fragile), leaving a flap to seal, and brush with melted butter. Fill with cooked pears and seal shut.

(4) Bake for about 45 minutes until the pastry is lightly browned and crisp – cover with greaseproof paper if it seems to be browning too quickly. Allow to cool slightly before turning out onto a plate and top with reserved pears. Cut in thick slices.

SORBETTO DI MOSCATO
Sorbet of muscat wine (serves 6–8)

There is a gelateria in front of Alba's train station that made this sorbet for people watching the parades. Although they used the elegant moscato d'Asti, any muscat will do – it need not be an expensive. Because of the alcohol the sorbet must be frozen at a very low temperature, and will still be softer than most ice-creams. Wonderful after a heavy meal.

4 oz/125 g white sugar
juice of 2 lemons
1 bottle moscato d'Asti wine (or another muscat wine)
2 egg whites
fresh mint leaves to decorate

Heat the sugar with the lemon juice and some of the wine until it dissolves. Stir into the remaining wine, pour into a container and freeze until slushy. Beat in the egg whites and refreeze until firm, stirring often. Beat hard an hour before serving (or whizz in a blender) and serve garnished with fresh mint leaves.

OUT OF THE
NOMAD'S TENT

The Pushkar Fair in

Rajasthan

At the full moon of Kartik Poornima every year, some 200,000 people travel to a camel fair in the little town of Pushkar that curls around a lake on the far side of the Nag Pahar, the Snake Mountain, on the edge of the great desert of Rajasthan.

The men have hawks' faces, scarred by the wind as if by knife wounds. They wear pillow-sized turbans in fuchsia pink and shades of orange; their women, in mirrored skirts of scarlet and amber with heavy silver embroidery, are paler, softer, very pretty. They cook over open fires and eat simple vegetarian food – from any supplies that are easily packed in a bullock cart or onto a camel.

With the people come tents, cooking pots, portable spices, dogs, cattle, poultry, ravishing curly-eared horses straight from a Moghul miniature, and lots and lots of camels.

The international set of tourists who come to look at them bring things too: cameras, soap, insect repellent, Dio-calm, malaria tablets, antiseptic wipes, sunburn lotion, dope, drink, and lots of toilet paper.

Perhaps surprisingly, the tourists do not detract from the fair's authenticity. 'Look, honey, isn't that snake-charmer/dancing girl/camel-driver just the cutest thing?' Presumably the fair has always attracted onlookers as well as participants, and the snake-charmers have come for a good laugh too.

ONE

In November in Rajasthan every traffic jam is a wedding.

The drive from Jaipur's négligé-pink palace to Pushkar should have taken about two hours, but each village had its party and its groom dressed in the finery of a maharajah (if for the first and last time in his life) being led through the streets on a white horse.

'Wedding is circus in this country,' said Hari, my driver, as we swerved close enough to a flower-decked wedding cart to count the eyelashes on the camel pulling it. 'Too many weddings, too many children, costing too much money.'

Hari was a madman from the Hindu Kush, a deranged driver in a country where people take pride in driving badly. In the first few miles on the road to Pushkar I counted six overturned tankers, two road-accident camels, and one bus that had crashed dramatically through the guard rail of a bridge some months before and hung there – half-on, half-off. When I pointed these out to Hari, he lifted his hands from the wheel and shrugged his shoulders in a fatalistic gesture, swivelling his face to nod sadly at me. My eyes were frozen on the bus full of horror-struck people hurtling towards us on our side of the road. At the last moment before a certain head-on collision Hari hurled the car through a gap between the bus and a herd of water buffalo.

'Oh yes, Miss,' he said calmly and sweetly. 'Very difficult driving here. Even I must guess what is a buffalo thinking.'

When I opened my eyes again we were out of the villages on a flat, straight road lined with white-barked eucalyptus groves and some trees that Hari called 'keem'. 'In summer we boil the leaves against malaria. And soap from them is making skin very soft also.'

Under the trees, flocks of vultures tore at unidentifiable carcasses and lifted into the air at our approach as slowly as bad luck. In the distance hung the Arrkavali Hills, the heat rising up from the road making them shiver, transparent as pale-blue gauze curtains. Women by the side of the road flung armfuls of wheat in front of us so that the car's weight would separate the grain from the chaff.

TWO

In Pushkar the fair was well under way. We inched through the town past the Pushkar Hotel, 'A Stay of Class in Piece', and the Everest Guest House, 'Cheep and Best', to the Tourist Tent Village, behind camel and bullock carts, elephants, Morris Oxfords, horses, painted buses.

Crowds of little boys ran up selling the same things they had been selling in Delhi, four hundred kilometres to the northeast. The patter was the same too. Only the little boys had changed.

'Miss Miss! Very good lock here Miss shape like tiger. Jus put key here pull tail – open! Push tail pull key – close! Best price twenty rupees Miss. Alright fifteen rupees. Alright. For you pretty Miss ten rupees.'

No Indians without passes were allowed inside the stockade of the Tourist Village, but all sorts of pale-skinned pickpockets and drug abusers mingled freely with the guests. A sign warned people to behave modestly: NO SHORTIES. NO HOLDING OF HANDS BETWEEN BOYS AND GIRLS IN THE TOWN. Boys with arms wrapped closely about each other's waists seemed to be perfectly acceptable, as were boys in the town dressed up as girls and performing mildly suggestive dances.

The advertised 'Luxurious Tented Accommodation' was an orange army tent lined with gaily-patterned cotton. Inside were two camp beds covered in spotless white linen, two grey quilts covered in horrible stains and craters, two deck chairs and an electric light bulb in a pot that lit up only when the darkness became completely impenetrable.

THREE

I left the Tourist Village the first morning, very early, stepping around the camera buff in his T-shirt – 'No Rugs, No knives. No puppets. No change, No nothing' – to brave a long row of stalls selling uglier, marginally less expensive versions of things I would avoid in London.

'Miss Miss! Hello – how are you? Are you healthy?
You want carpets?'

Seconds away from the street vendors in their
stacked Cuban heels, was the desert. A holy man
dressed like a monkey, with ash-whitened face, a
long tail, and tinsel in his hair walked by, eyes
closed, humming something to himself. A woman
lit her cigar through her veil. A painted elephant
begged bananas and pomegranates from a row of
stalls where I stopped for a cup of sweet Indian tea
with cardamom.

The white smoke of hundreds of breakfast
campfires drifted up into the dunes until it
vanished into the pale dawn sky. Groups of men
squatted around their fires, surrounded by the
mixed clutter of harness and cooking utensils and
round brass water pots. Horses whickered softly to
one another through their noses. A man scrubbed
his teeth with a frayed twig. His friend, in a turban
the colour of a badly tinted postcard sunset, dug a
round grey lump out of the ashes of his fire,

whacked it viciously several times with a stick and offered it to me.

The round lump, gritty with sand and ash but perfectly edible, turned out to be a sample of batti, a wholemeal bread remarkably similar in its lack of pretensions to some of the loaves tribal Pathans make on the border with Afghanistan.

I was touched by the man's generosity – he had given away a third of his breakfast – and, as is so often the case when travelling, it was a gesture impossible to repay. For a while we nodded idiotically at each other while he waited patiently for me to go so he could finish his meal.

Batti is bread in its embryonic state: unleavened, unadulterated, undisguised, primal; bread as it was before civilization invented 'cuisine' and tampered with the original concept of edible ballast. Local legend has it that this seminal form of baked fibre was invented by desert warriors who prepared the dough of wholemeal flour, water and salt, and buried small pieces of it in the sand, to be dug up after battle, bullet-hard from the baking heat of the sun. The bread was cracked open and quantities of ghee poured in to moisten it. Failing that it could always have been used as ammunition.

In Pushkar there was no excess ghee to use so lavishly: if you were poor, you dusted the ash off your batti and used it to mop up diced potatoes or dal cooked with cumin, ghee and chilli powder. If you had a

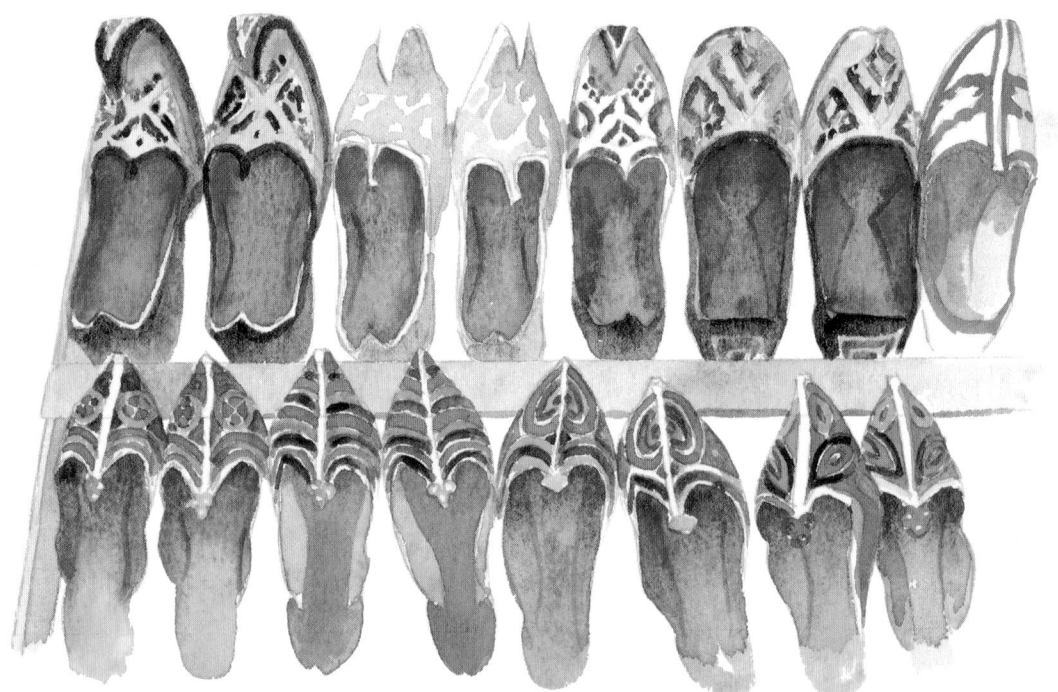

few rupees to spare in the bazaar, you paid for someone else to bake your bread, and you used it as a spoon for aloo matar, potatoes and peas simmered in a yoghurt sauce, or palag gobi, spinach dry-fried with spices and cauliflower pieces, or chovaleh, a black-eyed bean stew with while chillies, to which fresh spinach was added.

In the market you could buy peeled blood-orange carrots that stained your lips like the vampire's in a Dracula film, or crunchy matte-white mooli radish to munch with a squeeze of fresh lime and a dusting of pepper while you watched the camel races.

In some of the rudimentary cafés – long benches shaded by creaking, striped awnings – you could eat green and red chillies and tiny round aubergines dipped whole into a chickpea-flour batter (like the one on page 106) and deep-fried.

Cauliflowers, potatoes, garlic, the greens of spinach and bunched coriander leaf, but no tomatoes; to get the required tartness the cooks used a dried powder made from raw green mangoes, called amchoor.

I did not see vegetables being sun-dried, as would have been the case in Jodhpur. Vegetarian Maheshwari people there (who eschew garlic and onions because they heat the blood and excite passion) dry vegetables to preserve them through the hottest months. But there were trays of festive fried savouries: potato fritters stuffed with ground roasted lentils and fresh coriander; round dumplings made of cooked mung beans ground with chillies, 'sausages' of chickpea-flour dough, boiled, sliced and deep-fried in ghee to dip in a spicy curd sauce.

Cooking was done in a wok-shaped iron pan called a kadhai – for fast frying – or in a handi, a brass stew pot with a neck narrower than the base, whose top could be sealed with a cap of flour and water dough if the food was to be buried next to the fire and stewed for a long time.

The fuel for all the fires was dried camel dung, whether in Sanjay's Restaurant in town, in the clay ovens of the bazaar, or out in the desert. Depending on the nature of its drying and shape, it burned up fiercely to blend the flavours of spice and fat, or glowed with the steady heat needed to take the rawness off a yoghurt sauce without curdling it.

Girls with bare, supple stomachs and flirtatious eyes walked up and down the dunes all day selling different shapes of neatly displayed camel dung – round, flat, ovoid – from huge bowls balanced on their heads. There was a great trade in it: symmetrical rows, fenced in, dried in the sun, and small children scrabbled to get it fresh from the source.

New Delhi cynics had told me that in Pushkar these days there were

more diplomats than camels. Either they had never been to Pushkar or they had underestimated the camels. Hari mentioned 25,000 as a conservative guess when I asked him to quiz one of the owners.

'Are you sure, Hari? Twenty-five thousand seems a lot of camels.'

'Fifty thousand camels, Miss. Man says 50,000, but he can't count.' He shook his head dreamily. 'But never have I seen so many all in one place – and look at all the babies, also!'

Camels provided fuel, transport, income, shade, company. There were enough camels to stretch the threads of a new Silk Route from Rajasthan to China and back.

FOUR

A few time-warp flower children still sloped around the town, grey-skinned from too much Bang Lassi – the Pushkar milkshake of liquid yoghurt laced with hashish, a speciality of fair time, but they were only bit-players prowling around the sub-plots of the real story.

The protagonists were the people who had been coming to Pushkar once a year, every year from all over Rajasthan and Gujarat – for a chance to show off their Best Bullocks, Fattest Chickens, Swiftest Horses.

There were puppet shows and a ferris wheel for the children, bargains in silver jewellery, embroidered wall-hangings, cooking pots for their mothers; races and horsemanship trials and videos of birth-control methods for the fathers. I saw a group of turbanned men riveted by pictures of an IUD insertion. Rupees changed hands. Camels and cattle moved from one herd to another. A bullock escaped from his lap of honour and ran amok through the bazaar.

The hippies (mostly German and Scandinavian), the tourists in their funny shorts (English) or T-shirts with slogans (American) or designer Desert Wear (French) were like aliens from another planet.

On my last day at the fair a man in tennis shoes cajoled his white stallion into a spinning, snorting, prancing Lipizzaner dance outside the camel-racing ring, to the tune of Rajasthani bee-bop Charlie

Parker-style riffs over the loudspeaker. The horse lay down and played dead the man stretched out on top, hands folded behind his head. For a grand finale he galloped his horse at full speed and picked up a handkerchief from the sand with his teeth. What had begun as a private display for the benefit of a couple of us at the tea stall and one man selling camel-dung rakes ended with the applause of a huge crowd.

No challenger came forward from the onlookers. Like Pushkar itself, it was a hard act to follow.

RECIPES

PANEER
Fresh curd cheese

A woman in the bazaar talked of how the cafés use vinegar to make paneer, while in homes it is always lime juice, which makes an altogether softer curd. Milk is heated until just before boiling, the juice of a lime stirred in and the milk removed from heat. Within a few minutes the whey (clear liquid) will separate from the curd. The whey is drained off and used to bake breads, etc., and the curds are put to drain in a cloth, then weighted for about 10 minutes (for soft cheese) or up to an hour. This can then be sliced into little cubes, and is delicious deep-fried in a spice paste of turmeric or cumin, cooked with ground chillies and spinach, or in a tomato sauce such as this one:

Soften a chopped onion in hot ghee, turn heat high and sear several tomatoes and sweet pepper wedges in it so that the vegetables do not lose their shape. Stir in ½ tsp each turmeric and chilli powder, salt and pepper. Add paneer, stir-fry for a very few minutes and serve with phulkas.

CHOVALEH
Black-eyed beans with fresh spinach (serves 6)

At one of the tents in the bazaar on the edge of Pushkar they had big pots of cooked vegetables from which you could choose your own mix. They would then cook it with the appropriate sauce of fresh curds, whole chillies, fresh spinach or tiny aubergine. This recipe assumes you do not have the advantage of precooked food to hand. It is not spicy, but the whole chillies are available if you need some heat.

¾ lb/350 g black-eyed beans/peas, picked over and washed
2 tsp coriander seeds, 1 tsp cumin seeds
6 tbsp ghee
2 onions, finely chopped
4–6 garlic cloves, finely chopped
2 tsp mango powder, or 1 large crushed tomato
2 tsp ground ginger
1 tsp cayenne powder
1¼ tsp salt
6 fl oz/170 ml Greek yoghurt
1¾ pt/1 l water
¾ lb/350 g spinach, washed and roughly chopped
4 whole green chillies

(1) Bring beans to boil in 1¾ pt/1 l water with a pinch of bicarbonate of soda (to cut their explosive qualities). Boil hard 5 minutes, cover and remove from heat. Leave for 1 hour.

(2) Dry-fry the coriander and cumin seeds over medium heat until fragrant, grind to a powder. Heat ghee over medium-high heat in a heavy-based saucepan large enough to hold all the ingredients. Fry the onions in it until light brown (about 10 minutes), adding spoonfuls of water if the onions start to brown too quickly. Add the garlic and ground spices and stir-fry for a couple of minutes. Lower heat, pour in 4 tbsp water (and the tomato, if using) and stir in ¼ of the yoghurt until blended, adding the remaining yoghurt a little at a time. Pour in beans and liquid, half-cover and simmer over very gentle heat for 1 hour.

(3) Twenty minutes before the end of cooking, stir in spinach a handful at a time. Top with whole chillies, cover and finish cooking. Allow to sit for 10 minutes before serving. Serve with chapattis, parathas (page 108) or phulkas (page 188).

For a livelier mix, just before serving, melt 2 tbsp ghee with ½ tsp cayenne and 1 tsp cumin seeds and fry for 2 minutes. Mix in some garam masala (page 111) and pour over the beans.

PHULKAS
Flat breads (12 8 in/20 cm phulkas)*

Like chapattis, except that they are finished cooking over an open flame – these cannot be cooked on electricity. This puffs them dramatically, but they flatten out again.

12 oz/350 g chapatti or atta flour
(or 8 oz/250 g fine wholemeal flour and 4 oz/125 g strong bread flour)
sifted with good pinch of salt
approx 6–8 fl oz/185–225 ml warm water
a few tbsp melted ghee

(1) Add water to the flour slowly, just until the dough adheres enough to be kneaded (it should be quite soft and sticky). Mix and knead in a food processor (or on a floured surface for about 10 minutes), cover with a damp towel and leave to rest for 30 minutes.

(2) Knead the dough again for a minute or so until pliable and divide into 12 pieces. Roll each piece into balls, dust with flour and keep covered.

(3) Flatten each ball slightly and dust with flour, then roll out into a circle. Keep covered.

(4) Heat frying pan or griddle over medium high and dry-fry each phulk one at a time on both sides until several brown spots appear (about 30–40 seconds the first side and 20–30 the second). Then finish them off lying on an open flame for a few seconds each side (they will puff up), brush with melted ghee and keep warm, covered in a damp cloth.

*Phulkas can be made several hours ahead of time and reheated in a damp cloth.

KHAD
Layered 'cake' of spiced meat (serves 4–6 with other dishes)

Not all the people who came to Pushkar were vegetarian. As soon as I open the foil and release the savoury smells from this savoury mixture of spicy lamb layered with phulkas it brings back memories of the desert. 'Khad' means a hole in the ground – originally this cake was baked in the earth under charcoal and sand, no doubt for the same reasons as batti – nomads would not have time to have a clay oven.

6 phulkas (¹/₂ recipe on page 188)
7 fl oz/200 ml Greek yoghurt
1 lb/500 g ground lamb
2 big onions, 1 puréed with 4 garlic cloves, 1 finely chopped
1 in/2.5 cm thumb fresh ginger, peeled and ground
2 tsp ground coriander
1 tsp ground cayenne
¹/₄ tsp turmeric
1¹/₂ tsp salt
2 oz/60 g ghee
1 large potato, peeled and finely chopped
handful of chopped fresh coriander or mint
2 seeded and finely chopped green chillies
juice of 1 lemon

(1) Make and cook phulkas
(2) Whisk together yoghurt, meat, onion and garlic purée, ginger, coriander, cayenne, turmeric and salt. Preheat oven to 275°F/140°C.
(3) Heat ghee in a large frying pan, add chopped onions and fry until golden. Reduce heat, stir in meat mixture and simmer 5 minutes, then add potatoes and simmer until tender (about 30 minutes), adding a little water if necessary. Stir in remaining ingredients and remove from heat.
(4) Lay 1 phulka on a large sheet of greased aluminium foil and spread with meat. Stack another on top and continue up, finishing with a phulka on top. Wrap loosely and bake for 10 minutes one side, 10 the other. Serve cut in wedges like a cake with fresh mint or coriander chutney (page 107) and a salad of chopped tomatoes, onion, cucumber and coriander. Khad can be wrapped in foil greased and reheated in oven at a low temperature.

DHUANAAR
Smoking (of meat, vegetables)

In princely Rajasthani kitchens a technique called dhuanaar is used to simulate the deep smoky flavour imparted by the slow cooking over a fire used in the desert. ('Dhuan' means 'smoke'.) A small metal bowl with a glowing coal in it is set in the casserole with whatever dish has been cooked. A dry spice such as cloves or cinnamon is thrown over the coal and then melted ghee poured on to create smoke. The dish is closely covered until the smoke permeates the food. As few people in Western kitchens have access to glowing coals, I use a Chinese method of smoking.

Arrange the cooked meat or vegetables (it is very good with aubergines) in a heatproof dish that will fit into a steamer and still leave air space around it.

Line the base of a heavy pot with aluminium foil, and onto it put these ingredients: 10 cloves or a crumbled 1 in/2.5 cm stick of cinnamon, 6 tbsp flour, 3 tbsp brown sugar. Set the steamer above the mixture and turn the heat up high under the pan until smoke starts to appear (you might need to open a window). Immediately turn the heat down, cover the steamer tightly and leave for 10–15 minutes.

MAAS KE SULE

Smoked and marinated venison or lamb (serves 4–6 with other dishes)

The Rajasthani desert maharajahs were very fond of hunting – wild boar, deer, quail, duck, peacock – and this fondness inspired many game dishes. At the Rambaugh Palace Hotel in Jaipur, still the home of the old Maharani of Jaipur, I was told by the chef of great feasts eaten by the Rajputs in the old days. If you cannot find green papaya (which has great tenderizing properties) the venison will need a very long marination period – up to 48 hours, depending on the quality.

Marinade
1 onion, chopped
10 garlic cloves, chopped
2–3 tbsp ghee
8 fl oz/225 ml Greek yoghurt
3 tsp ground ginger
1 tsp ground cloves
1 tsp salt
1 tsp cayenne powder
1 green papaya, peeled and mashed (see note above)
2½ lb/1.25 kg venison or lamb, cut in 1½ in/4 cm cubes

Smoking ingredients (page 189)

(1) Fry the onions first and then the garlic in ghee until starting to caramelize. Purée together with all the marinade ingredients and thoroughly rub the meat with this mixture. Whisk enough water into the remaining marinade so that the meat is just covered and leave in a cool place for 14 hours (or 4 hours for lamb).
(2) Preheat the oven to 350°F/175°C/gas mark 4. Skewer the meat, leaving a little space between each lump, and cook for 30 minutes (15 for lamb), turning once and brushing with melted ghee. Smoke the meat in a steamer as mentioned on page 189 and serve with a selection of sweet chutneys (fresh mango, coriander, page 107), fresh yoghurt and some moist salad or vegetable dish, spicy potatoes cooked in yoghurt, say, and the spinach (page 108).

NOT DYING BUT DANCING

Days of the Dead in Oaxaca

Once a year, in Mexico, the dead live for a day.

In the Rufino Tamayo Museum in Oaxaca City there is a squat and malevolent stone figure wearing a skeleton mask, dated AD 200–750: 'God of Death, seated on his throne.' The Catholic priests, arriving in Mexico from Spain in the sixteenth century, took this pre-Hispanic cult of the dead and tied it to the Christian celebration of All Saints. The compromise was the Indians' Day of the Dead.

The state of Oaxaca is home to a fifth of all the native Indians in Mexico, three-quarters of whom speak Spanish as a foreign language. Teotitlán del Valle is the oldest village in the high, green Valley of Oaxaca, older than the nearby pyramids of Monte Alban, whose mountaintop was levelled to build them about 750 years before Christ.

In Teotitlán's church walls are stones from an early Zapotec temple, carved with figures once thought to be temple dancers high on the valley's magic mushrooms. Modern archaeologists disagree. They believe that the closed, dreaming Indian eyes and contorted limbs are not drugged, not dancing, but dying.

Thanks to the Spanish priests, the Indians no longer worship Xochiquetzal, goddess of beauty and love, or Xipe Totec, god of spring and the flayed, wearing his cloak of human skin to represent new growth. Instead they have Lazareth, and the Virgin of Guadeloupe; and Jesus Christ, wrapped in thorns and bleeding on the cross.

And there is no more god of death. At 3.00 p.m. on 1 November, the Dead, Los Muertos (Los Difuntos, to be more respectful), come to the Oaxaca Valley and stay for twenty-four hours. Families in every house honour their invisible guests at candlelit altars crowded with Los Difuntos' favourite dishes.

There is chocolate atole, Moctezuma's favourite, called in Oaxaca 'drink of the gods', and mezcal, drink of the people, and fruit, wild flowers, bread decorated with sugar skulls, figures of Christ and the Virgin and the local saints mixed up with plaster skeletons.

Failure to welcome your dead ancestors with the best food and drink may bring the tap of a bony finger in the middle of the night.

'You will know when Los Difuntos leave this valley,' said Hugo Santiago, a young Zapotec Indian from Teotitlán. His face was the replica of those carved into the side of the church. 'A big wind rises at

3.00 on the second and blows them on their way.'

I am not a believer in ghosts and miracles and magicians. I do not even read the horoscope page in the newspaper. But at exactly 3.00 on the afternoon of 2 November 1989, under a sky hard and blue as a stone, all the doors in Teotitlán del Valle slammed shut, the lid flew off the dustbin next to me, and a big wind rose up like a wave and blew through the village.

In Mexico, magic realism is the only kind of literature that makes perfect sense.

ONE

The thing you must remember when you eat deep-fried grasshoppers is to pull the legs off first so that the barbs on them do not cut you.

'You think them strange,' said a Zapotec friend. 'But grasshoppers are very clean – they eat only corn leaves. The grasshoppers are green first, and you boil them with epazote leaves (pigweed), when they turn red like lobsters. And then fry them in fat with garlic and salt and eat them with lime.'

Hoppers are as tasty with Mexican beer as the other local thirst-inducers – crisp salted sheets of pork rind, or garlic peanuts fried with wicked chillies no longer than a fingernail.

Oaxacans are good at things that go with beer, like mezcal, brewed in the valley from the leaves of the maguey cactus, bottled with genuine maguey worms for extra smokiness and served in little cups of green-glazed clay. A wedge of lime, a bottle of dark Dos Equis beer, and a saucer of earthy-tasting brick-red salt – those worms again, roasted and ground.

In Oaxaca this mezcal combo is so common that to order it you simply ask for 'el aperitivo'. I had it at El Capilla restaurant on the edge of Zaachila, where they serve it out of bamboo cups, and where you must arrive by 12.00 at the latest to get a table on their Thursday market day. I drank it many times in a café called El Biche Pobre, much favoured by the local police chief.

El Biche Pobre had a black velvet painting of The Last Supper on one wall. During Los Dias de Muertos they added an altar covered in marigolds and sugar skulls, as did almost all the cafés in town.

The café's speciality was a platter for two of 'botanas', Oaxacan snacks: crisp fluted cornmeal cups of creamy black-bean purée sprinkled with crumbs of fetta-like 'queso nuevo'; tiny balls of the prized local quesillo cheese – tightly wound strands like the inside of a golf ball – that flake into long meaty pieces with the texture of shredded chicken; mild green chillies stuffed with a sweet and sour mix of marinated pork and raisins; Oaxacan tamales of cornmeal and mole

negro steamed in corn husks; 'quesadillo' tortillas wrapped around fresh cheese and anisey epazote leaves.

I followed the police chief one day to Oaxaca's huge indoor Juárez Market, where the valley's famous ice-cream makers spun metal cylinders of fresh fruit and flower creams packed in salt and ice. There were flavours from avocado to rose petal and almond, and the local favourite, burnt milk with prickly pear (not a taste easily forgotten).

Juárez Market is named for Oaxaca's greatest hero, a Zapotec Indian born in a mountain village in 1806. Orphaned at three and educated by a Franciscan lay brother in Oaxaca City, Benito Juárez was three times president of Mexico.

For 500 pesos you can see the Franciscan's house where young Benito worked, its whitewashed rooms still preserved as they were in the last century. The kitchen is no different than the one in El Mesón Taquería on Oaxaca's main square. The same woodburning stove is set into a solid clay shelf, the same iron spit for meat hangs on a swinging chain over a coal fire. And if you sit long enough in a café on the square, an Indian looking not much different from Juárez will surely try to sell you the same crudely carved wooden spoons.

If, as they say, the souls of the dead come back to the house where they have lived, does Juárez come back to this place on the Days of the Dead, and does he pay the 500 pesos?

TWO

One afternoon I took the bus to Monte Alban. Mexican second-class buses, like all Third World transport, have a certain raffish charm. They run like this: you ask three people which is the bus to the market at Etla and you are given three different answers. You ask the driver of a bus with Etla written on the window in white paint if he goes to Etla. He laughs uproariously but waves you on. Inside there is a rich ripe smell of campfires and goats and boiled beans and earth.

You wait about thirty minutes while the bus fills, and as it does, someone shifts a sack of blue corn, a woman (they are all Indians) puts her basket on her head, a small child moves to its father's knee. If you have a friendly face, someone passes you a baby to hold, or a warm bowl of freshly ground chocolate, or a bag of tortillas. Or a chicken. Huge, anonymous wicker bundles are tied onto the roof with three live goats.

Then the driver gets out and washes off the old destination on the window and paints a new one.

The Monte Alban bus was dusty, of course, and very hot (the Indians believe that open windows let in a wind which may steal their soul) but comparatively civilized. It rumbled up the mountain road past houses made of twigs and mud and cardboard lashed together with straw, and fences of cactus interwoven with thorny branches.

These are the houses that Díaz built. Porfirio Díaz, anti-hero to Benito's hero, and President not long after his fellow Oaxacan, dragged the country into the Industrial Age at the expense of his people.

Thanks to Díaz, 15,000 tobacco workers died annually in northern Oaxaca and were replaced to die again – because it was cheaper to coerce poor men into slavery than to feed the ones already there. On the altar of Díaz put not water or mezcal, but Indian blood.

From the great pyramids on top of Monte Alban you could see the whole valley's grid of villages and corn fields and maguey plantations. Twelve different kinds of wildflower grew in the sunken stone court where Zapotec kings once played ball.

The long-nosed figures that dance or die on the walls of Monte Alban will sell you a rug now, woven in pre-Hispanic designs from The Alley of Columns' mosaics at nearby Mitla, or a cotton dress embroidered in the same seventeenth-century Zapotec folk patterns of vivid flowers and fabulous birds painted on the church walls at Tlacochahuaya. Oaxaca City is full of the products of their extraordinarily vivid imaginations.

In the week before Los Dias de Muertos, traditional skeleton toys started to appear in Oaxaca's markets and galleries in every imaginable guise, from skeleton wooden horses pulling skeleton carts with skeleton brides and grooms, to tiny clay skeletons sitting at word processors with crisp-packet holograms for screens.

A tall American gallery-owner told me that the Indians were excellent craftsmen holding on to centuries-old traditions with the grip of drowning men.

'Makes it interesting for us folks, o'course. But this is one of the poorest states in Mexico. Government sent teachers bilingual in Spanish and Indian languages out to the villagers so that at least they might qualify for Spanish-speaking jobs.' He shook his head.

'They threw those teachers out. Said, you're trying to destroy our culture. Mebbee so. But illiteracy runs about 30 per cent here.'

The zocalo is the heart of Oaxaca City, one of the most beautiful town squares in Mexico, full of trees and roses instead of cars, and busy with gardenia vendors, ice-cream makers on tricycles, and strolling families.

Northeast of the zocalo is the tourist side of the city: colonial buildings with ironwork balconies and classical carved doorways have become galleries, museums, hotels. Southwest, where earthquake damage in the one-storey pistachio and flesh-pink buildings is still vivid as scars, belongs to the Oaxaquenos. Wild West swing-doors open into mezcal cantinas from *Under the Volcano*, and small dark men sit inside,

raucous or silent according to their nature. Women are not welcome in the cantinas. They go instead to fill their baskets in shops selling fifty kinds of seeds and chillies for the rich sauces called moles. There are mills here that will grind seeds into moles for you, or turn raw corn into tortilla 'masa', and cocoa beans into chocolate.

At the chocolate grinders you can choose what percentage of raw sugar and cinnamon bark you want ground with your cocoa beans, the prices per kilo of spice, sugar and bean scrawled on the sacks. Senora wants to make mole negro? More chocolate, more cinnamon, less sugar. You want drinking chocolate? And what quality – the 5000 pesos a kilo or the 7000? The vendor scoops up his favourite blend, still soft from the grinder, and passes it to you to taste in a twist of brown paper.

Before Los Dias de Muertos, these streets were packed with shoppers and the pawnshops were packed as well – to pay for the feast. Juárez Market is for the city shoppers; the open Indian market, one of the largest of its kind in Mexico, is on the wrong side of the tracks next to the second-class bus station. It is a much bigger version of the Indian markets that happen each day in a different village all over the valley.

In the market you could buy every ingredient from the start of a day to its end. Ladies with flat panniers as big as tabletops on their heads patrolled the aisles, some with bouquets of onions and garlic, others with mounds of grasshoppers. One aisle was devoted to candles for the Days of the Dead, wrapped in silver and gold paper, or painted with images of the Virgin. A woman sat behind three sacks of corn – one of blue corn, one of yellow, one of white. Another woman brushed past with an armful of greenery, leaving behind the pepper-and-clove scent of fresh basil. Under a white sheet tied to a pick-up truck four women kept up a constant flow of conversation while they filled tortillas and rolled tamales. A young girl had her baby wrapped in a woven rebozo under one arm while she sold the big Oaxacan tortillas called clayudas from a basket over her other. If you stopped for an instant you were in someone's way, run over by a pig tied by one leg to a string, pecked by a chicken.

A woman behind a counter of fresh cheeses would lean out to hand you a rolled cheese the size of a marble. Señora – take this. Señora, it is good is it not? Another woman would break off a piece of chocolate, gritty with sugar and cinnamon. Señora, you want chillies for mole? You want oranges for the altar? Marigolds?

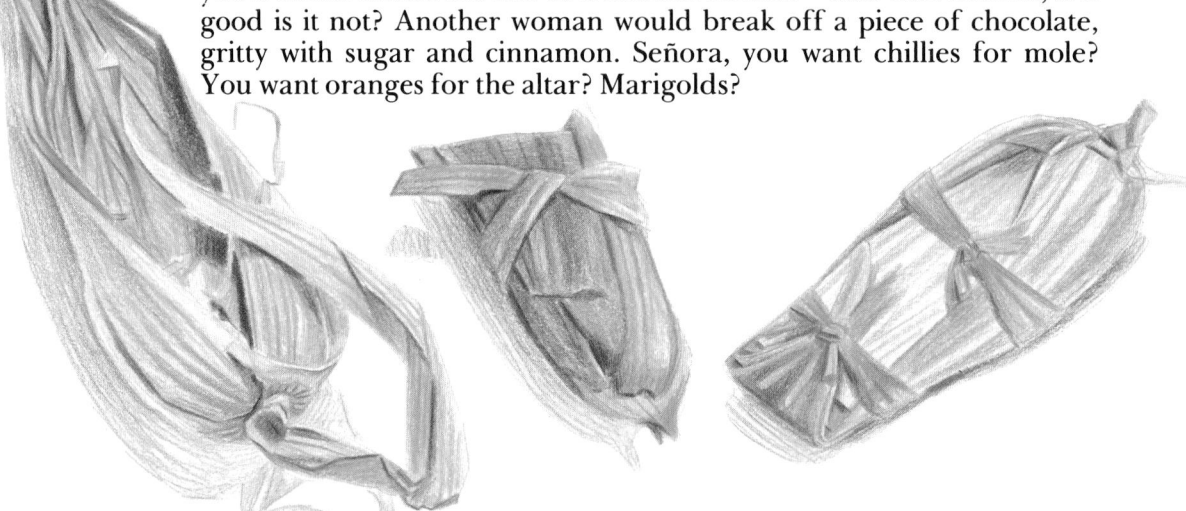

For the Days of the Dead, there were aisles of bread in the shape of people (souls), or loaves of every size with skulls and skeletons on them.

At the centre of the market, like the eye of a hurricane, were the little cafeterias called fondas painted in carnival colours. Indian men who had been unloading goods all morning sat in them drinking beer and eating chorizo and red-stained pork steak with black-bean purée.

I had a cup of chocolate at one turquoise fonda and it came with a brioche, 'Bread of the Dead', a sugar skull embedded in the crust. On the ground an old Indian man bit into a tortilla filled with grasshoppers.

On the night of 31 October, in two small cemeteries of a slummy Oaxaca suburb called XoXo, the people whose ancestors were buried there sat up all night to welcome their dead back. The air was thick with burning copal incense; there were crosses shaped from marigold petals on graves, tombs where candles glowed out of skulls and others with massed banks of lilies, gladioli, marigolds and coxcombs. Inside a ruined roofless church (1684 carved in its old stones) filled with tombs a radio sang out Mexican pop tunes.

'Welcome to our village,' said a man clutching a bottle of mezcal.

THREE

Hugo Santiago's sister Zoila invited my friend and I to spend the Days of the Dead in Teotitlán. We met her at 7.00 a.m., in Teotitlán's tiny market, next to a burro weighed down with the sugar cane used to make arches over the altars.

That morning we made tamales: softening corn leaves in warm water, squeezing each tortilla flat in a wooden press, folding the tortilla into the corn leaves with a spoonful of puréed chillies and some turkey and pork meat.

The tamales were steamed twenty at a time in a tall pot over an open wood fire in the courtyard.

'How often do you make these?' I asked.

'Only for fiestas,' said Zoila. 'Because they take so long. That is why Hugo's wife helps. It goes faster when we work together.'

In the afternoon we played a game called lotería, rather like bingo, using green walnuts and dried corn as money.

'I think they must be starving by now, our Dead,' said Hugo.

At three in the afternoon fireworks went off in the village and the church bells begin to ring. They would ring without ceasing for the next twenty-four hours. Inside the church there was an old human skull on the altar, and a clock that played an electronic version of 'No Place Like Home'. Zoila looked up. 'That is the signal that They have come. We can eat now.'

When we had finished the tamales, Zoila's husband killed a turkey for mole negro. Xenon was a big man, stout from beer drinking, without the fine Zapotec features. 'You want to watch?' he asked.

Two people held the turkey's legs. It made worried noises. Xenon stretched out its neck and plucked the throat of feathers. Then he stabbed the knife quickly into the skin and the blood squirted out into a little saucer while the turkey struggled and squawked. Xenon looked over at me and grinned. When the last bit of blood had dripped out, he cut off the turkey's head and Zoila slipped the congealed blood into a pot of boiling water, lifted it out in a piece, sliced it up and passed it round. The warm blood tasted just like fried liver.

That night we visited their ancestors' homes, fording a stream through the village and skirting tethered burros.

Some of the original adobe houses were buried behind centuries of additions, with walls built from the stones of old Zapotec temples that still had old stela carvings in them – worn now like the imprint on a well-used bar of soap.

To every house we took three 'pan de muertos' for each dead ancestor, a two-foot candle, chocolate atole, and bouquets of the wild 'flowers of the dead' – smelling sweetly of beeswax and rotting flesh.

We walked through gates in adobe walls, crossed cobbled yards where scarlet poinsettias bloomed next to old backstrap looms, and stepped into long rooms flickering with candlelight.

Visitors do not greet their hosts at first, but go to the altar, kneel and kiss it and light a candle, then add their bread offering to the piles.

It is traditional to have two big glasses of mezcal and a bottle of beer in each house, followed by three pan de muertos, and a cup of chocolate. Mezcal is hallucinatory as well as alcoholic. At midnight, after the fourth house, I studied three women with plaits to their waists and the faces of Aztec goddesses, slant-ing-eyed and inscrutable through the clouds of incense and the eerie light from a 25-watt bulb. I wondered what they whispered in their soft Zapotec

– stories of human sacrifice and long-lost Zapotec warriors?

Zoila noticed my interest. 'We usually talk about the weather.'

We slept on the floor, on rugs woven with Zapotec designs, with more rugs to cover us, and listened to the roar and buzz of country noises, and the distant laughter of people still going from house to house.

The next day Zoila offered us a thick, foaming drink of chocolate atole for breakfast. The Oaxaca Valley is full of chocolate makers, but only three other villages besides Teotitlán know the secret of making the chocolate for atole. Cocoa beans aged under earth for three months are dug up and washed, buried again for another three months, then ground with wheat, rice and cinnamon. That is not the end of it.

The atole chocolate must be kneaded with water until it is butter smooth, then whisked in a deep earthen bowl with a carved wooden beater, before it is beaten and scooped into another bowl as it froths.

Finally the chocolate froth is mixed with atole, the liquid that Indians boil up from corn dough – stirring in great ladles of froth until the drink rises up like a liquid soufflé. Zoila's skill at it came from her grandmother, who was known as 'Mother Chocolate'.

'But it took *hours*,' I said to Zoila.

'Yes,' she said. 'And if it did not, how would you know it was for a feast?'

At dusk, when the Dead had left, I walked to the cemetery with Hugo.

There was a warm, low November sun lighting the wooden crosses in the cemetery. Sliced oranges for the Dead lay open on tombs. Families sat around their ancestral plots eating and drinking mezcal and beer and chatting with their friends. From the little church came the high, wild beat of a Mexican brass band – fast and stirring and slightly out of tune – broken by a husky man's voice singing to a lost relative.

'We can sit on this grave that nobody is using,' said Hugo.

He was trying to produce a phonetic dictionary of Zapotec (the language is not a written one) so that he could tell potential rug importers what colours to ask for.

'You see, the old people here use wild flowers and weeds for dyes which do not seem to have any English or Spanish names. I must go directly to their botanical ones instead.'

Zapotec is an easy language in some ways, but many words have double meanings. Foreigners know 'Guelaguetza' as the name for the festival where Zapotec men in towering feathered headdresses perform a dance representing the Spanish conquest of Mexico.

'But that is not all it means,' said Hugo. 'It really refers to the whole system of mutual help which results in a big party that pays everyone back for their offerings.'

'Say you have a christening, or a new house, and I have four chickens. I might give you a chicken as a "guelaguetza". You will make a note to pay me back when you have something extra and I am in need.'

'So the guelaguetza is both the party and something you give to people who have less than you?'

'More than that. You might save up for a future christening by giving things away now.'

My friend and I left Hugo with his family and went to catch the last bus back to Oaxaca. Villagers were still arriving with baskets of food and games for the children and candles to light the graves. Outside the cemetery gate a man in a Batman T-shirt had set up a stall selling beer and mezcal. Behind his head a two-thousand-year-old stela reflected his profile, faithful as any mirror.

The Zapotec name for Teotitlán means 'Under the Stone', and refers to the mountain against which the village is pressed. Teotitlán is a later name given by the Nawatl people; it means 'The Place of Gods'.

They say that the Indians and their culture are dying out. Between 1976 and 1980, 94,000 people moved out of Oaxaca because of the lack of industry. When we bury our dead, they stay buried. But once a year, in Mexico, the dead get up to dance.

RECIPES

Breakfast on the first Day of the Dead: the brioches called pan de muertos, dipped in hot, cinnamony chocolate; then two bowls each, one of the thick maize drink called atole, the other of delicate turkey broth. A fresh green leaf of hoja santa had been placed in the soup bowl, and its strange flavour welled up with the hot liquid. With the broth, a spicy purée of roasted chillies, and a lace-edged embroidered cloth full of the huge, Oaxacan corn tortillas called clayudas.

A girl was sent to the local mill to buy freshly ground corn dough masa that is the basis of tortillas – and even of the old, old Mexican drink called atole. Little balls of the dough were flattened in a wooden press, filled with shredded turkey and pork, anointed with mild chilli sauce, and wrapped in leaves to be steamed over a fire in the courtyard. When the Dead arrived at 3.00, we toasted them with mezcal and chasers of Coronita beer, sharpened by licks of brick-red maguey-worm salt.

A few tamales were put on the altar for the Dead and we ate the rest in a rush, hungry from the long wait.

That night, more chocolate – and pan de muertos scented with orange-flower, and the next day a huge pot of turkey simmered in the mole negro seasoned with more than twenty-six seeds and spices, including bitter chocolate. In other homes people would finish the meal with the strange, ancient-tasting nicoatole, an almond and maize set custard, or with pumpkins simmered in honey, or with medlars, a fruit that is eaten when rotten and has a haunting chocolate flavour.

CHOCOLATE EN AGUA ESTILO OAXAQUENO

Oaxacan-style hot chocolate

This is a whiff of the warm chocolate smells that float in the back streets of Oaxaca. It comes from *Tradiciones Gastronómicas Oaxaquenas*, local recipes put together by Ana Maria Guzmán in Oaxaca in 1982. Chocolate in Oaxaca is whisked with hand-turned wooden beaters in green-glazed round-bottomed jugs.

(to serve 8)
4 oz/125 g bitter chocolate
½ oz/15 g ground cinnamon
½ oz/15 g ground almonds
6 oz/180 g light muscovado sugar

Add cold water to these ingredients to make a thin cream and heat over medium-low heat, stirring constantly until the chocolate and sugar dissolve. Whisk with a Mexican molinillo beater (or in a blender) until frothy.

PAN DE YEMA OR DE MUERTOS

Sweet egg brioche or Bread of the Dead (makes 2 medium loaves or 4–6 rolls)

A bread with a light, melting texture and sweet smell. It comes in small rolls to dip in chocolate or cinnamon coffee at the cafés in Oaxaca's Saturday market, or in huge loaves to offer on November altars. Pan de muertos has 2 tbsp orange-flower water, some grated orange zest, and ground aniseed to taste added to it. Both are stuck with sugarpaste skulls and pretty 'lost soul' faces bought in packets from the market during the Days of the Dead.

¾ oz/20 g fresh yeast (or equivalent dried)
1¼ lbs/600 g plain white flour

4 oz/125 g white sugar
4 oz/125 g unsalted butter, softened and cut in small pieces
¼ tsp salt
7 egg yolks (save a little for the glaze) and 2 whole eggs

(1) Dissolve yeast in half a teacup lukewarm water, and mix in a little of the flour to form a soft, loose dough. Cover tightly and leave in a warm place for 1 hour.

(2) Put the remaining flour in a large bowl, make a well in the centre, and into it put all the remaining ingredients, including the yeast batter. Mix it roughly into a firm (but sticky) dough and turn out onto a well-floured surface, kneading, lifting it and throwing it hard on the surface – until it starts to form air bubbles. Put in a bowl, cover with plastic film and leave in a warm place.

(3) When the dough has doubled (2–3 hours), divide into balls, depending on what size you want. Knead each ball of dough, folding them over and pressing down with the heels of your hands until air bubbles form again (about 5–10 minutes), and put balls into well-greased baking tins, seam side down. Cover with a cloth and leave again to double in size. Preheat oven to 275°F/140°C/gas mark 1.

(4) Cut a shallow slice across each loaf to allow them to expand, brush with beaten egg yolk, and bake for 30–40 minutes, or until they sound hollow when tapped.

Decorate the breads with sugarpaste faces and skulls, or with skull-shaped pieces of dough stuck onto the bread with beaten egg just before baking.

Don't throw stale bread out. It has a delicious taste and texture when toasted. Wonderful hot for breakfast with honey.

CAFÉ DE OLLA
Mexican cinnamon coffee in a clay pot

Heated in the same narrow-necked clay pot as Mexican chocolate and served in little glazed earthenware cups.

6 tbsp freshly ground coffee
3 cloves
1 cinnamon stick
raw brown sugar to taste (try muscovado)

Bring about 1¾ pt/1 l water to a boil. Add the cinnamon, and sugar to taste. Stir in the coffee, just until dissolved, and remove from heat. Leave to infuse for 3 minutes and strain into cups. Save any leftover coffee to make ice-cream.

HIGADITOS
Savoury egg mousse in broth (serves 8)

Traditional breakfast in Teotitlán for the second Day of the Dead – a recipe more curious than practical. Higaditos, an Indian word for heart and lungs, was once made with these organs from chicken or turkey. Now poultry broth is flavoured with tomatoes, sweet peppers, and the 'holy' herb, yerba santa, and while the broth is simmering, beaten eggs and shredded meat are poured in and gently pressed to one side to form a soft mousse. Each person is served a scoop of this in a ladleful of broth, and a spoonful of roasted chillies to spice it. With this round eggy cakes called marquesote and bowls of chocolate atole whipped to a froth.

● Yerba santa (or hoja santa/holy leaf) – Piper Sanctum, a member of the black pepper family. The large, soft leaves of this plant are used extensively in Oaxaca,

especially among the Indians. Yerba santa is almost impossible to find outside Mexico; it is also difficult to reproduce its complex spicy aniseed flavour, although some books suggest using a big handful of feathery fennel tops with ½ tsp black pepper to every 2 yerba santa leaves in a recipe.

CORN TORTILLAS

(about 15–16 oz/500 g dough makes 16 small or 12 large tortillas)

Tortillas come wrapped in a napkin to every meal, whether feast or fast, in Mexico. The same dough fried crisp becomes a tostada; when enriched with lard and pressed into an oval with fluted edges it is a memelita. Tortilla dough is made from ground large-kernelled corn, masa, bought fresh from the market or the local village mill. I have substituted a dough using masa harina* – a good nutty-flavoured alternative.

Mix 8 oz/250 g/1¾ cups masa harina with 11–12 fl oz/330–360 ml hot water and knead it until it forms a soft (but not sticky) dough – add more flour or water if necessary. Cover in plastic and leave for 30 minutes.

When ready to cook, roll the dough into 12–16 little balls and cover in plastic. Heat a heavy frying pan over medium heat. (The Zapotecs use a curved terracotta dish and cook the tortillas on the convex side.) Flatten each ball slightly between your hands, pat lightly with flour and place between 2 sheets of plastic. Flatten to about ¹⁄₁₆ in/0.25 cm thick in a tortilla press, if you have one, or under a wooden board. The thinner they are, the better, but more difficult to peel off the plastic.

Peel off the plastic carefully and cook the tortillas until their edges pull away from the pan (about 20–30 seconds), flip and cook reverse side until brown spots appear underneath (about 1 minute). Flip again for another 20–30 seconds – they will puff up – and wrap in a clean towel.

*Quaker makes a good brand. Do not substitute anything called cornmeal, cornflour, etc. – they are not the same thing.

To make quesadillas from tortillas, lay a few epazote†, basil or fennel leaves on a cooked tortilla, sprinkle over a mixture of fetta and mozzarella cheese (Oaxacans would use their quesillo cheese, with its meaty flavour), fold over, pinch the edges, and brown in hot oil.

†Epazote: Chenopodium ambrosioides, a member of a large family of succulent weeds; European cousins are much milder than those found in Mexico and the Americas. The pungent jagged leaf is also known as Mexican tea, wormseed, pigweed, and is a favourite flavouring for beans, quesadillas and moles in Oaxaca. Unfortunately there is no substitute for its pungent flavour (just as well, some would say). Use coriander or fresh fennel leaves instead.

TOSTADAS
Crisp-fried tortillas

Homemade tortilla chips have a harder crunch. To fry tortillas crisply, they need to be dried out (cooked tortillas left uncovered for an hour will do). The oil must be evenly hot (360°F/180°C/gas mark 4 – or when a piece of bread fries in 50 seconds) or the tortillas will be greasy. Fry until pale gold, drain on kitchen paper and sprinkle with salt, herbs (oregano and thyme are good) and ground chillies. Dip them into refried beans and new cheese, crumble them and use as a topping for stews.

TAMALES
Spiced corn dough steamed in leaves

Tamale-making should never be a solitary occupation. It is a real elbows-on-the-table, bottle-of-smoky-mezcal-in-the-hand sort of meal.

In Oaxaca I had two kinds of tamales: the city version – steamed corn dough filled with mole negro and shredded chicken (or sometimes fresh pineapple) emerging from its leaves like a fluffy cornbread; and the Zapotec – flattened corn tortilla folded to hold shredded turkey and pork and a spoonful of anise-flavoured sauce, and steamed in leaves more like an exotic ravioli dumpling. The Zapotec takes slightly longer to make, as tortillas must be flattened first, but less time to cook.

I use the inexpensive Chinese bamboo steamer baskets.

Be careful when handling chillies. Both oil from the skin (very hard to remove) and cooking fumes can hurt eyes and skin.

TAMALES/ZAPOTEC VERSION
(makes 16 small tamales)

16 dried corn husks
4–8 dried guajillos – a mildly hot, smoky chilli –
or other large dried red chillies and 2 large peeled tomatoes, seeded
5 yerba santa leaves, or a big handful of feathery fennel tops,
or handful fresh coriander
12–14 fl oz/360–400 ml good homemade chicken stock
1–2 sweet red peppers (optional)*
about 1¼ lb/750 g tortilla dough
salt to taste
shredded cooked flesh from ½ small free-range chicken (or
cooked turkey or pork)

(1) Submerge the corn husks in boiling water, weighting them with something heavy, and leave for several hours to soften.
(2) Seed and core chillies and toast on a dry pan or griddle until blackened and fragrant (but not burnt). Cover in boiling water and leave to soften for an hour. Drain and purée the chillies with herbs, stock, and just enough dough to make a thick sauce (about 4–6 oz/125–180g). Salt well.
  *Because it is impossible to get the smoky-flavoured Oaxacan chillies in Britain, I add grilled sweet red peppers – for flavour rather than authenticity.
(3) Follow tortilla recipe (page 205), flatten the dough, spoon on some sauce and a little chicken, fold in three and lay seam side down on softened corn husks. Fold the husk over to enclose the dough in an envelope, and tie.
(4) Line a large steamer with extra leaves, with a few air holes to prevent too much condensation. Lay the tamales around the edges, and steam for about 30 minutes, or until the leaves come away without sticking.

TAMALES/OAXACA CITY VERSION
(makes about 12)

12 cornhusks
Dough
9 oz/280 g masa harina
5 oz/150 g lard
1 tsp baking powder
½ tsp salt
11 fl oz/330 ml chicken stock
shredded cooked flesh from ½ free-range chicken
(or equivalent of turkey, pork, or picadillo)
6–9 fl oz/180–250 ml mole negro sauce

(1) Soften corn husks as in previous recipe. Purée the dough mixture with a spoonful of the mole sauce, adding more stock if necessary – a small lump of dough should float in cold water. Chill for 30 minutes.
(2) Line a large steamer with leaves, as previous recipe. Spread 3–4 tbsp of dough onto each corn husk, flattening the dough slightly. Add 2 tbsp of meat and a spoonful or two of sauce, wrapping the dough round to cover. Fold and tie the

husks quite loosely, as they need room to expand. Stack them loosely around the steamer, and steam for 1–1 ½ hours, until the leaf comes away cleanly.

Oaxacan tamales are also good made with the spicy meat 'picadillo' (page 211). Crush 3 large peeled tomatoes with the meat and then use as for the mole and chicken.

For breakfast masa dough is often steamed with shredded fresh pineapple instead of meat. You could try any variations – oranges, mango and chicken, raisins and ground pork.

MOLE NEGRO OAXAQUENO/OAXACAN BLACK MOLE
(serves 12–15)

Only in Mexico can one find the exotic smoky-tasting chillies necessary to make a true Oaxacan mole. Even in the USA some Oaxacan chillies are unheard of. And Mexican chocolate too is unique – ground with almonds, cinnamon and sugar. The substitutes I have suggested for the chillies change the character of this dish. It is still very good, a feast in itself – but it is not the same. So why cook mole negro at all outside Mexico? For the complexity of flavours, and to remember that in Oaxaca a dish that does not take time is not a feast.

10–12 lb/5–6 kg free-range turkey or
2 large free-range chickens (with gizzards),
cut in approx 4 in/10 cm pieces
2 onions, quartered
4 garlic cloves, halved
1 tbsp peppercorns
2 tsp dried oregano
3 large tomatoes, skinned, or 1 14 fl oz/400 ml tin tomatoes, drained
2½ oz/75 g Mexican chocolate, or bitter cooking chocolate
1 oz/30 g each raw almonds, walnuts, shelled pumpkin seeds,
sesame seeds (plus extra for garnish), toasted
1 in/2.5 cm cinnamon stick, ½ tsp cumin seeds, ½ tsp aniseed,
4 cloves, 8 peppercorns, dry-fried until fragrant, and ground
7 oz/200 g dried red chilhuacle (or ancho) chillies,
4 oz/125 g dried mulato negro chillies
or
10–15 large dried red chillies plus
1 tsp good chilli powder (with luck it will have some of
the smoky chillies in it)
about 6–8 tbsp vegetable oil or lard
1 onion, coarsely chopped
2–3 oz/60–90 g raisins or large stoned prunes
3 slices of dry pan de yema (or dry French bread)
salt to taste
4–6 tbsp sugar
2 avocado leaves (or bay leaves)

(1) Cut off the turkey neck and put in a large pan with the least meaty part of the back and all the innards (save the liver, to fry and eat separately). Cover with 5¼ pt/3 l cold water, bring slowly to the boil, skim, and add the onion, garlic, pepper and oregano. Simmer half-covered for 1½ hours.

(2) Crush the chocolate roughly and add to the tomatoes, toasted nuts, seeds and spices.

(3) Carefully seed and core the chillies, reserving about 2 tsp of their seeds. Chop or tear them into pieces, cover in boiling water and leave for 1 hour to soften.

(4) Heat the oil over medium heat in a large pan and brown the turkey pieces well on all sides. Set aside. Drain the chillies and fry on both sides in the oil until blackened and fragrant. Lift out with a slotted spoon. Add the onions to the pan, stirring until softened, then raisins, cooking until they are brown and puffed. Lift out with a slotted spoon and add to the tomatoes. Fry the bread until browned, add chilli seeds and continue cooking until bread is blackened but not charred on both sides (you may need more fat). Crush the bread and add to the tomatoes.

(5) Purée chillies (and chilli powder, if using) with about ¾ pt/400 ml turkey stock. Purée the tomato mixture with enough stock to make a smooth cream, sieve.

(6) Pour off almost all the fat, add the chillies to the pan and stir over high heat until dark and thickened. Add the tomato mixture and cook until it thickens as well, then pour in 1¾ pt/1 l stock and taste for sugar and salt. Add the turkey and avocado leaves and simmer gently, half-covered, for about an hour – or until the turkey is tender to a fork.

Serve the turkey mole in a big dish scattered with toasted sesame seeds and nuts, and soak up the juices with fresh corn tortillas.

It is worth making this the day before, since this will make the flavour much deeper and richer.

Always save some mole sauce and freeze to make tamales (page 206).

Fiestas in Oaxaca

Markets, especially during the build-up to the Days of the Dead, are an excuse for oil-drum braziers to be set up selling memelitas and tostadas and quesadillas; with hand-cranked fruit ices afterwards (especially good at the fondas in the Tlacolula market) – some of the best in the world. You might buy a round of cheese wrapped in sisal from one of tens of cheese stalls, and eat it with freshly made salsa from the next stall; or a bowl of the inevitable black beans cooked in clay pots.

Lining the road to the cemetery in XoXo was one stall after another selling freshly peeled and sliced fruit, rice cooked with plantains, stuffed chillies – to see the people through the long, candlelit night.

SALSA CAMPESINA
Country-style salsa

Mix together the following ingredients, leave for an hour for flavours to blend, and add the avocado just before serving (good with tortillas, cheese, grilled meats and fish):

1 lb/500 g ripe tomatoes, seeded and finely chopped
1 onion, peeled and finely chopped
3–5 fresh green chillies, seeded and finely chopped
1 handful of fresh coriander leaves, washed and chopped
juice of 1 lemon
a few sprigs of fresh oregano, chopped (or ½ tsp dried)
salt to taste
1 small avocado, chopped

SALSA OAXAQUENA
Oaxacan-style sauce

A classic smoky-flavoured sauce to serve with anything from roasted meats to sliced avocado or stuffed chillies (page 211). If you can't find the listed ingredients, follow instructions for the alternative salsa.

1 lb/500 g ripe tomatoes
3 dried 'pasillas' chillies
2 garlic cloves, unpeeled
½ onion, finely chopped
small handful fresh coriander, chopped

(1) If you can find really tasty fresh tomatoes, place them on a sheet of aluminium foil and roast them under a very hot grill for 12–15 minutes until they blacken and give off juice. Peel and mash the tomatoes with their juices.
(2) Roast the chillies and garlic in a dry frying pan until they start to burn. Peel the garlic and finely chop. Shred the chillies, discarding their seeds, and mix with tomatoes and garlic. If the sauce is very liquid, bubble it for a few minutes in a frying pan until it reduces. Mix with coriander and onions and salt to taste.

FRIJOLES DE LA OLLA
Beans boiled in a clay pot (serves 6 as a side dish)

It isn't necessary to cook these in an earthenware pot, although it does add an extra depth to their flavour. In Oaxaca this would always be made with lovely shiny black beans, very graphic against the toppings of white cheese and green coriander. The black beans I have cooked in Britain taste good, but do not seem to keep their colour.

12 oz/350 g black, pinto or kidney beans
1 large onion stuck with 8 cloves
4 tbsp lard, bacon drippings or vegetable oil
1½ tsp salt
2 epazote leaves, or big handful finely chopped
feathery tops of fennel bulb
1 tsp coarsely ground black pepper

Toppings
crumbled queso nuevo (or fetta cheese), chopped fresh coriander,
shredded pickled jalapeno chillies, grilled spring onions*

(1) Pick out any small stones or grub-eaten beans. Cover the beans in boiling water, bring back to the boil and boil hard for 5 minutes. Let stand for 2 hours and drain.
(2) Pour over 2¾ pt/1.6 l boiling water, add the onion and fat and bring to a very gentle boil. Simmer over low heat for 1–2 hours, or until tender. Just before the end of cooking, add the herbs and salt. Discard the onion, purée a cup of the beans with their liquid and stir back into them to thicken. Serve in little bowls topped with the cheese and herbs.
  *A delicious side dish often served in Oaxaca was whole green/spring onions that had been brushed with oil and then char-grilled until slightly blackened around the edges – to dip in coarse salt.
  Black beans are served in Oaxaca with scrambled eggs, chillies and tomatoes as a rustic breakfast.

ENFRIJOLADAS
Refried beans (serves 4–6 as a side dish)
Not the stiff, boring paste I have been served in bad Mexican restaurants, but a creamy purée – ideal for filling crisp tostadas or rolling into tortillas.

3 big cups (¹/₂ previous recipe) boiled beans
2 tbsp lard, bacon drippings or vegetable oil
1 onion, finely chopped
6 oz/180 g uncooked chorizo (or other spicy sausage),
skinned and crumbled
12–14 fl oz/360–400 ml good homemade stock
salt to taste
Toppings
fresh cheese (fetta, queso nuevo) to crumble on top,
chopped fresh coriander, deep-fried tortilla chips

Purée the black beans to a thick cream with a little stock. Heat the fat in a frying pan and fry the onion until soft, add the chorizo and brown well. Stir in the beans, and slowly add enough liquid to make a thick purée with the texture of whipped potatoes. Serve immediately with the toppings, or use to fill memelitas, tostadas, tortillas.

ARROZ CON PLATANO
Rice with plantains (serves 6)
Many times we ate at a plain family restaurant in an open courtyard where parrots shrieked in the trees and lizards clambered over warm stones. It was at Cabrera 47, south of the zocalo, and it served only a comida corrida (meal of the day). There were always botanas (snacks) to start, and the lovely cinnamony bread rolls that are called bolillos, and this lovely rice, simmered in broth from yesterday's meat, with whatever was the main course. Wonderful with mole.

10 oz/300 g long-grained rice
4 tbsp lard or vegetable oil
2 medium onions, finely chopped
1 cinnamon stick, slightly broken up
about 1³/₄ pt/1 l good homemade stock, heated to boiling
1¹/₂ tsp salt (depending on the saltiness of the stock)
1 large plantain, sliced thinly crosswise
handful of fresh coriander, coarsely chopped

(1) Wash the rice under cold running water until the water runs clear, cover in water and leave to soak for 15 minutes.
(2) Heat 3 tbsp fat in a saucepan and cook the onions and cinnamon in it until the onions are golden. Add the rice, drained, and continue cooking and stirring for another 5 minutes. Pour in 9 fl oz/250 ml water and cook until the rice absorbs it. Add salt and hot stock, cover tightly, and cook until the rice grains are soft and separate (about 10 minutes). In the meantime, cook the plantain over low heat in the remaining fat until it is well browned and tender. When the rice is cooked, leave it off the heat for another 10 minutes, then toss lightly with plantain and coriander.

CHILLIES RELLENOS
Stuffed chillies (serves 6–8)

Large mildly hot chillies are stuffed, deep fried, and sold as snacks in Oaxaca. They can be quickly prepared – stuffed with about 1 lb/500 g fresh crumbly cheese, or with refried beans – or they can be more elaborate, with the spicy meat mixture called picadillo (even this can be prepared well ahead of time and frozen in batches).

Oaxacan cooks use fresh chillies called poblano. When these or equivalent mildly hot chillies are unavailable, I use instead the smallest sweet peppers, adding 6–10 toasted hot dried chillies to the stuffing. A compromise, but a good one.

If you are short of time, omit the batter and deep-frying and just heat the peppers in the oven.

12 fresh chillies poblanos (or very small green peppers)

Picadillo
4 cloves, 1 cinnamon stick, roasted in a pan until fragrant and ground
2 tbsp lard or vegetable oil
1 medium onion, 4 garlic cloves, finely chopped
1 lb/500 g loin of pork, coarsely ground
2 oz/60 g each of pine nuts, flaked almonds (toasted), raisins and capers
1 lb/500 g tomatoes, skinned and chopped (or tinned, drained)
handful of black olives, chopped
1 tbsp sugar
1 tsp salt, or to taste
(6–10 small dried red chillies, seeded and toasted,
if using green peppers instead of poblanos)

To fry
1 egg, separated
4 oz/125 g flour sifted with ½ tsp salt
1 tbsp oil
just over ¼ pt/150 ml water
vegetable oil for deep-frying
18 fl oz/500 ml homemade tomato sauce (optional)

(1) Rub the chillies (or peppers) with oil and roast them over a flame or under a hot grill until the skins blacken. Peel them, leaving their stems on, and split them as little as possible down one side, just enough to empty the seeds. Cover in vinegar (not necessary for sweet peppers) and leave while you make the picadillo.
(2) Heat 2 tbsp fat in a frying pan, cook onion and garlic in it until they are transparent, then add meat and spices and continue cooking, stirring occasionally, until it is well browned. Drain off any excess fat, saving 2 tbsp in a separate saucepan.
(3) Heat reserved fat and fry nuts and raisins in it until golden. Stir in the capers, tomatoes, olives, sugar, and salt to taste, simmering down a little. Add meat and continue cooking and stirring until it is very thick. You may want to add a splash of vinegar to sharpen it.
(4) Drain the chillies and dry well. Stuff them with just enough picadillo (or plain cheese) so they can be lifted without spilling. Beat together the eggs, flour, salt, oil and water. Beat the egg white stiff and fold into the flour. Heat the oil until a piece of bread browns in 50 seconds, dip the chillies in batter and fry in the oil until very brown, a few at a time. Keep them warm. Serve with a few spoonfuls of warmed tomato sauce on each plate.

NIEVE DE LECHE QUEMADA
'Burnt' milk and brown sugar ice-cream (makes about 4 pints)

An intriguing smoky ice-cream, the most traditional in Oaxaca, often made with chunks of fresh prickly-pear in the city's famous 'nieve' (literally, 'snow') stalls. Theirs is the old-fashioned ice-cream – spun in tin cannisters packed with ice and salt – close to coarse Italian granita in texture. This recipe and the following one are based on some in Ana Maria Guzmán's book.

3½ pt/2 l whole milk
10 oz/300 g light muscovado (or other raw brown sugar)
3 cinnamon sticks

(1) Keep 1 large cup of milk aside and bring the rest to a rapid boil, skimming off any skin, until it smells strongly smoky and burnt – the milk should be burning on the bottom. Pour in the remaining milk, heated to boiling, with the sugar and cinnamon, and continue simmering for another 15 minutes. Strain through a sieve and allow to cool.

(2) Poor the cool milk into 2-pint/1 l cannisters and freeze, beating often, until the ice-cream holds its shape on a spoon. About an hour before serving, beat once more very hard to lighten it. Although less than traditional, I like this with dark chocolate grated over the top.

NIEVE DE LIMON VERDE
Fresh lime water ice (makes 3½–4 pt/2 l)

A lovely fresh palest-green ice. Serve it in hollowed-out lime shells with sliced strawberries.

juice and grated zest from 7 fresh limes
1¾ pt/1 l water
1 lb/500 g white sugar

Boil together the lime juice, water and sugar until the sugar is dissolved. Pour this over the lime zest, and leave to reach room temperature, then strain through a fine sieve. Continue as in previous recipe, making sure to beat very hard in last hour – it will be quite fluffy then (especially if you use a food processor).

VOICES OF CHRISTMAS PAST

—

*In Provence, Armagnac
and Canada*

· MARZIPAN · EEL ·

'Christmas is finished, man. What is it anyway – just an
excuse to spend, spend, spend.'
boy in Oxford Street, London, 1989

'Christmas, farewell; thy days I fear
And merry days are done:
So they may keep feasts all the year,
Our Saviour shall have none.'
History of the Rebellion, *1661*

Well, you know that Robert was a foundling? He was born in the north, but no
one knew his family and he could not even speak when the priest found him. So
the priest said, 'I will call you Robert Antilogus.' Antilogus being Latin for
'against language', you see.

When we were hiding him on our farm down here, when he was a member of
the Resistance during the war . . . well, he had no customs of his own, no
memories. All his Christmas memories start with our Provençal ones, with Le
Gros Souper on Christmas Eve, with our little carved santon figures, our thirteen
desserts, our vin d'orange – which I smuggled out to him where he hid in the
straw because we had too many German supporters hereabouts for him to join us
inside. He was very handsome, this Antilogus, very charmant, although he would
never go to church, not then, not now.

Paulette Antilogus, *farmer's wife, Vaison la Romaine, France*

After the midnight mass on Christmas Eve there are oysters and little sausages
grilled on the fire – you take a cool slippery oyster and then a bite of hot smoky
sausage and then another oyster.

Then what some call La Daube de la Saint-André, beef simmered for days in
red wine. I make mine thus: I do not brown the meat first, as they do further
towards the Pyrenees, because I use a very old recipe. I line a big pot of
earthenware with fatty pork rind, skin side down. Then a base of finely sliced
shallots, garlic, parsley, a layer of beef cut in chunks. I salt and pepper it well,
moisten it with some good local Madiran wine, and make another layer of
ground fatty pork, chopped onions, meat, etc., always being sure to season and
moisten it well with wine. I tuck in a bouquet garni, and a couple of cloves, and
the final layer is fat. I seal the pot with greaseproof paper and a tight lid.

It is important that you use a good cut of beef – ask your butcher for something
that does not shrink. You put the daube over a low flame (or in a very low oven –
about 225°F/110°C), so it cooks only very, very gently, for three hours; then cool
it and lift off any hard fat. You do this for three days, the final day being
Christmas Eve, when the meat will be melting and steeped in rich juices. For six
people I think you need not much more than 1.5 kg (3½ lb) of meat and about a
litre (1¾ pt) of wine.

With this we have the little cornmeal cakes called armottes – you mix twice the amount of cornmeal to plain flour and some salt and cook it in hot water until it stiffens (follow the quantities for the Piemontese cornmeal cake on page 176), then beat it with some melted duck or chicken fat, pour it into a greased tray, and when it cools, dip it in flour and fry it.

On Christmas Day there is foie gras instead of oysters, the daube reheated again – each reheating making it creamier and more delicious. And a big roasted chapon (castrated cockerel) that I have stuffed with parsley, liver, strips of fatty mountain ham, four sliced artichoke hearts, a chopped garlic clove and shallot, a couple of soupspoons of Armagnac, some foie gras, of course, and a pinch of truffle, if I have it.

Our cooks of Gascony are not known for their vegetables, but for myself, with my chapon rôti I like celeriac cooked for about fifteen minutes with a quarter of its weight in apples, then puréed with cream or butter and seasoned well.

After the roast there will be my own chocolate truffles, and prunes stuffed with toasted hazelnuts and chocolate mousse, and sometimes a pastis – our frilly apple pastry cake that looks like lace.

Huguette Méliet, *chef, Table des Cordeliers, Gascony, France*

First let me say about the big feast when all the families would get together every autumn to kill the pig.

For three days there would be a party: a long table covered in a white cloth under the lime trees outside, and my father making the black pudding, my uncle the hams and pâtés, my aunt the andouillettes . . .

You know, a feast in southwest France is something. First crudités and charcuterie, then maybe a poached hake with homemade garlic mayonnaise, then a dish in sauce – tripe perhaps – and a roast; cheese and a bitter winter greens salad dressed in vinaigrette, and finally two desserts.

Everyone had to stay until the very end, even the children – to get fat for the winter, so Gran'maman said.

At Christmas there was a lot of foie gras, of course, with glass after glass of cool, sweet Sauternes. And my parents used to eat a lot of oysters – maybe five, six dozen. So many that my father would have to buy them by the crate. With these you have sausages wrapped in crépinette and grilled so that the fat of the crépinette keeps the meat basted, and then a little red wine vinaigrette for flavour.

And finally a roast goose. And in the evening, because everyone is too full, just the bouillon from the poule au pot, cooked with vermicelli, and a salad of endives, and croutons of bread spread with foie gras fat and toasted on the fire.

You know we cook a lot on the cuttings from the vines, or on a fire of the Armagnac barrels? It gives a nutty flavour, like toasting hazelnuts or walnuts . . . a flavour to haunt you.

Bruno Loubet, *head chef, Four Seasons Restaurant, London, England*

Christmas was strictly religious for the Creoles. We all had to walk to midnight

mass on Christmas Eve, an' it was a long way to that old Cathedral. So Father, he would make a hot eggnog jes' before. Had to be the right amount o' whisky, jes' enough sugar, the right temperature. Papa Noel came down the chimney all right, but he never left me nothing I'd pay good money for now.
Tante Marie, *old Creole woman, New Orleans, Louisiana*

Before mass we would have boudin blanc grilled on the fire and served with a compote of apples, the apples cooked with sugar and lemon and a cinnamon stick, but not for so long that they lost their shape. After mass, back for coffee and sweet Christmas petits pains.

My mother, who is a cuisinière extraordinaire, usually roasts a pintade, a guinea fowl for Christmas Day, stuffed with spiced sausage. But most delicious are the dried figs heated in butter in the oven to soften them, then stuffed with a sweetened purée of tiny red berries called airelles (whortleberries or bilberries), and put around the pintade with whole chestnuts.

When it is served there is this beautiful golden brown bird, and the figs with their scarlet centre of berries, and the roasted chestnuts, and chestnuts puréed with some of the roasting juices as well . . . bon, ça, c'est vraiment vraiment délicieux!
Dominique Gantelme, *lawyer, Paris, France*

My mother used to make minced meat pies for Christmas with ground suet and meat and raisins and spice. You made it with what you had, really. And she always made two kinds of Christmas cake, one dark and one light. She died in September, and the next year, when I was eleven, I made the same cakes – but I iced them like wedding cakes, with silver beads and things, because I didn't know any better.

I remember that we only ever had the lights lit on the tree once, on Christmas night after the meal. Because they were candles, you know, set in tin holders – imagine the danger!

The doors to the living room would be closed and then a little while later we would go in, all the room in darkness except for this one sparkling vision of Christmas, very brief and magical.
Blanche Forbes, *housewife, Vancouver, Canada*

I stayed once in Pinhao, a remote town on the edge of the Douro valley in Portugal. Before the rail link, boats with butterfly sails made the journey downriver from here to Oporto, laden with barrels of new port.

The streets of Pinhao were muddy as a frontier city in the Wild West. There was one bar with swinging half-doors that reinforced the *High Noon* image. An old man waited inside behind a dusty counter on which stood two bottles of port, four bottles of unlabelled beer and a dusty can of Coke. When I asked what there was to drink he pointed sadly at the bottles. There was one long wooden trestle table and no other customers. A rooster was tied by one leg to the table.

Later I ate at the only restaurant in town. The cook was so delighted to have a stranger that she made a special Christmas sweet and came out to explain in halting French, our only common language. The crisp puffs of pastry rolled in cinnamon syrup were 'sonhos'.

'Sonhos – dreams,' the cook said. 'We call them that because they are sweet, and filled with air. And over too soon.'

As I walked back to the hotel the old man was in his bar waiting patiently. There were still no customers, and the rooster was gone.

In a restaurant in Old Nice there was a waitress of Russian extraction who swore that her grandmother knew Anastasia; or at least worked in a grand Nice villa for an even grander Russian duchess who exchanged jewelled eggs with the Russian royal family at Easter. After the Revolution, the duchess was reduced to penury, sold the villa, opened a caviare restaurant and lived on vodka and memories of better days. If my waitress's royal link seemed a little tenuous, her grandmother's stories of Russian Easter and Christmas feasts were not. A huge oval table would be laid with zakuski, a cold buffet of truly Siberian proportions. There would be bottles of vodka flavoured with pepper, lemon and orange peel and frozen to slippery viscosity; glossy bricks of pressed black caviare and silver buckets of chilled champagne – smoked eel, sturgeon and slivers of salmon layered with lemon slices; baby radishes, shredded beetroot and cucumber, all in sour cream; baskets of black rye breads sprinkled with seeds; herrings pickled in sweet wine marinade; carp in aspic; a whole roast suckling pig or a goose with apples, or ham cooked in hay and beer with spiced cherries; and best of all, so she said, the darkly Oriental-spiced Russian gingerbread with soured cream, and Ukrainian Medivnyk, a moist fruit cake so rich in raw sugar and buckwheat honey that in the streets of Kiev where it was sold even the bees came for a taste.

Vodka can be flavoured Russian-style by infusing a bottle with peel from a lemon or orange, or with any number of other herbs and spices: two teaspoons of slightly crushed coriander seed, a tablespoon of whole peppercorns, or a few spoonfuls of fruit-scented tea leaves (rosehip is delicious). Strain the vodka after twenty-four hours to avoid bitterness. The grand duchess, weeping into her caviare in Nice (perhaps by then she had been reduced to serving lumpfish roe), may have been nostalgic for the high old times in St Petersburg – but she was never, never bitter.

Christmas is a time for nostalgia. My Nice waitress's opulent Russian table reminded me of the feast prepared by a couple of friends who had lived for a long time in Denmark. To bring back the taste of

Copenhagen they held a traditional Danish Christmas Eve party.

The Scandinavians were responsible for the Russian zakuski table, a smorgasbord with caviare. As Lesley Chamberlain mentions in her book *The Food and Cooking of Russia*, it was Peter the Great, on one of his fact-finding tours of Europe, that brought back the idea of the zakuski table to Russia.

To start the meal we have a digestiv of Gammel Dansk, a fiery blend of thirty fruits and herbs. This must be served at room temperature to bring out the flavour, and then chased with cold beer – Carlsberg or Tuborg in their festive red and green bottles – and followed by Aalborg 'Jule Akvavit', special Christmas eau de vie, in iced glasses frosty from the freezer.

The toast with the Akvavit is 'Let it swim', which probably refers (in a country where the herring is so popular) to a wish that there may always be fish in the sea.

Now you must have a dark sweetish slice of rye bread spread with dripping and layered with herring, slices of hard-boiled eggs and pickled red onions. This you will do three times, first with herrings that have been pickled in a red wine marinade with onions and capers and cider vinegar, then with dilled herring, then with herrings in a curried cream. You can build your own herring breads with green peppers, capers – as you like.

These are not the sad, flabby excuses for herring that come in bottles of brine and are so appropriately called rollmops, darling, but fleshy, meaty-tasting fish with a firm texture.

Bryan Bale, *window dresser and wit, London, England*

After the herring there is bread and fresh prawns, mayonnaise, a tiny spoonful of glossy lumpfish eggs; then a warm liver pâté wrapped in crisp bacon and smothered in mushrooms; then roast pork with golden crackling interlaced with slices of orange and warm prunes, and red cabbage cooked with apples; more bread spread with something that sounds like 'feet' and piled with salami and fan-sliced gherkins, more 'feet', another kind of salami, onions, more gherkins.

Finally there is a cinnamony sponge cake soaked in kirsch and layered with what Bryan calls 'severely whipped cream' and melted

chocolate and toasted almonds.

Between each course there is more akvavit, more beer chasers. It becomes clear that Christmas in Denmark is celebrated, as Sybille Bedford once wrote, like Christmas in Mexico, France, Spain – like all the best feasts every-where – with barbarity and opulence.

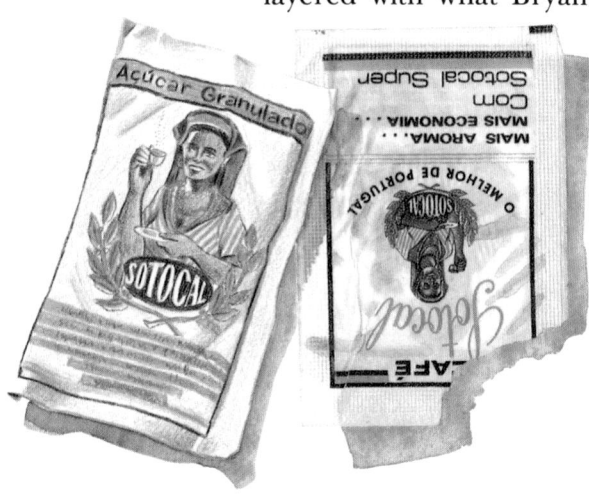

RECIPES

LA TORTIERE/SPICY FRENCH-CANADIAN MEAT PIE
(serves 6)

Strange that in Canada one should find still a recipe so close to the original highly spiced 'mincemeat' pies of early England and France.

Serve this traditional Christmas Eve pie with cranberry sauce and a bitter winter green salad dressed with mustardy vinaigrette, and glasses of cold cider or hot eggnog. In the past, before we had begun to worry about waistlines and cholesterol, it was the custom to have it with wedges of creamy homemade curd cheese as well.

My mother's trick to ensure that tender pastry does not break up is to keep a dishtowel permanently impregnated with flour, and roll the dough out on it so that it can be rolled up again easily.

Pastry
6 oz/180 g plain white flour
½ tsp salt
3 oz/90 g cold butter, plus extra 1 oz/30 g
1 oz/30 g cold chicken or bacon fat
4–5 tbsp very cold water

Cream sauce
10 fl oz/300 ml chicken stock/broth
5 fl oz/150 ml medium-dry apple cider
1 carrot, 1 small onion, piece celery, sliced; bouquet garni
1 oz/30 g butter
1 medium onion, finely chopped
1 oz white flour
6–8 tbsp thick cream

Meat base
8 oz/250 g ground veal
8 oz/250 g ground pork
4 oz/125 g dark field mushrooms, sliced
1 large tart apple, peeled and chopped
3 garlic cloves, finely chopped
large handful of raisins
juice and grated zest of 1 lemon
¾ tsp each cinnamon, allspice, nutmeg
salt and black pepper

(1) To make the pastry, put flour and salt into a large bowl, cut the butter and lard into small pieces and scatter over the top. Rub the fat into the flour with the tips of your fingers until the mixture looks like coarse crumbs. Sprinkle over just enough water to make the pastry bind (all this can be done in a food processor) and press the pastry into a ball. Wrap in cling film and chill for 1 hour. Then roll out into a rough rectangle on a floured surface, dot with extra butter and fold in three like a letter. Roll out again, fold in three, wrap in cling film and chill for another hour.
(2) To make the cream sauce, put the stock, cider, carrot, onion, celery and bouquet garni in a pan and bring to a low boil. Melt the butter in a saucepan and cook the chopped onion in it until soft and golden, then stir in the flour for 1

minute. Do not let it brown. Remove the pan from the heat and strain the boiling liquid into it, whisking until smooth. Return to moderate heat and simmer for 1 minute, stirring constantly. Stir in the cream by spoonfuls until the sauce is the consistency of very thick soup.

(3) Preheat the oven to 425°F/220°C/gas mark 7. In a large frying pan cook the meat, mushrooms, garlic and spices together, just until the meat is no longer pink. Stir in all remaining ingredients except the pastry, and season to taste with salt and freshly ground black pepper.

(4) Pour meat into an 11 in/28 cm round heatproof casserole. Roll out the pastry thinly, lay onto the meat and pinch the edges to seal. Cut three slashes in the top for steam to escape. Cut leftover pastry into holly-leaf shapes and stick on top of the pie, making 'berries' with red peppercorns or cranberries. Bake for 20–25 minutes, or until golden.

• An older French Canadian pastry for chicken or beef tortières or pot pies consists of grating raw potatoes, wrapping them in cloth, and squeezing hard to remove as much liquid and starch as possible. The resulting pulp is mixed with pork fat or suet to produce a melting crust.

HONEYED RUSSIAN GINGER CAKE

I was seduced by the magic of ginger cakes and breads from the first moment I read M.F.K. Fisher's description of Dijon's pain d'épice ... 'its flat strange odour, honey, cow dung, clove ...something unnameable but unmistakable ...'.

This rich, moist cake evolved from memories of Fisher's 'Take two pounds of old black honey, the older and blacker the better' and descriptions of the Russian honey cake sold by hawkers in the streets of Kiev. Honey and spice, our oldest sweet, the very essence of nostalgia. I like to bubble big spoonfuls of Seville orange marmalade with rum and pour the resulting sauce, still warm, over the dark cake.

3 oz/90 g butter
12 oz/350 g dark honey
3 oz/90 g rye flour
5 oz/150 g strong plain bread flour
pinch of salt
3 eggs, beaten
1½ tsp bicarbonate of soda
¾ tsp baking powder
6 fl oz/180 ml sour cream
grated zest of 1 large lemon
1 tsp each ground cinnamon, cloves, ginger, cardamom
½ tsp dry English mustard powder
2 big handfuls currants

(1) Heat together the butter and honey (use the darkest, strongest you can find) just to boiling, cool and then stir slowly into the two flours (sifted together with the salt). Mix the stiff dough thoroughly, cover tightly with cling film and leave in a cool, dry place for at least 24 hours, or up to a week. The longer you leave it, the richer it will taste.

(2) Preheat the oven to 300°F/150°C/gas mark 2. Butter a 3 in/8 cm deep, 7–8 in/18–20 cm loose-bottomed cake tin and line the base with buttered greaseproof paper.

(3) When ready to use, leave dough to soften at room temperature (the butter and honey will have hardened), then beat in the sour cream, bicarbonate of soda and baking powder until smooth, then all the remaining ingredients, beating very well until the batter is completely smooth. Pour it into the prepared tin and bake for 1¼ hours, or until a skewer inserted into the cake comes out dry.

(4) Allow the cake to cool before removing from tin. It tastes delicious at this point, but if you wrap in foil and leave in a cool but not cold place to age for at least 2 days it will taste even better. Cut in wedges and serve with sour cream or crème fraîche.

LE PASTIS GASCON/FRILLED APPLE PASTRY
(serves 4–6)

'I have a soft spot for the Gascon pastis, which I have watched being prepared at home and all over our province. My great-grandmother, Aurelie, prepared the pastry and the apples the night before, and I used to admire her from my viewpoint on the edge of the table where everything happened.'

Marie-Claude Gracia, *chef, Poudenas, southwestern France*

The pastry for this fragile pie, with its intricate petals of pastry, is essentially a stretched strudel dough, and I now side with Paula Wolfert, in her book *The Cooking of South-west France*, and agree that Greek filo pastry, fresh, when I can get it, or frozen when I cannot, makes a delicious substitute and substantially reduces the effort. My method is a mixture of Wolfert's American precision and Gracia's Gascon flexibility.

1½ lb/750 g large, tart apples, cored, peeled
and cut in thick pieces
Seeds scraped from 1 vanilla pod or scant ¼ tsp almond essence
½ tsp orange flower water
3 oz/90 g caster/fine white sugar, plus extra for sprinkling
approximately 4½ fl oz/125 ml Armagnac
3–4 oz/90–125 g butter, melted
10 sheets filo pastry, approximately 8 in/20 cm × 18 in/45 cm

(1) Layer the apples in a deep bowl with the vanilla seeds, orange-flower water, 3 oz/90 g sugar, and the Armagnac. Cover the bowl with cling film and leave for at least 24 hours, longer if possible.

(2) Preheat oven to 400°F/200°C/gas mark 6. Butter an 8–9 in/20–23 cm circle of greaseproof paper and lay in a greased 9½ in/24 cm loose-bottomed pie tin. Keep the pastry (thawed well, if using frozen) covered with a damp cloth. Take the first sheet, brush one side with melted butter, sprinkle with sugar, fold in half lengthwise and butter each side again. Place one end in the centre of the tin with the remainder overlapping the edge. Sprinkle with more sugar. Repeat with the remaining pastry sheets, buttering, sugaring, and overlapping in a circle so that the tin is completely covered.

(3) Drain the apples and pile in a circle in the centre, sprinkling with more sugar. Then take each pastry sheet one by one, twisting and crumpling it into the centre, roughly separating the double thickness out into a single thickness as you do – to form a 'petal'. The end result should be like a ruffly cabbage rose.

(4) Mix any remaining butter with equal quantities of apple liquid and brush

pastry surfaces with it. Sprinkle with more sugar. This will caramelize the pastry while it bakes. Bake for 20–30 minutes until crisp and golden brown. Lift carefully onto wire rack to cool slightly and sprinkle with more sugar before serving. This is wonderful with the Italian muscat ice-cream on page 178. Or you could beat Armagnac-soaked prunes into good vanilla ice-cream and re-freeze.

• Reduce leftover Armagnac-scented juices over high heat until syrupy and pour over ice-cream, or use to steep other fruit – prunes for the ice-cream, say.

• Wolfert recommends sprinkling toasted cake or bread crumbs mixed with sugar between the pastry layers if you want to prevent the base of the pie from soaking up too much liquid.

TARDY PUDDING
(serves 8)

Finally, a pudding that looks like a Christmas pudding, tastes like one, but is much lighter, and very fast. I like it with the whisky sauce given here, and scoops of the Mexican brown sugar ice-cream on page 212. Particularly festive with praline almonds scattered around its crown of holly.

6 oz/180 g butter
6 oz/180 g dark muscovado sugar
6 oz/180 g fresh brown breadcrumbs
3 eggs, beaten
3 tbsp orange marmalade
½ tsp bicarbonate of soda mixed with a spoonful of tepid water
large handful of raisins
large handful of toasted almonds
(optional) a few tbsp chopped candied peel
2 tbsp brandy
¾ tsp each cinnamon and allspice
Sauce
Juice of 3 lemons
6 tbsp marmalade
6 tbsp sweet sherry
6 tbsp Cointreau or other orange liqueur
½ tsp allspice
6 oz/180 g melted butter

(1) Cream together the butter and sugar, mix in the breadcrumbs, eggs and all other ingredients and pour into a buttered pudding basin or heatproof bowl, leaving 1 in/2.5 cm or so for the pudding to rise. Cover with buttered paper and a clean dishcloth and tie firmly. Steam for 2 hours in a double boiler. Turn out onto a warm plate and decorate with holly, ivy and pralined (or just toasted) almonds.
(2) To make the sauce: boil together the first five ingredients for a couple of minutes, then whisk in the butter and serve immediately, pouring some sauce over each pudding portion.

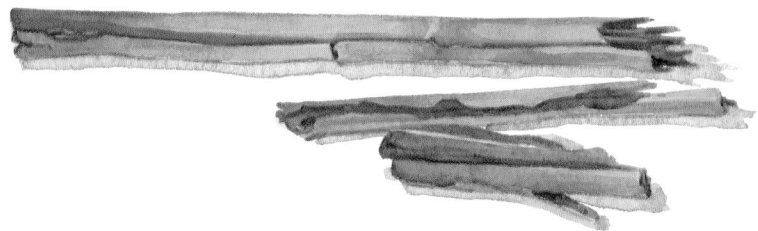

INDEX

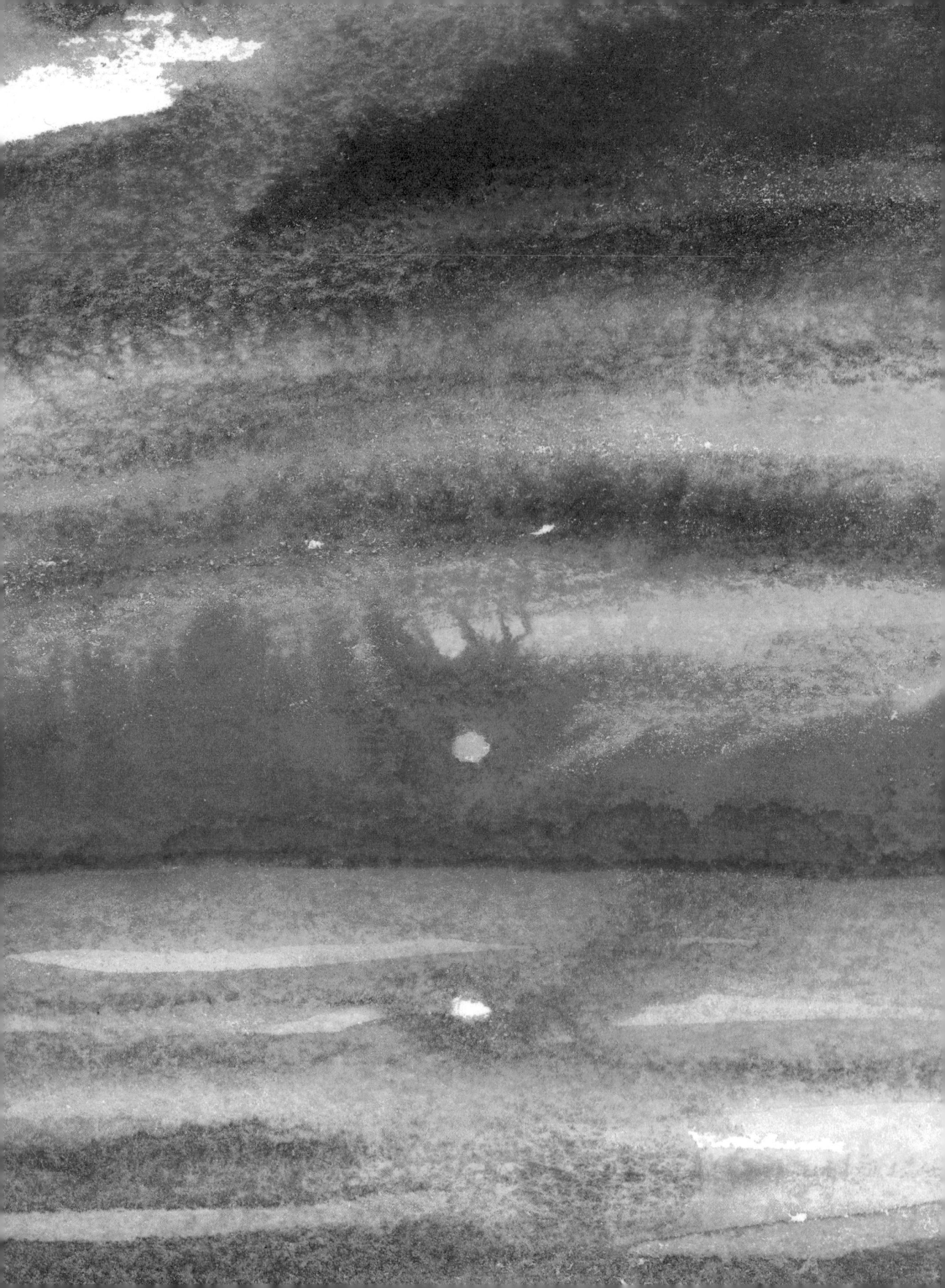